East Asian Perspectives on Silence in English Language Education

PSYCHOLOGY OF LANGUAGE LEARNING AND TEACHING

Series Editors: **Sarah Mercer**, *Universität Graz, Austria* and **Stephen Ryan**, *Waseda University, Japan*

This international, interdisciplinary book series explores the exciting, emerging field of Psychology of Language Learning and Teaching. It is a series that aims to bring together works which address a diverse range of psychological constructs from a multitude of empirical and theoretical perspectives, but always with a clear focus on their applications within the domain of language learning and teaching. The field is one that integrates various areas of research that have been traditionally discussed as distinct entities, such as motivation, identity, beliefs, strategies and self-regulation, and it also explores other less familiar concepts for a language education audience, such as emotions, the self and positive psychology approaches. In theoretical terms, the new field represents a dynamic interface between psychology and foreign language education and books in the series draw on work from diverse branches of psychology, while remaining determinedly focused on their pedagogic value. In methodological terms, sociocultural and complexity perspectives have drawn attention to the relationships between individuals and their social worlds, leading to a field now marked by methodological pluralism. In view of this, books encompassing quantitative, qualitative and mixed methods studies are all welcomed.

All books in this series are externally peer-reviewed.

Full details of all the books in this series and of all our other publications can be found on http://www.multilingual-matters.com, or by writing to Multilingual Matters, St Nicholas House, 31–34 High Street, Bristol BS1 2AW, UK.

PSYCHOLOGY OF LANGUAGE LEARNING AND TEACHING: 6

East Asian Perspectives on Silence in English Language Education

Edited by
Jim King and Seiko Harumi

MULTILINGUAL MATTERS
Bristol • Blue Ridge Summit

DOI https://doi.org/10.21832/KING6768
Library of Congress Cataloging in Publication Data
A catalog record for this book is available from the Library of Congress.
Names: King, Jim - editor. | Harumi, Seiko - editor.
Title: East Asian Perspectives on Silence in English Language Education/
Edited by Jim King and Seiko Harumi.
Description: Blue Ridge Summit: Multilingual Matters, 2020. | Series: Psychology of Language
   Learning and Teaching: 6 | Includes bibliographical references and index. | Summary: "This
   book provides a state-of-the-art account of current research on the relatively neglected,
   complex and ambiguous issue of silence within second language settings. The chapters use a
   range of theoretical approaches and research methodologies to explore silence within various
   educational contexts connected to Asia"-- Provided by publisher.
Identifiers: LCCN 2019045083 (print) | LCCN 2019045084 (ebook) |
   ISBN 9781788926751 (paperback) | ISBN 9781788926768 (hardback) |
   ISBN 9781788926775 (pdf) | ISBN 9781788926782 (epub) | ISBN 9781788926799 (kindle
   edition) Subjects: LCSH: Language and languages--Study and teaching--East Asia. | Second
   language acquisition--East Asia. | Linguistics--Study and teaching--East Asia. | English
   language--East Asia. | Language and culture--East Asia. | East Asia--Languages. | Classroom
   management. | Silence.
Classification: LCC P57.E18 A84 2020 (print) | LCC P57.E18 (ebook) | DDC 428.0071/05--
dc23
LC record available at https://lccn.loc.gov/2019045083
LC ebook record available at https://lccn.loc.gov/2019045084

British Library Cataloguing in Publication Data
A catalogue entry for this book is available from the British Library.

ISBN-13: 978-1-78892-676-8 (hbk)
ISBN-13: 978-1-78892-675-1 (pbk)

Multilingual Matters
UK: St Nicholas House, 31–34 High Street, Bristol BS1 2AW, UK.
USA: NBN, Blue Ridge Summit, PA, USA.

Website: www.multilingual-matters.com
Twitter: Multi_Ling_Mat
Facebook: https://www.facebook.com/multilingualmatters
Blog: www.channelviewpublications.wordpress.com

Copyright © 2020 Jim King, Seiko Harumi and the authors of individual chapters.

All rights reserved. No part of this work may be reproduced in any form or by any means
without permission in writing from the publisher.

The policy of Multilingual Matters/Channel View Publications is to use papers that are natural,
renewable and recyclable products, made from wood grown in sustainable forests. In the
manufacturing process of our books, and to further support our policy, preference is given to
printers that have FSC and PEFC Chain of Custody certification. The FSC and/or PEFC logos
will appear on those books where full certification has been granted to the printer concerned.

Typeset in Sabon and Frutiger by R. J. Footring Ltd, Derby, UK.

Contents

Figures		vii
Tables		viii
Contributors		ix
Acknowledgements		xii
Foreword: The Song of Silence Peter MacIntyre		xiii
1	East Asian Perspectives on Silence in English Language Education: An Introduction Seiko Harumi and Jim King	1
2	Silence, Talk and In-betweens: East Asian Students' Responses to Task Challenge in an Australian University Dat Bao	17
3	Approaches to Interacting with Classroom Silence: The Role of Teacher Talk Seiko Harumi	37
4	Silence and Anxiety in the English-Medium Classroom of Japanese Universities: A Longitudinal Intervention Study Jim King, Tomoko Yashima, Simon Humphries, Scott Aubrey and Maiko Ikeda	60
5	Examining L2 Learners' Silent Behaviour and Anxiety in the Classroom Using an Approach Based on Cognitive-Behavioural Theory Kate Maher	80
6	Communicative Language Teaching and Silence: Chinese (Pre-service) Teachers' Perspectives Michael Karas and Farahnaz Faez	105
7	Silence in Japanese Classrooms: Activities and Factors in Capacities to Speak English Simon Humphries, Nobuhiko Akamatsu, Takako Tanaka and Anne Burns	123

8 Willing Silence and Silent Willingness to Communicate
   (WTC) in the Chinese EFL Classroom: A Dynamic Systems
   Perspective   143
   Jian-E Peng

9 Conclusion: Silence in EFL Classrooms Revisited   166
   Amy B.M. Tsui and Rintaro Imafuku

Index   182

Figures

5.1	Cognitive-behavioural cycle	83
5.2	A cognitive-behavioural model of a silent L2 learner's social anxiety	85
5.3	The CBT model	90
5.4	CBT model of not initiating talk	93
5.5	CBT model of ending speaking turn	94
5.6	Cognitive-behavioural model of Mari's silence and anxiety in the foreign language classroom	95
5.7	Confidence graph	99
7.1	Model 1: Standardised estimates of factors influencing capacity to speak (CTS)	133
7.2	Model 2: Standardised model of underlying factors that fits the data	134
8.1	WTC fluctuations at group and individual levels in a 90-minute lesson	153
8.2	Attractor states of interplay of WTC and silence	160

Tables

2.1	Students' talk–silence preferences in task performance	24
4.1	Observation results across the three groups	67
5.1	Instruments from which interview items were drawn	88
7.1	Descriptive statistics of speaking activities in class and results of binomial tests	132
7.2	Descriptive statistics of students' perceived CTS for speaking activities in class and results of chi-square tests of independence	132
7.3	The reliability of internal consistency (Cronbach's alpha) for the latent variables in Models 1 and 2	133
7.4	Goodness-of-fit indices	134
8.1	Demographic information of the four focal students	148
8.2	Categories of observed behaviour in the modified Classroom Oral Participation Scheme (COPS)	149
8.3	Oral participation of the whole group	151
8.4	Focal students' classroom performance (on average)	152
8.5	Attractor states in the interaction of WTC and silence	160
9.1	Participation trajectories (percentage participation rate*) of four Japanese learners in PBL tutorials	173

Contributors

Editors

Jim King (PhD, University of Nottingham) is based at the University of Leicester, where he directs postgraduate courses in Applied Linguistics and TESOL. He is an International Research Fellow of the Japan Society for the Promotion of Science. Before entering academia, Jim taught in a wide variety of contexts around the world, including stints as a language teacher and teacher trainer in Australia, Poland, Hungary, Italy and Japan. His research interests centre around situated psychological aspects of foreign language education, with current projects focusing on L2 teachers' emotions and psychological resilience, and on the relationship between emotional engagement and language learner reticence. His books include the 2013 monograph *Silence in the Second Language Classroom*, the 2015 edited volume *The Dynamic Interplay Between Context and the Language Learner* (both published by Palgrave Macmillan) and *The Emotional Rollercoaster of Language Teaching* (co-edited with Christina Gkonou and Jean-Marc Dewaele, published by Multilingual Matters, 2020).

Seiko Harumi is a Lecturer in Japanese and Applied Linguistics (Education) at the School of Oriental and African Studies (SOAS), University of London. She holds a PhD in Applied Linguistics from the Institute of Education, University of London. She has taught English, Applied Linguistics and Japanese in Japan and currently teaches in the UK. Her academic interests lie in classroom silence, code-switching, classroom discourse, pragmatics, learner-centred reflective approaches in second language learning and language pedagogy. Her current research projects use conversational analysis to explore silence as an interactional strategy adopted by learners studying second languages. Seiko's published work includes the paper 'Classroom silence: Voices from Japanese EFL learners', which appeared in *ELT Journal* (2011).

Other authors

Nobuhiko Akamatsu is a Professor in the Department of English at Doshisha University, where he teaches TESOL and psycholinguistics. He holds a PhD (in second language education) from the Ontario Institute for Studies in Education (OISE) at the University of Toronto, and an MEd (TESOL) from the State University of New York at Buffalo.

Scott Aubrey is an Associate Professor in the Department of Curriculum and Instruction at the Chinese University of Hong Kong. His research and pedagogical interests include the areas of L2 motivation, task-based language teaching and computer-mediated L2 writing instruction.

Dat Bao is Senior Lecturer in Education at Monash University, Australia. He has previously worked with Leeds Metropolitan University in the UK, Cornell University in the US, the National University of Singapore and the Assumption University of Thailand. His expertise includes curriculum design, intercultural communication, materials development, literacies, creative pedagogy and visual pedagogy in language education. He is the author of *Understanding Silence and Reticence: Ways of Participating in Second Language Acquisition* (Bloomsbury, 2014); *Poetry for Education: Classroom Ideas That Inspire Creativity* (Xlibris, 2017); and *Creativity and Innovations in ELT Material Development: Looking Beyond the Current Design* (Multilingual Matters, 2018).

Anne Burns is Professor of TESOL at the University of New South Wales, Sydney, Australia, and Emeritus Professor at Aston University, Birmingham, UK. She is also an Honorary Professor at the University of Sydney and at the Education University of Hong Kong. She has been a visiting Professor at the University of Stockholm, Sweden, Thammasat University, Thailand, and Soka University, Japan.

Farahnaz Faez is Associate Professor in Applied Linguistics in the Faculty of Education at the University of Western Ontario, Canada. Her research interests include second language teaching and learning, language teacher education, teacher efficacy, teacher proficiency and non-native English-speaking teachers.

Simon Humphries is a Professor in the Faculty of Foreign Language Studies and Graduate School of Foreign Language Education and Research at Kansai University, where he teaches business communication (such as marketing and negotiation). He holds a PhD (in linguistics) from Macquarie University and MSc (TESOL) from Aston University.

Maiko Ikeda is Professor of Applied Linguistics in the Faculty of Foreign Language Studies, Kansai University, Japan. Her main research interests are L2 learner strategies, collaborative learning and teacher training. Her forthcoming publications include the co-authored paper 'Situated willingness to communicate in an L2', due to appear in *Language Teaching Research* .

Rintaro Imafuku is an Assistant Professor at the Medical Education Development Center at Gifu University, Japan. He received his MA from Monash University and his PhD from the University of Hong Kong. His research centres on learners' social interactions and group dynamics in enquiry-led education settings such as problem-based learning, interprofessional education, undergraduate research and professional identity formation.

Michael Karas is Assistant Professor in Applied Linguistics in the Faculty of Education at the University of Western Ontario. His research interests include learner silence, teacher self-efficacy, teacher cognition and language teacher proficiency. He has taught English in South Korea, China and Canada.

Kate Maher is an Assistant Professor in the Department of British and American Studies, Kyoto University of Foreign Studies, Japan. She is a PhD candidate at the University of Leicester, UK, under the supervision of Dr Jim King. Having worked in Japan teaching English for over 12 years and completing her MA in English education there, her main research interests are student silence, speaking-related language anxiety and psychological aspects of language learning in the Japanese university foreign language classroom.

Jian-E Peng is a Professor in the College of Liberal Arts, Shantou University, China. She holds a PhD from the University of Sydney. Her main works include a book, two book chapters, and a number of papers published in *Language Learning, TESOL Quarterly, System, Journal of English for Academic Purposes, Linguistics and Education, Asia-Pacific Education Researcher, Sage Open* and *University of Sydney Papers in TESOL*.

Takako Tanaka is an Associate Professor in the Department of English, Doshisha University. She holds an MA (TESOL) from the Institute of Education, University of London. Her research interests are L2 motivation and L2 reading motivation using mixed methods.

Amy B.M. Tsui is a Professor Emerita at Hong Kong University. She has published over 100 journal papers and book chapters, five authored books and four edited volumes on classroom discourse analysis, conversational analysis, language policy and teacher expertise.

Tomoko Yashima is Professor of Applied Linguistics and Intercultural Communication at Kansai University. She is the author of a number of books published in Japan, including *Motivation and Affect in Foreign Language Communication*. Her studies have been published in *Modern Language Journal, Language Learning, Psychological Reports* and the *International Journal of Intercultural Relations*.

Acknowledgements

This edited volume would not have been possible without the collaboration and support of key individuals at critical stages in its evolution. We are indebted to Laura Longworth at Multilingual Matters, who saw the potential of the project and has been unfailingly positive in her support since. We also owe great appreciation to a number of people who kindly agreed to read and comment upon early drafts of the studies contained in this book: thank you to Atsuko Aono, Sam Morris, Bill Snyder, Gerald Talandis Jr and Joseph Tomei. Your insightful feedback was invaluable. We are grateful to Kate Maher for her help with the book's index. Jim would like to acknowledge the support of a JSPS International Fellowship during the latter stages of the book's journey to publication. Finally, the editors would particularly like to express their special gratitude to our contributors, who have shared their new perspectives on the role of silence in second language education through what we feel are thought-provoking, state-of-the-art texts. It has been our pleasure and privilege to collaborate with such a wonderful group of scholars throughout the course of this project. Every publishing endeavour has its ups and downs (this one seemingly more than most!) and so we thank you all, both for your support and for your endurance through what has been quite a long publishing process.

Jim King and Seiko Harumi

Foreword: The Song of Silence

Most readers will be familiar with sheet music, the written form of the notes a musician plays. Written music has an interesting set of notations that does not have an analogous item in standard written text dedicated to silences or moments of rest. The musical notes to be played are shown on the staff alongside the prescribed silences, and the silences can be as complex as the notes themselves. Speech and music performance share a number of similarities, including that both are exquisite in the precision of their timing, especially among the silences. Composers write silences into the music very carefully, and musicians use those silences for a variety of artistic effects. Perhaps it is time we devoted more attention to how communicating with language artfully uses silences. The volume you are about to read is filled with observations about silence and its meanings.

Compared with studying spoken words, test scores or written text, at first glance studying silence might appear as if looking for something occult – not in the supernatural sense of the word but as something hidden from view. Yet a thoughtful approach to silence suggests that it is far more than simply the absence of speech. Silence itself is meaningful and communicative. Parables, expressions and well known quotations suggest that the persons wise among us have something to say about silence. First among them in my view – my mother told me to say nothing if I had nothing good to say, and that has proven to be sage advice. Searching the web for what thoughtful people had to say about silence produces a plethora of observations concerning the value and meaning of silence. Across the many inspiring quotes that are available there are at least two general themes.

The first theme is that silence communicates something meaningful. Silence is not merely the absence of speech: silence itself says something. *Psychology Today* has a webpage of quotes devoted to silence (see Sarkis, 2013). Among them is 'He who does not know how to be silent will not know how to speak' (Ausonius). Keywords used in other quotes to describe the positive side of silence include 'golden', 'perfect', 'strong', 'safe' and 'peaceful'. In classrooms of all types, teaching and learning require the active balancing of talking and silence across the whole group. Silence provides the necessary boundary for each person's meaningful speech. Without silences, the talk in a classroom would be a virtually incoherent wall of sound. Silence can be a most welcome thing.

The second theme among the quotes is more subtle and troublesome. A number of authors have suggested that silence is problematic when it is born out of fear and avoidance, as in a context where one could/should be speaking out about injustice in the world. *Psychology Today* quotes Martin Luther King Jr as saying 'In the end, we will remember not the words of our enemies, but the silence of our friends'. A reluctance to speak based on fear or apprehension is restrictive and at times can be quite debilitating. Language teachers might be especially troubled if a class is too reticent to speak when required. The silent learners who fear being less than perfect or losing face are depriving themselves of important learning opportunities, especially in the pursuit of language learning. Reticence based on fear is among the many reasons for silence, an unwelcome state with potentially enduring consequences.

The editors of this volume, King and Harumi, along with the contributors, deserve to have their work carefully considered. Applied linguistics, and studies of communication more generally, seem to have under-appreciated the many ways in which silence emerges in language learning and use. Although this volume contextualises the study of silence in East Asia, where the cultural dimensions of the work on silence have been a focus often attributed to influence by Confucian philosophy, the complex, interacting processes that dynamically create silence certainly extend beyond East Asian locations and Confucian philosophy. If silence is an inherently communicative, multidimensional phenomenon with nuanced meaning, it is so everywhere. The stereotype of Western classrooms being talkative, especially in contrast to East Asian classrooms, is a belief that needs to be examined more closely so that the meanings of silence can be better understood outside the Asian context. This volume contributes a necessary perspective to that pursuit. Language teachers around the world must deal with issues of talking and silence where different contexts will accentuate different processes. We can work towards identifying the commonalities among those processes within and across cultures, education systems, schools, classrooms and persons.

Thinking about silence in the context of individuals and their personality traits suggests the possibility of happy apples and anxious oranges. Some people talk more than others and some people are more comfortable with silence than others. The happy apples may be using silence to create a comfort zone for reading or thoughtful contemplation, or as an escape from a noisy world; for many people, silence is a welcome respite. For anxious oranges, silences are uncomfortable states to be avoided, and as the length of silence increases so does the perceived stress. When silence arises out of fear, anxiety, perfectionism, hesitations and so on, the teaching and learning process is disrupted. Conventional wisdom suggests that, in general, we should avoid comparing apples and oranges. The themes of meaningful versus avoidant silences identified above suggest some value in separating the positive and negative assumptions about silence, to avoid comparing the happy apples and anxious oranges. The patterns blending talk and silence in pleasant or unpleasant ways extend from the intrapersonal to intercultural relationships.

Perhaps we should take it as given from here on that silence – at its core – is an adaptive response constructed within context in a meaningful way. Taking silence as an active response, rather than the absence of an active response (talking), may lead to innovative approaches to creating the desired balance between the sound and the silence in the language classroom. Whereas such a balance has been coded explicitly into music, perhaps the present volume will remind teachers, learners and researchers to be more sensitive to the multiple, deliberate, adaptive and sometimes artistic purposes of silence.

Peter MacIntyre
Cape Breton University, Canada

Reference

Sarkis, S.A. (2013) 20 quotes on silence. *Psychology Today*. At https://www.psychologytoday.com/gb/blog/here-there-and-everywhere/201312/20-quotes-silence (last accessed February 2020).

1 East Asian Perspectives on Silence in English Language Education: An Introduction

Seiko Harumi and Jim King

How does silence function in second language learning? Do learners deliberately or perhaps unconsciously use silence as a strategy in the language classroom and, if so, why? When language students engage in second/foreign language (L2) learning, they use whatever resources they bring into classrooms. Silence may be one such interactional resource, used to signal the psychological or linguistic difficulties they encounter, or it may be an expression of solitary activity through reflection, enabling learners to process their own thoughts. It can also be viewed as an indicator of the social and cultural perspectives which can act as frameworks for second language acquisition. What is without doubt is that when we look closely at this issue, it is clear that learner silence is a complex and multifaceted phenomenon that emerges from a whole gamut of sources and hence defies easy generalisations. This book offers an insight into this complexity in order to build a better awareness and deeper understanding of the silent episodes which occur within East Asian language classrooms and beyond.

This introductory chapter argues the case for why education-oriented research into the relatively neglected issue of silence has the potential to have a significant impact not only on second language acquisition (SLA) theorists, but also on classroom practitioners and education policy planners alike. The chapter sets out the main goals of the collection, provides a historical overview of silence-oriented research since the 1980s, illustrates a wide range of definitions of silence and considers some of the fundamental issues and questions surrounding the topic of language learning silence by highlighting the significance of contextual factors. It also discusses the methodological challenges and approaches to data collection used in the study of silence. For example, how best can the multi-formed phenomenon of silence be defined by researchers working within specific contexts, and should silence be considered a positive or a negative phenomenon in education? This first chapter in the collection also provides a detailed overview of each of the studies that make up the edited volume.

Why a Book on Silence?

The topic of silence has great relevance both for academics researching international education and SLA, and for language teachers in their daily interactions with learners. It is only quite recently that recognition has grown around the crucial role that silence plays in the L2 classroom, particularly within East Asian contexts, and this nascent awareness has led to some innovative research focusing on silence both as a barrier to successful learning and as a resource that may in some cases facilitate language acquisition. Silence is a pedagogical issue that touches all who teach. However, its key role in language classroom practices has not been fully explored. Over the last few decades, the multiple meanings and uses of silence in L2 contexts has increasingly begun to draw the attention of researchers and practitioners, who have revealed its hidden dimensions and pedagogical value in enhanced classroom interaction.

There are two main reasons why this volume focuses on the use of silence by East Asian learners specifically. Firstly, despite a growing number of recent empirical studies and a trend towards a more communicative approach in classroom practice, the silence of East Asian learners is still considered by many practitioners to be something entirely problematic and to be a niche topic for researchers both in mono- and multilingual settings. While this book helps challenge the stereotype of the silent, passive East Asian learner, it also provides an acknowledgement that learners' backgrounds, in conjunction with other variables, do play a role in shaping classroom discourse behaviour. The key here is to base one's conclusions about silence on reliable, empirical research. This volume presents the results of such research and, as it does so in a contextually valid manner, we can learn much about the silences of language learners in other settings too. Wherever there is L2 learning, there are sure to be some silent learners. Secondly, prior to the appearance of this book, no single collection of studies focusing on East Asian learners had attempted to show a complete picture of classroom silence seen from interdisciplinary perspectives and using a range of theoretical approaches. With this in mind, the idea for the current collection emerged from discussions between the editors following a talk organised by the Japan Foundation in London (see King, 2016a). As applied linguistics researchers who share a fascination with silence in language education, we were becoming increasingly aware of the groundswell of interest in this topic and the need to share a state-of-the-art account of current research on silence within L2 settings. We were delighted that such a strong and internationally diverse set of applied linguistics researchers responded to our endeavours and embraced our theme to make this book possible.

The volume's scope includes work that is informed by cognitive, sociocultural and interactional perspectives. It brings together empirical works that explore silence in a wide range of educational settings and that collectively illustrate the diversity of innovative theoretical approaches. Some of our contributors offer a fresh perspective on ways to facilitate classroom interaction while at the same time embracing the phenomenon of silence. The book touches upon key pedagogical concepts, such as teacher cognition, the role of L2 task features, classroom interactional approaches, pedagogical intervention and socialisation, willingness to communicate (WTC), as well as other psychological and sociocultural factors. Taken together, the collection's findings and insights on pedagogical implications drawn from its empirical studies will help researchers and classroom practitioners to gain a thorough understanding of key issues related to silence in relevant and diverse educational contexts.

Silence: A Historical Sketch and Conceptualisations

Silence is an issue that touches all who teach. Whether encouraging reticent learners to participate or having to quieten the boisterous, silence plays a key role in educators' daily classroom practices. Silence in the L2 classroom has been perceived as a complex, ambiguous, yet meaningful communicative resource. Recent perspectives on classroom silence have shed light on the significant roles it has played in second language education, focusing on its varied roles across cultures and aiming to understand its often fuzzy and multilayered meanings and functions. This research has also considered a range of strategies for responding to silence, taking into account its ambiguity and different uses by learners and teachers alike, as well as exploring ways that silence might be utilised as a linguistic resource to facilitate learning.

Research since the early 1980s has tended to draw attention to culture-specific and group-based usages of silence through ethnographic studies, often from intercultural perspectives (e.g. Gilmore, 1985; Lebra, 1987; Philips, 1972; Saville-Troike, 1985). At a micro-level, sociocultural differences in the expected length and tolerance of pauses and silences have been extensively discussed from interactional perspectives (e.g. Scollon & Scollon, 1981; Tannen, 1985). At around the same time, further studies on classroom silence conceptualised it as a teacher's waiting time after posing a question or otherwise soliciting a response (e.g. Rowe, 1986; Shrum, 1985; see also Smith & King, 2017); these began to raise awareness of the facilitative role of silence in educational contexts as a pedagogical strategy for increasing the quality and quantity of learner talk. What was clear from this early work was that silence takes on a variety of forms, from the micro-silences of pauses and hesitations, to the macro-silences of non-participation in communicative events, through to the subtler silences of under-elaboration and topic avoidance.

Among these early studies, those focusing on the use of silence in intercultural communication offered an intriguing perspective on how silence fulfils various communicative roles, depending on the specific culture and communicative setting in which it occurs. The studies provided a fresh perspective on how misunderstandings can occur when participants from different cultural backgrounds interact. These misunderstandings can be traced to different cultural expectations and interpretations in the use of silence and talk during interaction (Lehtonen & Sajavaara, 1985; Nakane, 2012; Spencer-Oatey & Franklin, 2009; Tannen, 1985). While the length of pauses and silences in interaction can be a source of cultural misconceptions, the mismatch of expectation and tolerance of the pace of overall interaction, turn-taking practices and meanings attributed to communicative style can result in serious misunderstanding or negative stereotypes (Scollon & Scollon, 2012). For example, the ethnographic study by Scollon and Scollon (1981) found that Anglo-American English speakers considered the longer silences of Athabaskan Indian people to indicate that they were being uncooperative and therefore regarded this use of silence negatively, as a sign of interactional failure. The Athabaskans, on the other hand, considered the talkativeness of Anglo-American English speakers to be rude and aggressive. Similar interactional misconceptions are illustrated by Tannen (1985), who observed how the avoidance of silence during a Thanksgiving dinner by two New Yorkers of Jewish background was interpreted as dominance rather than cooperation in interaction by other participants from differing cultural backgrounds. Illustrating that the idea of the silent 'East' and talkative 'West' is a somewhat simplistic generalisation, longer uses of silence by Finnish people, when compared with Anglo-Americans, were reported by Lehtonen and Sajavaara in their 1985 study (see also Sajavaara & Lehtonen, 1997). Carbaugh (2005) argues that Finns may not intend to convey lack of interest in communication through the use of longer silences.

Tolerance of silence has been studied from intercultural perspectives in varied situational contexts. For example, in business settings, Yamada (1997) reported longer use of silence, lasting around five seconds, by the Japanese participants in a formal Japanese business meeting, compared with less than one second in the case of a US business meeting. Also in an intercultural business context, a lack of familiarity with other participants' communicative style was explored by Fujio (2004), who reported that Japanese managers tended to be able to tolerate longer silences than their North American colleagues, who saw silence as a sign of discomfort and frustration. Although few in number, some studies have been conducted on the use of silence in intercultural communication in wider sociocultural contexts and in other languages. Mushin and Gardner (2009) analysed inter-turn pauses among Garrwa language speakers from Aboriginal communities in Australia and found that a 1.5-second gap indicated trouble in communication. Interestingly, this seems to mirror Watts' (1997) conversation analysis of British interactants, in which he suggests 1.5 seconds is the central point on a continuum between 1.3 and 1.7 seconds, after which silence becomes marked (cf. Jefferson, 1989).

Looking at academic contexts, Turner and Hiraga's study (2003) on tacit interactional style and lack of initiation by Japanese international students in tutorial sessions in British academic contexts explored silence as a source of misunderstanding, in this case interpreted by UK academics as lack of willingness to communicate as part of study procedures. This finding mirrors Nakane's (2007) research, which explored the use of silence by Japanese overseas students in Australia and illustrates how their use of silence was interpreted in a negative way by Australian lecturers, who saw the absence of talk as a sign of withdrawal from interaction. Similarly, a study by Harumi (1999) illustrated British informants' negative interpretations of the video-recorded classroom silences displayed by Japanese learners of English, seeing them as signs of boredom or lack of interest.

Some non-Japanese English language teachers express the desire to have faster interactional exchanges with Japanese students; when these are not forthcoming, feelings of frustration can result (King, 2016b; Morris & King, 2018). This phenomenon is also reported by Harumi in Chapter 3 of this book. On the other hand, silence may be regarded as an invisible or unmarked phenomenon, as explored by Morita (2004) in a study on Asian students' academic discourse in a Canadian university. Morita illustrates how students actively negotiated multiple roles and identities in the classroom, even when they appeared passive or withdrawn. This reflects King and Aono's (2017: 494–495) idea of the 'active state of silence', in which learners may not be producing talk but are nevertheless cognitively engaged. In a recent study on silence in the intercultural collaboration of a Dutch and a Chinese university as part of a scientific international research project, the Dutch researchers attributed Chinese researchers' silence in everyday conversation to a lack of communication (Verouden & van der Sanden, 2018). For example, failing immediately to provide feedback or to reply to comments was interpreted as detrimental to collaboration when seen from a Dutch point of view, as was silencing the voices of subordinates (2018: 145). In Chapter 6 of this collection, Karas and Faez observe similar societal roles of teachers, who are seen as figures of authority in L2 classrooms, triggering the use of silence by learners in Chinese contexts.

Recognition of the crucial role that silence plays in the L2 classroom has also inspired research into multiple aspects of second language learning and amply demonstrates its relevance to evidence-based language teaching. Pioneering research outside the field of applied linguistics paved the way for methodologically and conceptually varied empirical L2-oriented studies from the 1990s onwards, which situated silent behaviour within various specific educational contexts. In particular, increasing attention was paid to reticent language learners in East Asia (e.g. Bao, 2014; Harumi, 2011; King, 2013a, 2013b; Liu, 2009; Tsui, 1996) as well as to overseas East Asian international students (e.g. Liu, 2002; Nakane, 2007).

A small number of scholars have chosen to explore the facilitative role of silence and learners' silent periods in mainstream and second language education (e.g. Granger, 2004; Jaworski & Sachdev, 1998; Li, 2001; Reda, 2009), while others have considered silence as an example of invisible pragmatic transfer which becomes a possible source of misunderstanding (Nakane, 2007). By focusing on silence's varied communicative and social meanings in L2 classrooms across cultures, a key theme to emerge in research is how participants' perceptions of silence may differ significantly. While some may interpret silence as a space for critical reflection and the absorption of content, others within the SLA community acknowledge that non-participatory silence by language learners has the potential to impede L2 development by limiting target language interaction and output. In light of this, an increasing number of studies have been carried out to seek better pedagogical practices aimed at enhancing the oral participation of silent learners (Talandis & Stout, 2015; Yashima *et al.*, 2016; Zhang & Head, 2010).

Given the historical development of research perspectives on silence, a growing body of recent studies on its role in second language education has applied varied perspectives on its conceptualisations (e.g. Bao, 2014; King, 2013a, 2013b; Smith & King, 2017, 2018) as both an inhibitive and a facilitative element in interaction. More specifically, Bao has stressed the need to draw attention to the distinctive roles of silence as a voluntary productive communicative resource able to enhance L2 learning opportunities as 'modes of learning' (Bao, 2014: 2) and of reticence as withdrawal from learning. Following this distinction between silence and reticence, this collection further conceptualises and approaches silence as a phenomenon through multiple formats.

Overview of the Collection: Understanding Contexts and Methodological Approaches

To close this introductory chapter, we illustrate the scope of the collection and provide a detailed overview of each individual study, further highlighting the rich variety of research that can be found in subsequent chapters by focusing on the role of context and methodological approaches in each study.

Awareness of the interaction between the use of silence and contextual factors is indispensable to an understanding of the nature of silence. Just as silence has been variously defined in this collection, there are also different ways to understanding context (see King, 2015) and its significance to the study of silence. In this collection there are three broad areas encompassing essential contextual factors, seen through analytical lenses which closely relate to the use of silence by learners in L2 classrooms: psychological, cultural and immediate educational settings. Below we illustrate why understanding context is essential to the exploration of silences, which serve as unmarked and invisible practices in L2 learning and discuss methodological approaches which have the potential to explore silence within multilayered contexts and to enhance learners' active participation in L2 learning.

The collection includes the following studies: an interpretive case study on the interplay of task complexity and Asian learner silence in an Australian university (Bao); conversational analysis of teacher talk and interaction with the silence of Japanese students learning English as a foreign language (EFL) (Harumi); a longitudinal intervention study aiming to enhance Japanese EFL learners' oral participation from a complexity perspective (King et al.); a mixed-methods study on anxiety and silence using a cognitive-behavioural model (Maher); a cognition study exploring Chinese language teachers' perceptions of silence and communicative language teaching (CLT) (Karas & Faez); a study on Japanese high-school learners' perceptions of their capacity to speak (CTS) (Humphries et al.) in EFL contexts; and an investigation from a dynamic systems perspective on the interplay of silence and willingness to communicate (WTC) in Chinese EFL classrooms (Peng). A final commentary on the collection is provided by Amy Tsui and Rintaro Imafuku.

In Chapter 2, the collection's first empirical contribution, Bao presents interpretive case studies examining task complexity and learner silence through in-depth interview data. These involved 10 postgraduate students from various East Asian backgrounds (Chinese, Mongolian, Korean and Japanese learners) in an Australian university, and explore the role of silence as a mode of learning. Bao conceptualises silence as a mode of learning by focusing on the nature of classroom tasks. This entails the examination of task orientation, differentiating modes of learning which involve talk, silence or something in-between (a kind of hybridity of talk and silence that can include inner, private speech), forming a sequence within the learning process. This study sheds light on the interaction between the nature of tasks and learner silence as immediate educational, contextual and cultural factors, revealing learners' inner-speech dynamics, manifested in the metacognitive process of self-discovery through the interview process. Bao's findings demonstrate a clear relationship between various aspects of tasks and learners' choice of verbal or reflective responses and he concludes that learners' preferred modes of participation involve reflection and articulation. Bao also explores learners' movement between these modes as part of the process of task design. The study also emphasises the essential role of teacher flexibility, supportive attitudes and innovative pedagogical strategies, which enhance learners' learning experience through the optimum engagement of tasks and also the need to improve task design. The investigation's insights into the interplay between task and silence urges a reappraisal of the significance of task design in teaching practice and the need for educators to understand learners' uses of silence.

In the collection's next chapter, Harumi employs a mixed-methods research design to focus on the silences which occur during dyadic interactions within EFL classrooms in Japanese universities. Harumi specifically examines the use of silence from an interactional perspective and conceptualises the facilitative role of silence as an interactional resource by engaging in microanalysis of turn-taking systems, mindful of the potential for learners to maintain interaction and achieve L2 output with the support of teachers in order to create space for learning in Japanese tertiary EFL contexts. In order to examine the role of teacher talk as a key immediate educational contextual and also cultural factor, her study uses questionnaires with open-ended items to investigate how teachers working in this context react to instances of silence when they encounter them. She discovers that, within her sample, some teachers had experienced a degree of discomfort resulting from different interactional norms on silence when experiencing silent episodes (cf. King & Aono, 2017) but, on the whole, did not perceive these episodes entirely negatively. The teachers revealed a variety of techniques for responding to silence: from increasing their wait time to five seconds, to providing further linguistic support for learners (e.g. in the manner of reformulations). Harumi's discussion of teachers' perceptions of learner silence within Japanese EFL contexts and their pedagogical approaches for dealing with it indicate that, in varying degrees, teachers are also aware of the cultural expectations of classroom interaction as it occurs within Japanese EFL classes. Echoing themes of social inhibition explored elsewhere in the book (e.g. King *et al.*, Chapter 4; Maher, Chapter 5), she observes that learners are extremely conscious of peer evaluation and that teachers use various strategies and responses to avoid pressurising learners to interact in English but also to support learner oral output. Taking the stance that silence (of more than one second) can be an interactional resource which has the potential to provide a shared space for learning, Harumi then delves deeper into student silence, wait time and teacher talk by using conversation analysis to scrutinise eight hours of classroom interaction video data. The study provides important empirical evidence of the pedagogical strategies and interactional patterns that accompany instances of silence within Japanese EFL tertiary contexts.

In order to tackle non-participatory learner silence from a psychological and complexity perspective, the longitudinal intervention study by King, Yashima, Humphries, Aubrey and Ikeda reported in Chapter 4 examines three key interrelated areas: students' anxiety coping strategies; the improvement of interpersonal dynamics and social collaboration among students; and encouragement to engage in target language interaction. In their study, silence has been defined as anxiety-driven social inhibition in the classroom and learners' avoidance of talk. This aspect of silence has been problematised as a social aspect of foreign language anxiety heavily influenced by group dynamics in Japanese tertiary contexts (King, 2014; King & Smith, 2017), suggesting the possibility of improved oral participation through pedagogical interventions which encourage improved peer relationships. Drawing data from structured classroom observations of 71 students and learners' self-report reflections, stimulated recall interviews and teacher reflections over the course of an academic semester, this study extensively explores the effects on classroom discourse of a multi-strategy intervention enhanced through socialisation strategies outside the classroom in addition to in-class activities. The findings suggest that key factors which trigger learner silence are learners' anxiety in the use of English and their social inhibition within immediate social groups. The study illustrates the overall improvement of social dynamics in the classroom after a series of interventions, which consequently enhanced learners' oral participation. This study also emphasises the significance of other factors, such as task demands, topic choice and teachers' roles in shaping classroom discourse participation. This innovative and insightful approach towards learner silence sheds light on the significant role of pedagogical interventions, both within and outside the classroom, which have the potential to improve social dynamics among learners and enhance their oral participation in the L2 classroom.

In Chapter 5, Maher also explores silence from a psychological perspective and presents an innovative study using concepts drawn from cognitive-behavioural theory (CBT), adopting a cognitive-behavioural model (King, 2014) to explore how an anxious student's thought patterns can be modified in such a way as to encourage a reduction in anxiety and a corresponding increase in oral participation in the target language. In this study, silence expressed as individual fear of verbal participation in L2 within a cycle of negative thoughts among university students in Japanese EFL contexts is explored. The chapter focuses on Mari (pseudonym), whose tendency to remain silent in her English language lesson while blushing, wringing her hands and keeping her head lowered caught the attention of Maher during a series of classroom observations conducted at a university in Japan. Maher recounts how she worked with Mari during a succession of CBT-style interviews to raise the student's awareness of how a negative cycle of thoughts, behaviours, emotions and bodily sensations was feeding her silent behaviour. The study suggests that confidence to speak can be built as students become more aware of such negative cycles and are encouraged to relate them to their core beliefs about language learning. Rather than suggesting that silently anxious learners are in some way mentally ill, the use of CBT-style interviews actually has the potential to empower students and liberate them from silent behaviour which they previously had no control over. This study therefore suggests that CBT-style interviews can be a useful tool for enhancing L2 participation. This approach not only reveals contextual factors which affect learners' psychological states and subsequent oral participation but also suggests ways to overcome obstacles by encouraging learners to set goals. Both Maher's research and King et al.'s in Chapter 4 deal with learner anxiety and illustrate that tackling silence-inducing affective factors is possible through focused interventions which facilitate social and psychological contextual improvement.

In Chapter 6, Karas and Faez investigate the role of silence in the CLT classroom from the perspectives of 91 Chinese pre-service teachers in Canada. They also consider both the macro- and the micro-level positive uses of silences using sociocultural, interactive and cognitive perspectives. This includes silence used to show respect for the teacher, reflecting sociocultural values in Chinese educational contexts at a societal level, as well as associated interactional values which involve allowing others to speak or time for cognitive processing and listening, acting as a productive approach to learning. They also explore the pros and cons of introducing CLT in China (cf. Jin & Cortazzi, 2002), and potential methods to support learners who prefer silent learning strategies in CLT classrooms. Thus, this study explores perspectives of Chinese teachers on the role of silence in the CLT classroom where the implementation of this pedagogical approach is considered problematic due to various impediments influenced by sociocultural beliefs and factors such as students' preference for silent learning strategies and societal expectations of teachers' roles. Despite practical constraints such as class size and the Chinese education system's focus on examinations, the participants' responses illustrate the productive use of silence in L2 learning, with its focus on group discussion and written reflection. However, by discussing pedagogical approaches as well as the post-writing reflections, teachers in their study were able to offer a range of pedagogical strategies which may be well suited to East Asian CLT classrooms. The participants' highly positive attitudes towards the use of silence and its productive role in L2 learning suggests that various strategies can be utilised to support silent learners in the CLT classroom. This study raises our awareness of the relevance of the practical pedagogical roles of learner silence, not only in China but also in other settings where similar issues persist, revealing the interplay between CLT used as a pedagogical approach and the uses of silence as a learning strategy. The study also illustrates the important role of teachers' perceptions in dealing with dilemmas and possibilities in L2 pedagogy (see also Harumi, Chapter 3) by reflecting on their own teaching contexts.

In contrast, Humphries, Akamatsu, Tanaka and Burns take a quite different approach in their study reported in Chapter 7, preferring to focus on student perceptions rather than on those of teachers. They make the valid point that research on learner silence has tended to focus on undergraduates, with pre-tertiary contexts relatively unexplored – a non-linguistics-oriented exception to this being Yoneyama's (2009) excellent investigation into silence as a form of resistance in Japanese high schools. Thus, the research they present here explores how Japanese high school students perceive their capacity to speak (CTS) English during various classroom activities, such as when responding to teachers' simple questions, engaging in group discussion, or reading aloud from a textbook. This study defines silence relative to the learners' CTS. It focuses on classroom situations and activities which directly influence the use of target language speech or silence within Japanese high school contexts. Humphries and his colleagues adopt a structural equation modelling (SEM) approach to test the influence of contextual factors through an online survey, and find that confidence and classroom support are the key factors which influenced their participants' CTS. Their study emphasises the need to nurture learners' confidence to enable them to progress in target language oral participation. Using an online questionnaire, data were gathered from 260 participants attending five different high schools to provide insights into the kinds of target language activities that learners believed either helped or hindered them in speaking English in class. By looking at levels of structure and preparation time for speaking activities, the study also indicates that cognitively demanding activities can induce more silent responses. Interestingly, the survey's findings play down the role that motivation and anxiety play in learner silence and instead emphasise the importance of confidence and classroom support for encouraging talk in the classroom.

Turning to the role of immediate educational contextual factors, two studies in this collection (Bao, Chapter 2; Humphries *et al.*, Chapter 7) explore the central roles of tasks and activities in dealing with classroom silence. These are the immediate contextual factors which teachers encounter directly and constantly in daily teaching practice. These studies suggest that the type of task and its nature can significantly influence the learner's choice of responses (cf. Yashima *et al.*, 2016) and emphasise the need for teachers to be aware of this when dealing with silence. Further, Harumi's conversational analytic study reported in Chapter 3 explores the ways teachers respond to learner silence and also further support their L2 output by utilising various types of responses, including calibrated wait time. These three chapters, which explore the immediate classroom educational contextual factors outlined above, demonstrate the crucial role that activities and teachers play during silence events and emphasise the need for teachers to listen to silence within the moment-to-moment shifting interactions of the classroom so as to better understand and respond to students' needs.

The next chapter in the collection is Peng's partial replication of King's (2013a, 2013b) study which used structured observation to measure the levels of oral participation and silence within EFL classrooms from a psychological perspective. Peng's investigation explores how silence and a lack of willingness to communicate (see MacIntyre et al., 1998) interact as two separate systems serving to drive Chinese learners of English towards various discourse behaviours within the L2 classroom. Peng examines the interplay of two essential concepts: on the one hand, willingness to communicate, seen as readiness to contribute to verbal participation; and on the other, silence perceived as reticence in Chinese university learning environments. Thus, in this study Peng considers that 'exploring the interplay of WTC and silence as two complex dynamic systems in the L2 class can unveil a fuller picture of students' classroom communication psychology' (Peng, this volume, p. 146). Peng employs the Classroom Oral Participation Scheme (COPS) instrument (see also King et al., Chapter 4; Maher, Chapter 5) to good effect in order to form a picture of classroom discourse patterns within three Chinese university English language classrooms. Silence and the construct of second language willingness to communicate (L2 WTC) are intimately linked and Peng's ambitious research attempts to study the two phenomena in an integrated, contextually sensitive manner. Her study uses data from multiple sources: students' own appraisals of their WTC, structured classroom observation and also interviews. This study defines five types of silence, which Peng suggests form together in a psychological tapestry in which silence can interact with complex psychological parameters. Drawing on data from classroom transcripts, student self-reports of dynamically changing WTC levels and stimulated recall interviews with learners following specific silent episodes, the research helps to uncover the complex relationship between Chinese students' L2 WTC, silence and situated classroom communication psychology.

Rounding off this collection of *East Asian Perspectives on Silence in English Language Education* is Tsui and Imafuku's concluding chapter, which takes stock of the empirical studies described above and highlights the shared themes, particularly relating to sociocultural values, that are apparent across the collection's papers. Viewing 'classroom silence' through the prism of learner reticence, they argue that our collection provides further evidence of the complexity of L2 learner and teacher silence and call for more longitudinal research on the complex interplay of factors which shape oral participation in educational contexts. To illustrate this point, Tsui and Imafuku draw upon data from a longitudinal study of the participation of individual students attending tutorials at a Japanese university and discuss parallels between their own findings in this L1 context and findings in the collection's L2-focused studies, emphasising the role that social dynamics play in shaping learner silence.

Thus, the definitions of silence in this collection clearly demonstrate great diversity in the way silence is conceptualised. As we emphasise above, the nature of silence is complex, multidimensional and fuzzy in L2 learning contexts. However, this variety of definitions works to illustrate how silence can be demystified when conceptualisation, observation and analysis are carefully applied. Whether or not silence is considered an inhibitive or facilitative element in L2 learning, these studies share an understanding that silence can be conceptualised as a significant part of learners' engagement in L2 learning, and can thus be 'viewed in ways of participating in situated practices' (Taguchi, 2015: 7). Moreover, another commonly recognised feature of silence illustrated in this book is the way it can function as a fuzzy process of learning which may involve shifting silent learning styles and transitions of attitudes and perceptions which are shaped by sociocultural interactional exchanges within L2 classrooms and beyond. This begs the question: how can we apply these different perspectives on silence to specific learning and teaching practice situations? To shed some light on this, we have discussed the role of contextual factors in how silence has been defined in the collection, by looking at the way each study explores silence from various methodological perspectives in order to deepen understanding of its use and also to enhance L2 learning within each context.

Self-reflection/Discussion Questions

(1) Have you experienced silence in your daily life recently? What was the situation and who else was present? How did the silence make you feel? Do you think it signified anything? If so, what?
(2) This chapter discusses the various ways in which silence can be defined. Think about a language-learning setting that you are familiar with. How would you define the silence that occurs in this setting? Do you see it as a negative or a positive phenomenon? Why?
(3) Some people believe there is a dichotomy with the silent East on one side and the garrulous West on the other. What do you think of this idea? Is it just a gross generalisation or do you think there is some truth to it? When discussing your ideas, think carefully about the context in which silences may occur.
(4) This chapter deliberates on the difficulties associated with effectively researching the ambiguous phenomenon of language-learner silence. Think about a language-education setting that you are familiar with. What are your ideas about the best ways to research silence in that particular context?

Recommended Reading

Edited volumes which focus on the topic of silence are, without doubt, few and far between. Two that are worth consulting are as follows:

Tannen, D. and Saville-Troike, M. (eds) (1985) *Perspectives on Silence*. Norwood, NJ: Ablex.

Despite its age, Tannen and Saville-Troike's book is often cited, as it contains a fascinating collection of still-relevant studies on the role of silence in human communication. Look out in particular for Gilmore's study of silence and sulking within a US high school, and Lehtonen and Sajavaara's contemplation of 'the silent Finn'.

Jaworski, A. (ed.) (1997) *Silence: Interdisciplinary Perspectives*. Berlin: Mouton de Gruyter.

Jaworski's book looks at silence across an exceptionally wide range of genres and domains. Chapters include discussions relating to how silence connects with such diverse areas as fine art, religion, literature, music and professional discourse. A highlight is Sifianou's chapter, which considers the role of silence in expressing politeness during Greek and English interactions. Some of her ideas have relevance for the L2 classroom in certain East Asian contexts.

References

Bao, D. (2014) *Understanding Silence and Reticence*. London: Bloomsbury.
Carbaugh, D.A. (2005) *Cultures in Conversation*. Mahwah, NJ: Lawrence Erlbaum.
Fujio, M. (2004) Silence during intercultural communication: A case study. *Corporate Communications* 9, 331–338.
Gilmore, P. (1985) Silence and sulking: Emotional displays in the classroom. In D. Tannen and M. Saville-Troike (eds) *Perspectives on Silence* (pp. 139–162). Norwood, NJ: Ablex.
Granger, C. (2004) *Silence in Second Language Learning: A Psychoanalytic Reading*. Clevedon: Multilingual Matters.
Harumi, S. (1999) The use of silence by Japanese learners of English in cross-cultural communication and its pedagogical implication. Unpublished PhD thesis, University of London.
Harumi, S. (2011) Classroom silence: Voices from Japanese EFL learners. *ELT Journal* 65 (3), 260–269.
Jaworski, A. and Sachdev, I. (1998) Beliefs about silence in the classroom. *Language and Education* 12 (4), 273–292.
Jefferson, G. (1989) Preliminary notes on a possible metric which provides for a 'standard maximum' silence of approximately one second in conversation. In D. Roger and P. Bull (eds) *Conversation: An Interdisciplinary Perspective* (pp. 166–196). Clevedon: Multilingual Matters.
Jin, L. and Cortazzi, M. (2002) English language teaching in China: A bridge to the future. *Asia Pacific Journal of Education* 22 (2), 53–64.
King, J. (2013a) *Silence in the Second Language Classroom*. Basingstoke: Palgrave Macmillan.
King, J. (2013b) Silence in the second language classrooms of Japanese universities. *Applied Linguistics* 34 (3), 325–434.
King, J. (2014) Fear of the true self: Social anxiety and the silent behaviour of Japanese learners of English. In K. Csizér and M. Magid (eds) *The Impact of Self-concept on Language Learning* (pp. 232–249). Bristol: Multilingual Matters.
King, J. (2015) An introduction to the dynamic interplay between context and the language learner. In J. King (ed.) *The Dynamic Interplay Between Context and the Language Learner* (pp. 1–10). Basingstoke: Palgrave Macmillan.

King, J. (2016a) Do I lose if I talk? Silence in higher education in Japan and the UK. Invited talk, Japan Foundation, 16 November, London, UK.
King, J. (2016b) 'It's time, put on the smile, it's time!' The emotional labour of second language teaching within a Japanese university. In C. Gkonou, D. Tatzl and S. Mercer (eds) *New Directions in Language Learning Psychology* (pp. 97–112). Dordrecht: Springer.
King, J. and Aono, A. (2017) Talk, silence and anxiety during one-to-one tutorials: A cross-cultural comparative study of Japan and UK undergraduates' tolerance of silence. *Asia Pacific Education Review* 18 (4), 489–499.
King, J. and Smith, L. (2017) Social anxiety and silence in Japan's tertiary foreign language classrooms. In C. Gkonou, M. Daubney and J.-M. Dewaele (eds) *New Insights into Language Anxiety: Theory, Research and Educational Implications* (pp. 92–110). Bristol: Multilingual Matters.
Lebra, T.S. (1987) The cultural significance of silence in Japanese communication. *Multilingua* 6 (4), 343–357.
Lehtonen, J. and Sajavaara, K. (1985) The silent Fin. In D. Tannen and M. Saville-Troike (eds) *Perspectives on Silence* (pp. 193–204). Norwood, NJ: Ablex.
Li, H. (2001) Silences and silencing silences. In *Philosophy of Education Studies Yearbook* (pp. 157–165). Champaign, IL: University of Illinois Press.
Liu, J. (2002) Negotiating silence in American classrooms: Three Chinese cases. *Language and Intercultural Communication* 2 (1), 37–54.
Liu, M. (2009) *Reticence and Anxiety in Oral English Lessons*. Bern: Peter Lang.
MacIntyre, P., Clément, R., Dörnyei, Z. and Noels, K. (1998) Conceptualizing willingness to communicate in a L2: A situated model of confidence and affiliation. *Modern Language Journal* 82, 545–562.
Morita, N. (2004) Discourse socialization through oral classroom activities in a TESL graduate program. *TESOL Quarterly* 42, 541–566.
Morris, S. and King, J. (2018) Teacher frustration and emotional labour of second language teaching. In S. Mercer and K. Kostoulas (eds) *Language Teacher Psychology* (pp. 141–157). Bristol: Multilingual Matters.
Mushin, I. and Gardner, R. (2009) Silence is talk: Conversational silence in Australian Aboriginal talk-in-interaction. *Journal of Pragmatics* 41 (10), 2033–2052.
Nakane, I. (2007) *Silence in Intercultural Communication: Perceptions and Performance in the Classroom*. Amsterdam: John Benjamins.
Nakane, I. (2012) Silence. In C.B. Paulston, S.F. Kiesling and S. Rangel (eds) *The Handbook of Intercultural Discourse and Communication* (pp. 158–179). Oxford: Blackwell.
Philips, S.U. (1972) Participant structures and communicative competence: Warm Springs children in community and classroom. In C.B. Cazden, V.P. John and D. Hymes (eds) *Functions of Language in the Classroom* (pp. 370–394). Prospect Heights, IL: Waveland Press.
Reda, M.M. (2009) *Between Speaking and Silence: A Study of Quiet Students*. Albany, NY: State University of New York Press.
Rowe, M.B. (1986) Wait time: Slowing down may be a way of speeding up! *Journal of Teacher Education* 37 (1), 43–50.
Sajavaara, K. and Lehtonen, J. (1997) The silent Finn revisited. In A. Jaworski (ed.) *Silence: Interdisciplinary Perspectives* (pp. 263–283). Berlin: Mouton de Gruyter.
Saville-Troike, M. (1985) The place of silence in an integrated theory of communication. In D. Tannen and M. Saville-Troike (eds) *Perspectives on Silence* (pp. 3–18). Norwood, NJ: Ablex.
Scollon, R. and Scollon, S. (1981) *Narrative, Literacy, and Face in Interethnic Communication*. Norwood, NJ: Ablex.
Scollon, R. and Scollon, S. (2012) *Intercultural Communication: A Discourse Approach*. Oxford: Wiley-Blackwell.

Shrum, J.L. (1985) Wait-time and the use of target or native languages. *Foreign Language Annals* 18 (4), 305–314.

Smith, L. and King, J. (2017) A dynamic systems approach to wait time in the second language classroom. *System* 68, 1–14.

Smith, L. and King, J. (2018) Silence in the foreign language classroom: The emotional challenges for L2 teachers. In J.D. Martinez Agudo (ed.) *Emotions in Second Language Teaching* (pp. 323–340). Dordrecht: Springer.

Spencer-Oatey, H. and Franklin, P. (2009) *Intercultural Interaction: A Multidisciplinary Approach to Intercultural Communication*. Basingstoke: Palgrave Macmillan.

Taguchi, N. (2015) *Developing Interactional Competence in a Japanese Study Abroad Context*. Bristol: Multilingual Matters.

Talandis Jr, G. and Stout, M. (2015) Getting EFL students to speak: An action research approach. *ELT Journal* 69 (1), 11–25.

Tannen, D. (1985) Silence: Anything but. In D. Tannen and M. Saville-Troike (eds) *Perspectives on Silence* (pp. 93–11). Norwood, NJ: Ablex.

Tsui, A. (1996) Reticence and second language anxiety. In K. Bailey and D. Nunan (eds) *Voices from the Language Classroom* (pp. 145–167). New York: Cambridge University Press.

Turner, J. and Hiraga, M. (2003) Misunderstanding teaching and learning. In J. House, G. Kasper and S. Ross (eds) *Misunderstandings in Social Life: Discourse Approaches to Problematic Talk*. London: Pearson Education.

Verouden, N.W. and van der Sanden, M.C.A. (2018) Silence in intercultural collaboration: A Sino-Dutch research centre. *Advances in Applied Sociology* 8, 125–151.

Watts, R.J. (1997) Silence and the acquisition of status in verbal interaction. In A. Jaworski (ed.) *Silence: Interdisciplinary Perspectives* (pp. 87–115). Berlin: Mouton de Gruyter.

Yamada, H. (1997) *Different Games, Different Rules: Why American and Japanese Misunderstand Each Other*. New York: Oxford University Press.

Yashima, T., Ikeda, M. and Nakahira, S. (2016) Talk and silence in an EFL classroom: Interplay of learners and context. In J. King (ed.) *The Dynamic Interplay Between Context and the Language Learner* (pp. 104–126). Basingstoke: Palgrave Macmillan.

Yoneyama, S. (1999) *The Japanese High School: Silence and Resistance*. New York: Routledge.

Zhang, X. and Head, K. (2010) Dealing with learner reticence in the speaking class. *ELT Journal* 64 (1), 1–9.

2 Silence, Talk and In-betweens: East Asian Students' Responses to Task Challenge in an Australian University

Dat Bao

> Silence can be colonized by talk, of course, but meaning cannot.
> Zembylas and Michaelides (2004: 207)

Introduction

The epigraph suggests that while talk might dominate as an utterance system, silence can operate as a productive system of its own. In many cases, the structure of silence between talk intervals that enhances articulation. Because of this, in reviewing silence, it would be unreasonable to remove talk from the background of the discussion, simply because without the presence of talk, one cannot recognise how silence occurs. This project investigates students' ways of responding to classroom tasks and documents their justification when a decision on participating modes is made. Based on this, recommendations are offered on task design. Being able to comprehend the rationale behind decisions to cope with a task will benefit tasks in optimising students' learning strengths.

To understand classroom silence is one step forward in uncovering the learning mechanism. As educators, we need to 'hear' and interpret silence attentively, not only from experience but also on the foundation of research, without which we might, in the words of Zembylas and Michaelides (2004: 207), happen to conduct 'teaching with ignorance'. Although the current discourse has expressed appreciation for the silent mode of learning (see, for example, Creelman, 2017) and has recognised students' choices to be either silent or verbal, not much research has unpacked the process of students' verbal or non-verbal behaviour as tactically influenced by task characteristics. This chapter responds to this gap through an empirical project that sheds light on the relationship between the nature of the task and students' responses in either spoken or reflective ways.

Research Focus

The project examines students' perceptions, attitudes and experiences in coping with the classroom tasks, which are related to both language learning and subject content. The study includes three main research questions:

(1) What kinds of classroom task tend to trigger more silent processing from students? Why?
(2) What kinds of classroom task tend to elicit more spontaneous verbal responses from students? Why?
(3) Does tension occur, during students' task performance, in the choice between the silent and verbal learning modes? How?

Discourse on Silence and Tasks

Historically, as far as task dynamics is concerned, verbal participation has received more favourable attention than silent behaviour across many educational settings. While theories related to task performance, including the interaction hypothesis (Long, 1996), peer interactive tasks (Ohta, 2001) and teacher–learner communication (Hall & Walsh, 2002), analyse the complexity of talk in detailed components such as initiation, guidance and response, learners' inner-speech dynamics has been largely ignored. Although classroom discussion in many educational settings privileges a more verbal over a silent form of engagement, recent research discourse in silence studies has recognised the productive use of both talk and silence (see, for example, Bao, 2014) and has confronted the hierarchy regarding which of the two modes is superior in the learning process.

In much discourse on second language acquisition (SLA), it is talk, not silence, that receives recognition as language output. However, to assume that output must always be audible or visible represents a narrow way of understanding learners' progression. Depending on how silence is employed, the occurrence of inner speech in the learner's system deserves to be viewed as a type of production, especially when ideas or thoughts are taking shape in the mind. According to Innocenti (2002: 62), the words that form our inner speech, before being spoken out loud, exist as auditory or visual information in our consciousness. Ridgway (2009: 49) also observes that 'thinking in a language provides practice which is arguably as good as speaking it. Processes as important as automatization continue to operate and one's proficiency continues to develop.' Such silent incubation of ideas is, in fact, common among students. Research has provided evidence that many students practise spontaneously speaking to themselves for years without realising that they have such skills and habits (De Guerrero, 1991). These observations and insights suggest that learners' mental processes do produce output that needs to be explored through further research. How the proactive mind copes with the everyday classroom task has yet to be fully understood.

One clear example of meaningfully employed silence, in relation to tasks, is narrated in a research study by Ollin (2008), in which the researcher realised that many students need more processing time, especially when they are exposed to new experiences. What happens during such moments is that students work out ways to settle in by absorbing information, coordinating the hands and the brain, enjoying the involvement, and not wishing to be interrupted. In another study, Carless (2004) reported a thought-provoking incident when primary school students resisted talk for a good reason and decided to work in silence. During a lesson, the teacher gave students a survey form and asked them to verbally exchange information about how their friends travelled to school every day. Most students in that class went to school on foot and this was already known to them all. As a result, many did not find any use in talking. Instead, they quietly wrote down the answer on the survey sheet. Silence in this case was authentically employed, simply because there was no rationale for talking. These anecdotes demonstrate that task construction is not always about serving verbal interaction but should take into account when learners need to speak and when they do not need to. In many cases, it is the purpose of a task that decides the responding mode. Such dynamics deserve more research effort since, at the moment, the field of silence studies does not have adequate knowledge in this area.

According to German psychologist and philosopher Wilhelm Wundt (1832–1920), language is a mental product comprising two dimensions: an internal domain and an outer domain. The internal domain handles a mental process filled with imageries and silent speech (Reisberg *et al.*, 1991), which then get transformed into linguistic elements (Segalowitz & Trofimovich, 2012). Since language production is heavily monitored by the inner formulation system, focusing on speech production alone would amount to only a partial understanding of output. While silent formulation of ideas supports verbal articulation, which is a logical pattern outlined in the speech production model proposed by Levelt (1989), little in SLA research has documented how preverbal messages are processed in the mind. The research gap gets wider when it comes to how silence functions in response to the multidimensional dynamics of task types.

The process of mental rehearsal, according to empirical research by De Guerrero (1991), has seven characteristics: it can be ideational (creating thoughts), mnemonic (memorising or retrieving words from memory), textual (organising structure of a text), instructional (applying linguistic rules), evaluative (monitoring and self-correcting language), interpersonal (visualising how to talk with others) and intrapersonal (practising inner speech). Although this analysis provides a helpful understanding of how the mind works in silence, for a long time little scholarly effort has been made to connect these functions with task events. While the connection between silence and tasks has been widely acknowledged, in-depth research into the procedural dynamics of this relationship remains uncommon.

Contextualisation is another helpful element in our understanding of how silence occurs during task performance. In a large-scale study by King (2013b) in Japanese university settings, it was realised that silence occurs rather unproductively, a phenomenon that is closely connected to the culture of the system. Students in the study were noticed to disengage, feel confused, leave the talking responsibility to the lecturer, withdraw into themselves and keep to their own cliques. Such behaviour, however, might not be stable across all contexts. Researchers have noted that when silence is shifted to a different setting, such as Australia, where task performance is expected to embrace more verbal involvement, many Japanese students negotiate their silent behaviour either by opening up more than when they are in Japan or by employing silence in more strategic ways. Such observations have been documented, for example, by Nakane (2007), who emphasises the need to reconstruct and reinterpret silence within its cultural context, and by Bao (2014), who recognises how the practice of harmony becomes negotiated: if harmony requires quietness in the Japanese context, to achieve harmony in the Australian context might require more verbal effort so that one can fit into the social environment. The present project is founded upon the awareness that learners' response to classroom tasks is a question of both individual preferences and the sociocultural environment. The discussion also appeals for teachers' thoughtful tolerance and understanding of individual choices when it comes to students' favourite learning modes and resources.

In examining the connection between silence and task, the current discourse has also recognised a distinction between on-task and off-task silence. The former often has meaningful purpose, serving what Harumi (2010: 268) refers to as 'reflective or interpretative tasks'; the latter tends to represent boredom and inattention, which is sometimes known as the silence of disengagement (King, 2013a). Within the humble body of literature on the silence–task relationship, classroom silence has been examined from an ecological perspective and with narrative references to task characteristics (see, for example, King, 2016; Svalberg & Askham, 2013; Yashima et al., 2013). One example of tasks that involve silence, provided by King (2013a), is non-verbal activities which do not require verbalisation, such as listening to audio or performing silent reflection during a task.

Understanding silence with connection to task design is important because, as Stickler et al. (2007) explain, task design has a strong influence on the amount of speaking or non-speaking participation. It has been argued that the impact of a task can be altered by facilitating or constraining factors in the classroom situation (Messick, 1989). For instance, allowing time for rehearsal is a supporting factor that would pave the way for more open discussion (Yashima et al., 2013). Scholars such as King (2016); Svalberg and Askham (2013) and Yashima et al. (2013), among others, based on empirical research have recognised task design and group dynamics as influential factors in how much students remain silent. For example, tasks might generate silence due to learning difficulty (Svalberg & Askham, 2013). In many cases, even when tasks are developed with a spoken focus in mind, classroom situations might change their nature. For instance, it might be difficult for a class to share thoughts when students do not know each other well enough (Yashima et al., 2013) or when peers already know information about each other and there is no need to find out any more (Carless, 2004). Such silent responses might not benefit L2 development (see, for example, King, 2016; Mackey, 2002).

Participants

The study involved 10 postgraduate students from various East Asian backgrounds attending an Australian university. The reason for selecting these participants was that many lecturers had remarked that these students' classroom behaviour seemed strikingly different from that of their Australian counterparts. While many other groups such as European, North American, Latino American, South Asian, Australian, New Zealander and Pacific Islander students seemed to get along during classroom discussion in verbal communication and spontaneous talk, many East Asians were noticed to exercise more caution in spoken participation. To explore how this target group coped with classroom tasks would assist teachers in inclusive pedagogy, with a special focus on task design and task management.

Recruitment to the project was voluntary – participants were those who wished to join it. The small sample allows for qualitative analysis rather than representative significance. The choice of postgraduate level comes from the researcher's workplace and access to students, but it was also hoped that participants' rich experience and thinking maturity (they were pursuing an advanced academic degree) could help bring complex, thoughtful data into the study. The selection of four groups of nationalities, rather than one, came from the need for diverse participant backgrounds to give a variety of perspectives. To maintain some degree of regional consistency in sampling, mainly East Asian students were involved, rather than a scattered sampling with 10 participants from various continents. In the selection process, there were no biased or stereotypical assumptions by the researcher that these groups of participants would be silent learners. As the data will show, participants demonstrated a variety of verbal and non-verbal preferences in their learning styles.

The 10 participants included three Chinese students (Cheng, Lainie and Ranran), three Japanese (Masae, Sayo and Setsuko), three Korean (Areum, Insuk and Sujo) and one Mongolian (Baasanjav) student, who were pursuing a master's degree in education at various Australian universities. They shared similar experiences in using English as the target language in the Australian academic context. The sample comprised one man and nine women, aged between 25 and 50 years. They all had had higher education experiences both in their own countries and in Australia. Hopefully, with academic history that stretches beyond one educational setting, their reflection on the learning process might take on some degree of contextual complexity.

Research Methodology

This study, which takes a phenomenological stance through investigation of learners' experience and reflection on it, attempts to bring intuitive ways of behaving to the surface of consciousness. The data embrace metacognitive clarification of participants' perceptions, thoughts, awareness, emotions and other aspects of how the mind copes with classroom tasks both in words and in silent thinking. The research procedure involves documenting participants' description of their experience from the first-person point of view, contextualising such narratives in participants' context of both their classroom and the broader academic setting, and analysing data to seek patterns, issues and influential factors in both silent and verbal practice.

The project employed a semi-structured interview as the primary data-collection tool and utilised interpretive discourse analysis, in the words of Denzin and Lincoln (2011: 4), to 'make the world visible'. One semi-structured interview was conducted with each individual participant, who shared thoughts on how their verbal and silent learning modes worked together in response to classroom tasks. Data are analysed from participant's viewpoints with comments from the researcher's scholarly knowledge. Methods of analysis and interpretation are inspired by Creswell (2008) for in-depth exploration of individuals, Moran (2000) and Sokolowski (2000) in the need to position participants' views in their own context, and Merriam (2009) in respecting how participants experience and make sense of the world around them.

Data Collection

Ten in-depth interviews were conducted, either in a face-to-face setting, mostly on a university campus, or in an online mode such as email communication, depending on whether participants were in Australia or overseas at the time of data collection. No classroom observation was conducted. Participants were invited to share their overall experience with tasks as much as they could recollect. The focus was on how they would cope with tasks, without having to remember any definite time frame and without having to mention any particular lesson or type of class (for example, the class did not have to be a language or English class but could be of any academic content). Three main questions were planned for each interview. They were the same as mentioned in the section 'Research focus' presented above, that is: what task types trigger more silent processing, what task types trigger more verbal responses, and when does tension occur between the choices to speak or to remain silent?

Due to the complex content and intellectual nature of the data, the sessions became mentally demanding as participants engaged with psycholinguistic, cognitive and meta-cognitive processes regarding how the mind functions to optimise learning efficiency. Interviewees not only scrutinised their own learning system but also envisaged how that system tactically interacted with task characteristics. On the foundation of academic ethics, when stressful moments took place during data collection, the researcher would invite the participant to take a break or consider quitting the session altogether. In the end, while most of the participants performed their best to provide personal insights, two of them, feeling intellectually worn out, seemed to oversimplify their responses in the second half of the interview. This behaviour was shown during face-to-face interviews when participants reduced the length of their answers; when that happened, the researcher would try to close the discussion as soon as possible. In an online interview setting, such as via email or on a chat application, when participants systematically began to type shorter answers, the researcher understood that it could be about time to try to close the conversation.

Data Presentation and Discussion

Table 2.1 documents the dynamic relationship between the silence–talk decision and task types. The table has three components: a list of task types, students' preference for learning mode in each, and the most common responses to each of the task types. This section provides detailed explanation of how these components are presented in Table 2.1.

First, the 'task types' column lists activities that emerged during the interview. Some of these tasks were mentioned by the researcher to explore how participants coped with various tasks; others were brought up by the participants themselves as they reflected on their own experience. In other words, the various task types were contributed by both the interviewer and the interviewees. Such mention of tasks mainly served to facilitate discussion rather than to present any organised system of task design. The shade coding on these tasks shows the main response from students, indicating that the activity may be performed through talk (light grey), silence (light grey), both talk and silence (dark grey), changeable modes or uncertainty about which mode to select (white). For example, the white shade (such as in the case of Sayo) shows that the participant's responses to tasks tended to vary with regard to whether activities should

Table 2.1 Students' talk–silence preferences in task performance

No.	Task types	Cheng (Chin.)	Lainie (Chin.)	Ranran (Chin.)	Masae (Jap.)	Sayo (Jap.)	Setsuko (Jap.)	Aerum (Kor.)	Insuk (Kor.)	Sujo (Kor.)	Baasanjav (Mong.)
1	Fluency tasks, tasks for oral development, spontaneous tasks	0	T	T-S	T	T	T	T-S	T	T	T
2	Rehearsal tasks for oral presentation	0	T-S	T	T	T	T	T-S	S-T	T-S	T-S
3	Exploratory tasks that involve discussion	T	S	T-S	T	T	T	T-S	T	T	T
4	Communication and feedback tasks	T	T	T	T	T	T-S	T-S	T	T	T
5	Collaborative projects (poster, video, summary)	0	T	T	T	T	T	T	S	T-S	T
6	Independent tasks (reading, answering questions)	S	T	S	S	S	S	S	S	S	T-S
7	Pre-task – preparations, gathering information	0	T	S	S	S	S	S	S	S	S
8	Post-tasks/follow-up tasks for sharing further thoughts	0	S	T-S	S	T	T	T	S-T	T	T
9	Deductive tasks – form-focused grammar exercises	0	T	S	S	S	T	S	S	T-S	S
10	Discovery/inductive tasks – noticing or generating rules	0	T	S	S	S	S	T-S	S	S	T-S
11	Creative/problem-solving tasks – choice, preferences, attitudes, viewpoints, solutions	T-S	T	T-S	S	S	T	T-S	S-T	T-S	T-S
12	Other: group report, movie or book discussion, video project, forum discussion, excursion, gallery or museum visit	T-S	0	T-S	0	T-S	0	T-S	S-T	T	T

T = Talk; S = Silence; T – S = Talk and silence;* S – T = Silence and talk;* 0 = No particular preference.
Shading codes that denote preferences:
Light grey: Either talk or Silence; Dark grey: Talk and Silence/Silence and talk; White: Uncertain about choices.

*'Talk and silence' and 'Silence and talk' are participants' words indicating sequences.

be conducted mainly in talk or in silence. The white shade also indicates that students did not respond to the item, as they felt unsure about what to say or when they failed to remember how they coped with a certain task during actual classroom events.

The second component denotes students' preferences for learning modes. The shade code on each of the participants' names show us whether the student preferred to employ silence (light grey), talk (light grey), or both (dark grey); and in one case (Sayo), preferred one or the other without mixing these modes together (white).

The third component represents the most selected response to each of the task types, that is, to employ silence or talk, or a blend of both modes. Interestingly, there is clear disparity among students in how they responded to a task. Take problem-solving tasks as an example (in row 11), which is highlighted in dark grey to suggest mixed responses. While two students (Sayo and Masae, both Japanese) preferred to solve a problem mostly in silence, two others (Lainie, Chinese, and Setsuko, Japanese) wished to deal with this task type by talking aloud, while six students (Cheng and Ranran, Chinese; Areum, Insuk and Sujo, Korean; and Baasanjav, Mongolian) wanted to deal with a problem by performing both in silence and talking. To sum up, these three components shape the initial overview of the data. More in-depth, qualitative analysis will be discussed in the next section.

Classroom tasks that trigger silent processing

Four types of task that facilitate the silent learning mode are independent tasks (which allow students to work individually without much exchange of ideas, such as reading and writing work), pre-tasks or preparations (which involve gathering of information from the internet, reflecting on one's own experiences, making choices based on preferences, and noting down comments), deductive tasks (which involve written responses to form-focused language exercises) and discovery or deductive tasks (which require observing and thinking to draw on rules, functions and methods).

Some common features among these task types include offering personal space and wait time, not requiring peer interaction, challenging the mind, inviting personal reflection, asking for a written response and organising the cognitive processing of rules or methods. Such instructions encourage students to work alone and produce output such as a written summary, an idea, an account of experience or solutions to problems. As Sujo reveals: 'Tasks with thoughtful, complex and demanding content will keep me in quiet thinking; those that require formal presentation in front of the class also prompt me to prepare my ideas in silence.'

Classroom tasks that elicit verbalisation

Five task types that require more talk include fluency tasks (which involve spontaneous responses for verbal skills development), exploratory tasks (which involve peer discussion), communication and feedback tasks (which involve mutual support), collaborative projects (such as producing a poster, a video clip or a summary) and post-tasks (which follow up a main task for sharing further thoughts). The common characteristic of these activities is that they involve collaborating with classmates rather than functioning alone, with clear emphasis on fluency, rehearsal, communication, collaboration and sharing. They prompt talk by requiring quick, spontaneous answers or reactions, which focus on the process rather than outcome and are often not of a cognitively demanding type. As Sujo and Areum (Korean) elaborate, tasks that match their knowledge and experience will give them the confidence to speak out more. Tasks of an informal nature that require no right or wrong answer also make them feel relaxed enough to participate.

Classroom tasks that involve both silence and talk

Tasks that involve both modes of response often contain various layers or components, which require alternation between silence and talk. It is important to note that participants' responses tend to indicate two different sequences of combination between silence and talk: sometimes talk comes first but at other times silence does so. To make this distinction in the data, the two expressions 'Talk–Silence' and 'Silence–Talk' in this chapter often do not mean the same thing. For example, a rehearsal activity for oral presentation will require silent work to be followed by speech. A discussion task with a follow-up reflection component might require some talk first and then silent thinking later. A problem-solving task might demand some thinking time before good ideas can be shared with peers.

Other tasks that might involve both silence and talk at different stages are exchanges of attitudes, viewpoints, preferences and experiences. Other group-based activities and team projects, such as making a movie or a poster, or joining a trip, also take place through both individual thinking and peer consultation. Compared with activities that require an immediate response, these types demand team cooperation and mutual feedback; they also involve extended durations of time and multiple steps to be completed. In general, activities of a multi-component nature and activities with a focus on both process and outcome are likely to engage students in both learning modes.

Silence is often employed for processing input and for practising internal speech, which is a common pattern whereby content comprehension precedes speech production. A closer reading into the data, however, reveals that the combination of talk and silence seems more complicated than that. Some participants referred to this process as 'talk and silence' while others call it 'silence and talk'. They also indicated that the amount of talk and of silence might vary from one task to another, depending on the degree of challenge and how they respond to it. Along this line, there are at least two ways of understanding the in-between of silence and talk: first, this hybridity takes on a mobile nature, when students practise switching modes between silence and talk in any sequence as required by sub-tasks and in response to the moment-to-moment changing classroom situation; second, in-betweens occur when silence and talk merge into constructs that are neither public talk nor complete silence, such as when students whisper to themselves (inner speech), whisper to the person next to them (individual speech), or talk to a peer without intending to share with other peers (insider speech). According to participants, these forms of speech might not be the kind of contribution expected by the lecturer or peers in the class. Sujo and Insuk (both Korean) felt that the ways in which students respond to tasks can be a blend between silence and words that are diverse in amount, timing and sequence. As they explained, during a task, students might quietly follow teacher instruction or might ask a question, think about the issue or check understanding, quietly take notes or talk to a peer. There is no fixed way how one would combine silence with talk but it all depends on students' mood, ability and classroom situations. Arguably, silent participation might represent students' favoured or an unfavoured mode of learning, and so might talk. Since talk and silence share surprisingly similar features, the dichotomy between them should be re-evaluated so that these two domains do not have to exclude one another but work collaboratively for mutual benefit.

Task-associated factors that influence silence and talk

Although task types are intended to affect students' decisions to speak or remain silent, they are not the only determining factor. A range of other elements were revealed by participants, including task content, task challenge, peer dynamics, teacher management of tasks, and the individual teacher's receptivity and policy. Each of these capacities, which is closely related to the ecology of task conduct, will be unpacked further in this discussion.

Task content plays a role in students' willingness to speak out or quietly to gather more thoughts. The data show that if the content seems controversial, sensitive, embarrassing or offensive, students would rather remain quiet in order to avoid discomfort. Task content that students enjoy, find familiar and can connect their experience with will enable more verbal sharing. Sujo (Korean) commented: 'When tasks are more related to my life experience, I might openly share my ideas. But if a task stretches beyond my cultural knowledge and interest, I would rather observe and listen.'

Task challenge was mentioned by four participants (Lainie, Chinese; Sayo and Masae, Japanese; Areum, Korean) as a factor that decides whether more processing time is required or spontaneous participation is possible. Sayo reflected: 'Some tasks make me think more deeply than other tasks and it is important that the class should have this space.' Areum commented: 'The pace of thinking may vary among students. Different students need different silent reflection time and the teacher might need to take this into consideration.' Both students felt that when tasks require detailed and accurate responses, silence works best in preparing them to achieve those effects.

Peer dynamics is an intricate factor that comprises ability, participation style, viewpoint and emotion. Half of the participants (Lainie, Ranran, Masae, Baasanjav and Sujo) thought it affected classroom response. Students do not treat a task independently but respond to the involvement of others. For example, aggressive, talkative and domineering peers might put off others from talking. If students' views contradict or differ greatly, some might refrain from articulating their thoughts. In addition, during group tasks, positive feeling about group membership, such as respect and support, is an important factor in students' openness towards each other. As Masae (Japanese) and Baasanjav (Mongolian) elaborated, if some group members are too fluent and clever, the rest might feel intimidated and become quieter than they usually are. Sujo (Korean) revealed:

> It's not that I can plan whether to contribute or not. Sometimes my desire to speak gets discouraged by highly eloquent peers. At other times, my silence gets disturbed by the lecturer's pressure to join a verbal discussion. In that way, my practice varies depending on classroom situations, peer influence and lecturer expectation.

This situation calls for a more socially inclusive pedagogy which recognises how verbal involvement is sometimes used as a way of excluding classroom members who are not prone to spontaneous verbal discourse. Educational processes will be most meaningful when the teacher is aware of how talk and silence, respectively or in combination, can help students learn and overcome difficulty. Teacher management of tasks plays a mediating role in students' willingness to be articulate or reflective. Lainie (Chinese) shared an example of how well a lecturer handled a task:

> In one of my class activities, our lecturer prepared a worksheet with some questions. He asked each student to walk around and collect answers from five different classmates. At the end, we shared some of the best answers with everyone. This opportunity of collecting and sharing perspectives was helpful and exciting.

The way teachers monitor silent learning should be as helpful as the way they monitor talk. Sayo (Japanese) believed that if teachers asked students to think about an issue, they should be able to follow through with that request. She believed that not following up on students' silent processing is a poor pedagogical decision. Sayo shared an anecdote:

> During one class, our teacher asked us: 'What kinds of skills and qualities make a good leader?' After students tried hard to come up with their responses, one commented that a good leader should care about the opinions of others. The teacher, however, simply acknowledged the contribution without commenting and swiftly moved to the next part of the lesson. From that moment on, I became less passionate in contributing to the discussion topic.

In many cases, the thinking time and the opportunity for verbal participation need to go well together. If teachers do not provide sufficient wait time for students' silent thinking, that might reduce the quality of the discussion dramatically when students' thoughts are not ready for sharing. Ranran (Chinese) recalled: 'Sometimes, my classmates and I come up with brilliant ideas and get ready to participate. The lecturer, however, fails to notice our enthusiasm and that makes us lose interest in the lesson easily and quickly.' These episodes suggest that it is essential for teachers to be able to allocate processing time, monitor it well, follow up on it in a timely manner, demonstrate receptivity and organise discussion to a sufficient extent.

Teacher receptivity supports task management skills, can inspire student engagement and influence the openness to an exchange of views. This event shared by Cheng (Chinese) is a case in point:

> During a lesson, the teacher asked a challenging question, to which nobody responded. After a moment of classroom silence, he decided to nominate the best student in the class. When this student failed to answer the question, the teacher gave up and moved on to the next part of the lesson. I felt frustrated because I kind of knew the answer but was never given the opportunity to share my thoughts. If my teacher is more helpful and open-minded, the whole class would want to participate more.

According to Cheng and Baasanjav (Mongolian), the teacher's biased assumption (such as who could and who could not answer a difficult question) might prevent a great discussion from happening. Sayo (Japanese) believed that the teacher should openly welcome differences, so that students feel comfortable contradicting one another if need be. She thought that in many Japanese classrooms everyone cared so much about keeping harmony that discussions became a boring routine.

A shift in ways of learning

Some participants valued their overseas study and wished to make the best use of it by speaking out more than keeping quiet, which is uncommon in their own nature and home context. For example, Areum (Korean) often practised her verbal communication skills as much as possible during class discussion, which she did by combining listening and thinking with speaking as her mode of participation. Insuk (Korean), reflecting on how much she had changed during her study in Australia, realised how much she had modified her learning styles to become more articulate. Issues such as face-saving, shyness and cultural harmony, which were important factors in her classroom back in Korea, were no longer her concern in the Australian context. She revealed:

> I'm willing to go through challenges to unlock my verbal competence. Being able to join the group in open discussions and sharing my own opinions without fear of being judged is my way of responding to inclusive education in Australia. I'm only silent when preparing to talk; after that I will try to speak out. I would feel frustrated if my classmates all participate in class discussions while I'm not capable of doing so.

Four participants, Areum, Insuk, Sujo and Baasanjav, expressed a similar transference towards a more articulate learning behaviour. They felt that silence earned them less support than words in the dominant culture of the Australian classroom, which is a highly context-bound decision: while it seems perfectly fine to silently perform a task in a Korean or Mongolian classroom, the same behaviour in an Australian classroom could be subject to unfavourable judgement.

As the data suggest, the most unexpected finding from this study is that silence is not the dominant or preferred learning mode during task performance. The reason for this, as indicated by the data, comes from the context of the Australian classroom, where verbal participation is expected, coupled with the students' decisions to adjust their own learning style to fit into the host academic context. It is interesting to note that, for most participants, a positive experience with a classroom task often helped them speak up and expand their usual ways, while a poor experience was one that kept them silent against their will.

As Table 2.1 reveals, all the students in the project preferred talk over silence to a considerable extent. In particular, out of a total of 120 responses to tasks, there are 46 (38.3%) talk choices, 29 in-betweens (24.2%), 34 silence choices (28.3%) and 10 uncertain decisions (8.3%). In other words, while 75 responses (62.5%) involve the need to speak out and in-betweens, only 34 responses (28.3%) denote the wish to keep silent. This suggests that the need for verbalisation among participants is much greater than the need for silent processing. This finding seems uncommon, as it reveals East Asian students' preference for more verbal articulation than mental processing. In particular, three participants (Lainie, Chinese; Setsuko, Japanese; and Baasanjav, Mongolian) tended to employ more talk than silence during most activities, while three others (Ranran, Chinese; Areum and Sujo, Korean) resorted to both learning modes. One participant (Sayo, Japanese) preferred a balance between talk and silence; and two participants (Masae, Japanaese; Insuk, Korea), while making some effort to develop verbal skills, continued to value the impact of the silent learning mode.

Recommendations for Task Design

Task developers might consider providing explicit suggestions for silent processing, verbal responses or self-talk when necessary. One example provided by Wilkinson and Olliver-Gray (2006) is an instruction that guides students to write down how they feel during exam time and then compare their responses with peers. Stickler *et al.* (2007) suggest that task designers can specify which part of a task does not involve speaking and can allocate specific moments when students are expected to reflect or silently type their thoughts. Such instructions show the evidence that materials developers can consider including learning strategies to assist students in coping with the learning process.

Sometimes, to avoid disrupting students' productive silent processing, teachers also need to keep silent to ensure that the shared space is observed and respected. It is noted that experienced teachers tend to use silence in their pedagogy more than novice teachers (Vassilopoulos & Konstantinidis, 2012), perhaps because it takes a great deal of time in observing classroom behaviour over one's career (Gilmore, 1985) before one can understand the need for shared silence. Silence may not benefit learning unless teachers monitor the ways in which learning takes place before, during and after the productive silent moment. This requires thoughtful task design, clear expectation and a well planned management procedure. Such a procedure includes explicit instruction, appropriate wait time, timely support, relevant follow-up strategies and effective assessment policy. All these strategies should be included in task design, with guidance for teachers to use the material.

The challenge of the pedagogy above is that silence, unfortunately, might not be favoured by all members of a learning community, depending on who shares the learning environment and its broader social norms. It is therefore important for teachers to handle diverse preferences, with clear expectations when conducting multiple sub-tasks that allow various learning modes to come into play.

Concluding Remarks

It is interesting to note that most participants in this project perceived their use of silence as a form of engagement. There was no mention of disengaged or off-task silence in the data of this project; instead, participants were acutely aware that they were in control of their learning decisions. This research outcome seems distinct from some empirical studies where learner silence is sometimes recognised as undesirable classroom behaviour (see, for example, Cheng, 2000). Such choice denotes a self-regulated significance whereby students take control of their learning development and act, which Wright (2012) refers to as learner agency and Pavlenko and Lantolf (2000: 169) view as the foundation on which 'ultimate attainment' in learning is built.

The silence–talk relationship remains a highly multidimensional area for research. This is because ways of reasoning within this topic can never be linear: a task designed for talk may not lead to talk; and likewise, a task designed for silence may not result in silence. In a classroom-based study, Moran (2016) discovered that within cooperative learning tasks, there are always students who keep talking constantly and there are always others who frequently remain quiet. To some extent, the nature of a task might not decide the nature of participation. Calling a task 'cooperative' does not mean that all participants in that task will cooperate in a pedagogically envisioned way.

Such irregularity, whether we like it or not, shapes the dynamics of task performance, which is what keeps task development continually challenging. Once I was told this anecdote. An eloquent student told a classmate: 'I can train you to become more confident at speaking in front of the class'. The other student replied: 'I can train you to become better at listening to others'. As can be inferred from this exchange, since different individuals have their own prioritised ways of learning, it is hard to assume everyone will benefit from learning in the same manner. In many cases, not talking in class may not denote low confidence but could mean one simply feels confident enough to contemplate a less assertive disposition.

Teachers need to be unbiased about the various ways in which students respond to the demand of a task and should not hold on to any pre-determined expectations, such as assuming that talk is the natural route of learning. In many cases, it is teachers' flexibility, supportive attitudes and innovative pedagogical strategies that improve task design by allowing both mental and verbal rehearsal to reach its optimum. Although many communicative tasks may expect learners to switch to an impulsive learning mode, during the actual classroom process some learners might choose to handle them in a more reflective manner. This is because some might need more self-monitoring time than others before verbal exchange can take place. When this happens, the quality of classroom tasks should not be measured by how much speaking occurs but by the depth of learner engagement.

Silence as mental rehearsal provides conditions for self-directed learning, which may be either connected to or independent from the teaching. Pedagogy founded on a profound understanding of productive silence can liberate learners from the constraint of having to produce impulsive, low-quality participation. Silence needs to be managed with acute awareness of why, how, when and how long students need it to support their own learning and when the verbal mode of learning should take over. Obligatory talk can be frustrating when learners are required to publicise their half-baked thoughts when they are unprepared to do so. Silence training should be organised to include reflectivity, concentration, outcome and avoidance of idle, unproductive moments – the same way that talk needs to be directed to enhance learning rather than become mere social time in the classroom. The structure of learning might fundamentally change when this knowledge is applied so that learners can employ both silence and talk as learning tools in conscious, informed ways.

Self-reflection/Discussion Questions

(1) Classroom tasks sometimes exhibit a stimulating quality that inspires students' thinking. At other times, they might have a routine and humdrum characteristic. When you are inspired, do you find yourself spending more time in silent thinking or do you speak out more with others? Why is that the case?
(2) Arguably, learners' silent processing might occur quietly or at times it might develop into the occasional verbal articulation. For example, some reflective students prefer to work quietly on a written task, while their reflective counterparts might switch learning modes and share their thought with peers, especially when the task seems to require some exchange of ideas. Have you ever experienced such moments of adjusting your participation mode? What factors might have influenced such modification?
(3) What can you say about the relationship between students' verbal versus silent learning mode and the teacher's style of task management? This question is raised because it has been observed that a student's preference for a learning mode is not always individually permanent, but in many cases is conditional on the ecological progress of classroom discussion. Such a classroom process might involve a range of factors, such as the teacher's task management, task types, peer interaction, classroom mood, seating arrangement and technology, among others. If you do not wish to discuss learning modes in relation to task management, feel free to select another factor which you feel might influence your choice of learning mode.
(4) Empirical research has found that peer influence is a factor which governs how much a learner is willing to participate in classroom discussion (see, for example, Bao, 2014). However, findings from various case studies are often so diverse that they show no consistent formula with regard to what personality leads to talk or to silence. You might wish to reflect on your individual inclination in working with peers. To what extent does your decision to speak out or to remain quiet

during a discussion have to do with your peers' behaviour? What kind of peers might influence you to be more articulate and what kind of peers tend to keep you more silent? It would be interesting to compare your thinking with another learner/colleague and see how your views differ.

Recommended Reading

Wilkinson, L. and Olliver-Gray, Y. (2006) The significance of silence: Differences in meaning, learning styles, and teaching strategies in cross-cultural settings. *Psychologia* 49 (2), 74–88.

This research article, which examines Chinese students in the educational context of a New Zealand university, highlights the need for classroom tasks to have a clear structure. It was found that such explicit arrangement would set up students' expectation for an open climate of ideas sharing and scaffold classroom participation, and help students maintain some degree of verbal participation if they wished.

Ridgway, A.J. (2009) The inner voice. *International Journal of English Studies* 9 (2), 45–58.

Following up on Brian Tomlinson's (2003) appeal for pedagogical attentiveness to the inner voice in every language learner, the article discusses this phenomenon from a cognitive psychological perspective. Ridgway emphasises the importance of this construct in connecting with short-term memory and in facilitating both text comprehension and the production of new language.

Ollin, R. (2008) Silent pedagogy and rethinking classroom practice: Structuring teaching through silence rather than talk. *Cambridge Journal of Education* 38 (2), 265–280.

The article, which is based on a qualitative study, examines silence from a teacher perspective. It identifies a range of silences and how they are productively employed in classroom pedagogy. The discussion can be connected with a study by Bao (2014) which investigated teachers' use of silence in the Philippine classroom context. The use of self-talk among teachers, which is currently under-researched, represents another exciting topic for enquiry along the silence theme.

Bao, D. (2014) *Understanding Silence and Reticence: Ways of Participating in Second Language Acquisition*. London: Bloomsbury.

Founded on empirical research, this book provides a range of perspectives on how the silent mode of learning is practised differently in Australian, Chinese, Japanese, Korean and Vietnamese education cultures. In an approach known as silent engagement pedagogy (SEP), Bao offers suggestions for how teaching and learning can help learners who prefer to spend some time in quiet mental processing before sharing ideas in classroom discussion.

Acknowledgements

The author would like to thank the participants in the project: Cheng Guan, Xiaofang Shang and Ranran Liu from China; Masae Maki, Sayo Tanaka and Setsuko Nashiyama from Japan; Areum Lee, Insuk Han and Sujo Lee from Korea; Baasanjav Tserendagva from Mongolia. Without your kind support, this project would have been impossible.

References

Bao, D. (2014) *Understanding Silence and Reticence: Ways of Participating in Second Language Acquisition*. London: Bloomsbury.
Carless, D. (2004) Issues in teachers' reinterpretation of a task-based innovation in primary school. *TESOL Quarterly* 38 (4), 639–662.
Cheng, X.T. (2000) Asian students' reticence revisited. *System* 28, 435–446.
Creelman, A. (2017) *Silent Learners – A Guide*. Copenhagen: Nordic Council of Ministers. At http://lnu.divaportal.org/smash/get/diva2:1171709/FULLTEXT01.pdf (accessed 6 November 2018).
Creswell, J.W. (2007) *Qualitative Research Design: Choosing Among the Five Approaches*. Thousand Oaks, CA: Sage Publications.
Creswell, J.W. (2008) *Educational Research: Planning, Conducting and Evaluating Quantitative and Qualitative Research* (3rd edn). Upper Saddle River, NJ: Pearson/Merrill Prentice Hall.
De Guerrero, M.C.M. (1991) The nature of inner speech in mental rehearsal of the second language. Unpublished doctoral dissertation. Inter American University, San Juan, PR.
Denzin, N.K. and Lincoln, Y.S. (2011) Th*e Sage Handbook of Qualitative Inquiry* (4th edn). Thousand Oaks, CA: Sage Publications.
Gilmore, P. (1985) Silence and sulking: Emotional displays in the classroom. In D. Tannen and M. Saville-Troike (eds) *Perspectives on Silence* (pp. 139–162). Norwood, NJ: Ablex.
Hall, J.K. and Walsh, M. (2002) The links between teacher–student interaction and language learning. *Annual Review of Applied Linguistics* 22, 186–203.
Harumi, S. (2010) Classroom silence: Voices from Japanese EFL learners. *ETL Journal* 65 (3), 260–269.
Innocenti, D. (2002) The mind's eyes view: Teaching students how to sensualize language. In K.S. Fleckenstein, L.T. Calendrillo and D. A. Worley (eds) *Language and Image in the Reading–Writing Classroom: Teaching Vision* (pp. 59–69). Mahwah, NJ: Lawrence Erlbaum Associates.
King, J. (2013a) Silence in the second language classrooms of Japanese universities. *Applied Linguistics* 34 (3), 325–343.
King, J. (2013b) *Silence in the Second Language Classroom*. London: Palgrave Macmillan.
King, J. (2016) *The Dynamic Interplay Between Context and the Language Learner*. New York: Palgrave Macmillan.
Levelt, W.J.M. (1989) *Speaking: From Intention to Articulation*. Cambridge, MA: MIT Press.
Long, M.H. (1996) The role of the linguistic environment in second language acquisition.

In W.C. Ritchie and T.K. Bhatia (eds) *Handbook of Research on Language Acquisition* (pp. 413–468). New York: Academic Press.

Mackey, A. (2002) Beyond production: Learners' perceptions about interactional processes. *International Journal of Educational Research* 37 (3/4), 379–394.

Merriam, S.B. (2009) *Qualitative Research: A Guide to Design and Implementation*. San Francisco, CA: Jossey-Bass.

Messick, S. (1989) Validity. In R.L. Linn (ed.) *Educational Measurement* (3rd edn) (pp. 13–104). New York: American Council on Education and Macmillan.

Moran, D. (2000) *Introduction to Phenomenology*. London: Routledge.

Moran, H. (2016) Listening to their silence: The learning experiences of quiet students in a middle school environment. Unpublished master's thesis, University of Canterbury, Christchurch, New Zealand.

Nakane, I. (2007) *Silence in Intercultural Communication: Perception and Performance in the Classroom*. Amsterdam: John Benjamins.

Ohta, A.S. (2001) *Second Language Acquisition Processes in the Classrooms: Learning Japanese*. Mahwah, NJ: Lawrence Erlbaum Associates.

Ollin, R. (2008) Silent pedagogy and rethinking classroom practice: Structuring teaching through silence rather than talk. *Cambridge Journal of Education* 38 (2), 265–280.

Pavlenko, A. and Lantolf, J.P. (2000) Second language learning as participation and the (re)construction of selves. In J.P. Lantof (ed.) *Sociocultural Theory and Second Language Learning* (pp. 155–177). New York: Oxford University Press.

Reisberg, D., Wilson, M. and Smith, J.D. (1991) Auditory imagery and inner speech. In R. Logie and M. Denis (eds) *Advances in Psychology* (pp. 59–81). Amsterdam: Elsevier.

Ridgway, A.J. (2009) The inner voice. *International Journal of English Studies* 9 (2), 45–58.

Segalowitz, N. and Trofimovich, P. (2012) Second language processing. In S.M. Gass and A. Mackey (eds) *The Routledge Handbook of Second Language Acquisition* (pp. 179–92). London: Routledge.

Sokolowski, R. (2000) *Introduction to Phenomenology*. Cambridge: Cambridge University Press.

Stickler, U., Batstone, C., Duensing, A. and Heins, B. (2007) Distant classmates: Speech silence in online and telephone language tutorials. *European Journal of Open, Distance and E-learning* 10 (2). At http://www.eurodl.org/?p=archives&year=2007&halfyear=2&..&article=277 (accessed 19 November 2018).

Svalberg, A. and Askham, J. (2013) A dynamic perspective on student language teachers' different learning pathways in a collaborative context. In J. King (ed.) *The Dynamic Interplay Between Context and the Language Learner* (pp. 172–193). New York: Palgrave Macmillan.

Tomlinson, B. (2003) Helping learners to develop an effective L2 inner voice. *RELC Journal* 34 (2), 178–194.

Vassilopoulos, S. and Konstantinidis, G. (2012) Teacher use of silence in elementary education. *Journal of Teaching and Learning* 8 (1), 91–105.

Wilkinson, L. and Olliver-Gray, Y. (2006) The significance of silence: Differences in meaning, learning styles, and teaching strategies in cross-cultural settings. *Psychologia* 49 (2), 74–88.

Wright, L. (2012) *Second Language Learner and Social Agency*. Bristol: Multilingual Matters.

Yashima, T., Ikeda, M. and Nakahira, S. (2013) Talk and silence in an EFL classroom: Interplay of learners and context. In J. King (ed.) *The Dynamic Interplay Between Context and the Language Learner* (pp. 104–126). New York: Palgrave Macmillan.

Zembylas, M. and Michaelides, P. (2004) The sound of silence in pedagogy. *Educational Theory* 54 (2), 193–210.

3 Approaches to Interacting with Classroom Silence: The Role of Teacher Talk

Seiko Harumi

Introduction

Teachers regularly encounter silence in L2 classrooms. The decision of the teacher on how to interact with learner silence can have a profound impact for future turns and pedagogical steps that follow the interaction. For many decades, this moment of silence at 'the crossroads of interactional concerns' (Park, 2017: 123) has been considered problematic in Japanese EFL contexts (Anderson, 1993; King, 2013) and it can still be considered troublesome due to its high frequency, lengthy moments and learners' frequent inability to give verbal accounts of why they are silent, which makes it difficult for teachers to address the nature of the silence they encounter. As reflected in previous studies (Sacks *et al.*, 1974), silences in spoken interaction have primarily negative connotations, especially when fluency and spontaneous turn exchanges in dialogic interaction are the norm. However, diversity of cultural expectations on the value of silences (Bao, 2014) calls for an exploration of its pedagogical role within specific sociocultural contexts, and classroom silence in Japanese EFL contexts, which is highly valued by learners and teachers at Japanese educational contexts, is no exception.

Nevertheless, in Japanese EFL contexts, pedagogical attention in L2 learning has been drawn to imperfect or deficient models of interaction (Hall *et al.*, 2011) and also to learners' immediate reaction to the question asked, characterised as 'missing replies' (Hosoda, 2014) or lack of initiative as a sign of non-participation. However, recent studies (Hauser, 2010; Hawkins, 2015) assert that more attention should be paid to the overall quality of interaction, which has potential 'extendability' (Schegloff, 1968: 1084) in L2 learning, supporting Hall *et al.*'s (2011) account, focusing less on learners' limitations and more on their attempts to accomplish interactional goals through speech. From this perspective, it is vital to shed light on other facilitative dimensions of classroom silence – seen as an interactional resource – before re-examining its role within diverse notions of speaking competence. The silences this study focuses on are therefore relatively micro-level, occurring at turn-taking junctures, and do not include non-participation during whole-group speaking tasks.

Interestingly, Chavez observes that research examining 'the precise connections between teacher and learner talk', while revealing 'how exactly teachers shape the conversational spaces of their students' (Chavez, 2016: 137), remains lacking. This is in spite of the fact that some studies (Nakane, 2005; Walsh, 2011) claim that the way teachers interact or negotiate with learner silence should be considered a fundamental contributor to L2 learning. Further, Harumi's (2011) study, which examined pedagogical support expectations of intermediate-level Japanese EFL learners opting to remain silent in L2 classroom interaction, concluded that 27.3% ($n = 197$) of learners specifically expected teachers to adjust their questioning strategies and wait time. Voices raised by learners themselves also suggest this is a pedagogical approach needing further exploration to contribute to L2 learning. As these studies indicate, examination of this aspect of teacher–learner interaction with reference to the use of classroom silence in L2 learning, while illustrating interactional pattern mechanisms, also deepens our understanding of the role of silence within L2 contexts.

This study therefore argues that the use of classroom silence in relation to teacher talk warrants further close analysis as an indispensable interactional resource contributing to L2 learning, exploring the use of wait time and teacher talk with reference to learners' classroom silence in Japanese EFL contexts. In this study, wait time is defined as the vocally silent moments after a question is initiated by the teacher before the student responds or the teacher provides further initiation. It examines the specific context of tertiary-level oral conversation classes where students have limited proficiency. This has involved first studying teachers' perceptions of their own strategies when encountering learner silence in L2 contexts, elicited through a questionnaire survey. Second, the study also demonstrates teachers' responsiveness to learner silence through conversational analysis (CA) as a main analytical framework, aiming to illustrate the interactional patterns which emerge through the sequential analysis of the turn organisation of dyadic interactions between a teacher and individual students in teacher-fronted classes. In order to articulate the interactional process, this study defines classroom silence as an interactional resource able to promote collaborative interaction in L2 learning and also considers a starting point where learners can potentially develop ways to express themselves further with scaffolded teacher assistance through wait time and teacher talk, fostering L2 learning opportunities.

Classroom Silence and Teacher Talk

Facilitative use of silence in L2 classroom

The place of silence in L2 classrooms has been re-examined in recent years, with a focus on pedagogical values attached to its use, seen from teachers' and learners' perspectives, although undeniably it can still have a negative influence on spoken interaction as reticence, possibly leading to communication breakdown. Nevertheless, from various pedagogical perspectives, the facilitative role of classroom silence as 'mode of learning' (Bao, 2014: 2) or an interactional resource can be illustrated as a space for learning, for example by providing opportunities for attentive listening, thinking and reformulating ideas. Previous studies (Bao, 2014; Gardner, 2007; Liu, 2002; Walsh, 2011) have illustrated three key analytical perspectives on facilitative classroom silences: (1) as a learning tool for individual reflection; (2) as desirable interactional space between turns; and (3) as pedagogical strategy for teachers to enhance interaction fostering L2 learning opportunities.

First, examining classroom silence as a reflective tool for learners' own learning space, there are studies in multilingual settings where Asian EFL learners' classroom silence, regarded as a learning process, and listening served as an essential learning strategy. McPake and Powney's (1998) study in a UK mainstream primary school where Japanese students' silence was initially considered obstructive to local teachers' participatory learning styles illustrated that teachers' in-depth long-term observations came to evaluate it positively as a space for individual reflection contributing to L2 learning.

Second, from an interactional perspective, the use of silence as a process of interaction rather than as a final outcome of learner output has been emphasised (Gardner, 2007; Lee, 2007). Gardner (2007: 58) specifically highlights difficulties L2 learners experience in dialogic interaction and argues that 'broken' starts and 'delay' in answering quickly become accountable actions in themselves in subsequent turn exchanges. Further, Lee's (2007) study in American tertiary educational contexts advocates the importance of the feedback move, the third turn by the teacher in the initiation–response–feedback (IRF) sequence (Sinclair & Coulthard, 1975), which determines whether 'collective silences' can function as facilitative turns.

Finally, emerging awareness of the educational role of silence as wait time has highlighted it as an essential pedagogical tool both in subject-based classrooms (Ingram & Elliott, 2015; Rowe, 1986) and in L2 contexts (Maroni, 2011; Smith & King, 2017; Tsui, 1996). Teachers' general tendencies to fill the gaps between their questions and learner replies have been frequently observed (Tsui, 1996; Walsh, 2011) and more regular use of extended wait time has been recommended as a strategy to increase opportunities and space for learning (Walsh & Li, 2013). Earlier studies (Rowe, 1986) examined extended wait time as a method to promote learning and concluded that training teachers to increase wait times to three seconds had the positive effect of longer learner-initiated replies. Although more recent studies involve various contextual and methodological approaches and have suggested some favourable uses of wait time in specific contexts, they nevertheless indicate five key factors closely correlated to the use of wait time: (1) learners' proficiency levels (Hosoda, 2014); (2) learners' degree of (un)willingness to communicate, or confidence (Zarrinabadi, 2014); (3) availability of non-verbal cues or visual image such as embodied actions (Kozar, 2016); (4) turn-taking organisation (Ingram & Elliott, 2015); and (5) pedagogical support, including alternative use of questions and elicitation strategies. While appraising these five factors, studies indicate closer and more direct relationships between the use of wait time and question type, as the content of questions naturally determines the level of cognitive workload required for learners to prepare replies. While Tsui's (1996) study found that learners' familiarity with answering particular types of questions or with interactional organisation in specific local contexts is closely related to wait time effectiveness, other research (Smith & King, 2017: 11) suggested a correlation between extended wait time and longer student responses, but also found that 'lower-level cognitive questions served various purposes' in discourse, and concluded that alternation of question types can be 'an indirect means of manipulating wait time'. Similar pedagogical approaches recommended by Ingram and Elliott (2015) emphasise the importance of teachers' ability to use a range of elicitation repertoires and wait times and utilise them according to context. The effect of extended wait time involves not only the actual length as 'a production strategy' (Ingram & Elliott, 2015) but also other factors.

Perspectives emerging from these studies rendered the necessity for articulated pedagogical focus to shape learners' L2 learning (Walsh, 2011) in similar learning contexts where teachers intend to utilise the effective use of wait time to enhance L2 learning. However, the link between the silence learners create and the wait time, which is the domain of the teacher, has not been explicitly investigated in order to understand how they are interactively related (Schegloff, 2000) as facilitative interactional resources within turn-taking systems. The present study aims to illustrate this relationship.

Classroom silence as interactional resource

In order to closely analyse this process of decision making, the concept of classroom interactional competence (CIC) – defined as teachers' and learners' ability to use interaction as a tool for mediating and assisting learning (Walsh, 2011: 158) – must be examined as an indispensable aspect of learning. The fundamental principle lies in both learners' and teachers' decision-making ability to select appropriate interactional resources and use them to facilitate co-construction of meaning and shape appropriate space for L2 learning so that learners can participate and contribute to class conversation and receive relevant feedback on their contributions. CIC regards interaction as a tool for creating a shared space for learning, maximising learning opportunities. In order to explore how CIC can be applied to L2 learning, types of interactional resources evidenced in previous studies will be illustrated.

First, the use of various interactional resources by teachers has recently gained more attention. For instance, the use of increased wait time to afford and promote learners' learning space while extending learner turns has been considered as one such resource (Walsh, 2011). Additionally, the use of multilingual resources such as L1, embodied actions and awareness of (un)willingness to communicate are also evidenced as interactional resources in other studies (Sert, 2015, 2017) as a part of CIC. Likewise, the use of CIC suggests it is vital to be aware of a wide range of teaching strategies and utilise appropriate interactional resources in a timely manner to facilitate L2 learning. Further, recent studies (Seedhouse, 2011; Sert, 2017) have also started paying more attention to the role of various interactional resources used by learners of limited proficiency, such as vowel-marking, as situated resources for initiating word search or forward-oriented repair (Carroll, 2000), the use of L1 and reactive tokens (Hauser, 2010). These studies broadened the scope of analysis of CIC to articulate the quality of interaction produced in L2 classrooms by observing how learners use these resources to maintain and advance interaction. That is, interactional resources learners already have, and utilise, non-linguistic cues such as paralinguistic devices, including silence, embodied action and code choices described above, are considered important interactional resources in L2 classrooms.

Second, it is necessary to refer to a key concept, closely related to CIC: the notion of interactional competence (IC) (Hall, 2007; Young, 2008). This emphasises the role of collaborative interaction in the situated context. It has been specifically characterised as 'acquisition of knowledge of specific social-context, the ability to deploy and recognize context specific patterns including the use of non-verbal cues and the ability to repair problems within interactional work' (Hall *et al.*, 2011: 12). What is prominent in this notion of IC is the ability to repair problems in specific contexts as a key feature of spoken interaction, focusing on how participants process interactions. Repair has been defined by ten Have (2007) as 'a set of practices to deal with various kinds of troubles' when interacting, while Hall (2007) considers the role of repair in restoring understanding among participants as a fundamental interactional resource. That is, repair not only involves solving linguistic problems in interaction but also includes the ability to maintain interaction by restoring mutual understanding through pedagogic engagement. Within this scope, classroom silence, often considered troublesome, can also be considered a potential resource to enhance L2 learning opportunities. The challenge is to discover how this repair sequence in talk-in-interaction involving learner silence can be a bridge to L2 learning.

Further, in order to analyse its interactional process within CA, this study focuses on two fundamental aspects of turn organisation, to examine it as a learning opportunity. First, four configurations of repair in the turn sequence studied by Schegloff et al. (1977) and Hall (2007) offer a useful analytical lens to examine the extent to which self-initiation is enhanced within interaction. These configurations are: self-initiated self-repair (SISR), other-initiated self-repair (OISR), self-initiated other-repair (SIOR) and other-initiated other-repair (OIOR). Among these, SISR is considered the optimal arrangement, in which the person who produces the trouble initiates the repair and completes its work. Regarding this, McHoul (1990) and van Lier (1984) claim that teachers should create opportunities for learners to engage in self-initiated repair, even by delaying OIOR, to enable learners to enhance learning opportunities by themselves. That is, stances which encourage successful autonomous interaction by learners through self-monitoring are prioritised over spontaneous turn exchanges as pedagogical goals. Other studies (Schegloff et al., 1977; Schegloff, 2000) also claim that the right of the speaker who was the cause of the trouble to perform possible self-repair should be respected. Van Compernolle (2011) also emphasises the importance of SISR, which can potentially shape developmentally appropriate assistance, as ultimately teachers acting as mediators can only hypothesise learners' problems.

Another fundamental turn organisation is adjacency pairs, units of conversation and functionally related to each other as question and answer. Hutchby and Wooffitt (1998: 40) claim that 'on the production of a first pair part, the second part becomes relevant in analysis and remains relevant even if it is not produced in the next serial turn'. That is, even if there is no response in the immediate next turn, which is normally expected, absence of answer, denoted a 'noticeable absence' by Hutchby and Wooffitt (1998: 45), also becomes 'conditional relevance' (Schegloff, 1968: 1084). In this respect, the use of classroom silence itself can be considered part of interactional processes contributing to relevant answers in repair sequences where L2 learning can be promoted beyond the next turn through teacher talk. Thus, from an interactional perspective, exploration of repair types and the use of adjacency pairs provide opportunities to understand how learners and teachers co-create potential learning opportunities.

Adopting CA as a main analytical tool, this study therefore also considers factors examined in previous studies when analysing wait time and teaching strategies utilised by teachers in L2 contexts. Among these, particular attention will be paid to the mechanism of turn organisation, including use of adjacency pairs and the types of repair associated with turn distribution in repair sequences, as an indication of engagement and involvement in L2 learning, and its turn-by-turn progress towards accomplishment in L2 output. Thus, the process of enabling learners to produce L2 output as a potential level of interactional accomplishment used to express themselves will be explored, making reference to classroom silence and support provided by teachers' scaffolding through wait time and teacher talk. Perceptions of the use of teaching strategies expressed by teachers through questionnaire surveys will also be used to deepen understanding of pedagogical approaches within the specific contexts.

Interacting with Classroom Silence: Methodology and Data Analysis

Research contexts and procedure

To illustrate the complex, multifaceted nature of silence, a mixed-methods approach (Hashemi, 2013) and qualitative data analysis were adopted. This study drew on two data sets. The first was an open-ended questionnaire survey on the use of teaching strategies when encountering learners' silence, administered to 56 tertiary-level native English teachers from five different private universities, whose teaching experiences ranged from one to 25 years. Open-ended questions were considered more revealing than pre-categorised answers, as teachers' perceptions could be elicited more deeply for qualitative analysis. The second data set comprised eight hours of video-recorded classroom interaction from three different oral communication classes taught by different English teachers. Based on the questionnaire survey responses, three experienced teachers were selected for the further investigation in order to learn how they interacted with learner silences, leading to L2 output. Learners' proficiency level ranged from B1 to B2 within the Common European Framework of Reference for Languages (CEFR).

Initial classroom interaction analysis selected silences exceeding one second during dyadic interaction between a class teacher and nominated individual students in teacher-fronted classes. The focus of the analysis was the moment when students were required to answer questions at the initial stage of a conversation. The second stage of analysis further explored subsequent turn exchanges and selected representative extracts in which the initial use of lengthy silence was successfully bridged to L2 output with scaffolded help through teacher talk, or ended unsuccessfully.

Data Analysis

Analysis of questionnaire survey

The survey uses open-ended questions on reactions to learners' classroom silence and the use of teaching strategies to facilitate oral interaction when teachers encounter learner silence. This part of the enquiry aimed to elicit teachers' views on learner silence and their own teaching strategies with reference to wait time. It explored the ways teachers perceive their attempts to facilitate L2 learning. Two questions were asked: (1) Do you feel uncomfortable if your students do not answer your questions immediately? (2) If your students remain silent, what do you do?

Teachers' reactions to the first question varied and correlated with the length of their teaching experience in Japanese EFL contexts. Their responses indicated that the majority of newly qualified teachers needed at least 0.6 years to learn how to deal with learner silence and understand its meaning in local contexts. Overall, whereas 31.4% of teachers indicated they did not feel uncomfortable, 5.7% said they did, and the remainder qualified their responses as follows: (1) at first, 26.7%; (2) occasionally, 17.1%; (3) slightly, 8.6%; (4) accustomed, 8.5%; and (5) depending on the situation, 2.0%. This suggests the majority of teachers felt frustration at some stages of their teaching experience in Japanese EFL contexts, although its frequency and consistency varied. The study also indicated that teachers' frustration stems from familiarity and understanding of the local context, involving 'prolonged emotional challenges tackling both the sources of silence itself as well as their [teachers'] own emotional reactions to it', as illustrated in the study by Morris and King (2018: 441). That frustration also led to adjusted pedagogical approaches, as demonstrated by participants' responses, such as: 'I wish the pace of the lesson was quicker but I am learning to give them time to think' (participant teacher 3). Other responses indicated awareness of specific social and contextual situations involving 'groupism' or 'peer pressure' (Anderson, 1993), such as: 'I do not feel uncomfortable because it is not appropriate for Japanese students to answer immediately. They need to have the support, approval and encouragement of their immediate peers' (participant teacher 6).

As for the second question, on teachers' own strategies, four types of approach emerged: linguistic support (reformulations, explanations, new question), 26%; wait time, 12.9%; affective support (encouragement to talk, not to put the student on the spot), 20.4%; support with turn-taking (change the dynamics of discourse by moving to another student, change the formation of discourse into peer interaction), 25.9%; and 'other' (adjustment of own teaching style), 14.8%. Their replies indicate that wait time is a frequently used technique, and four teachers said they try to wait five seconds (Hosoda, 2014) as a standard practice to elicit learner responses. Changing the dynamics of class discourse from one-to-one interaction with a nominated student to peer-oriented interaction seems to be a frequently used technique, as well as some adjustment of teaching style. These four pedagogical outlooks mirror teachers' general repair or elicitation strategies through linguistic support and wait time in previous studies, but more specific approaches involving affective and interactional organisation in interaction were also considered. Although this questionnaire survey did not specifically examine the role of learners' embodied actions or use of visual signs, teachers may unconsciously take these into account when choosing elicitation techniques. This indicates that non-verbal cues during collaborative interaction warrant further investigation to understand their role in classroom discourse.

Conversation analysis

Eight hours of video-recorded data were used to analyse the interaction between individual teachers and nominated individual students in teacher-fronted classes, when interaction was initiated by a teacher's question and was followed by learner silence and subsequent turn exchanges. The data were analysed through CA, focusing on turn organisation around wait time, turn design, turn sequence and types of repair used by teachers and learners. Following analysis of all relevant transcripts, four types of frequently used successful turn-exchange patterns emerged, along with one pattern that was unsuccessful despite teachers' perseverance.

1. Scaffolding through direct prompts and content feedback

In this extract, the nominated student is expected to supply her own sentence using a grammatical structure just learnt in class. (A key to extract notation is provided in Appendix 1 at the end of this chapter.)

Extract 3.1
01→T: gratitude is one of the best way of linking people (.) one of the best way of X is?
02 S: (1.3)
        + looking at the teacher
03→T: give us an example, Yamada(.) <X is the best way of>?
                ((name of student))
04 S: (2.5)
        +leaning her head slightly towards left, however not looking down
05→T: for instance?
06 S: (1.2) °running°(0.5) °running°=
07→T: =↑<u>dan</u>cing?(.) what?
        ((teacher experiencing difficulty to understand the words uttered by the student))

```
08    S:   (0.8) running.(.) running.
09→ T:   (.) ↑o::::h,(.) running.
10▶ S:   (2.3) running(.) is the best way of keeping your health.
11    T:   (.) very good example. (.) are you a good runner?
12    S:   (2.3)
13         [+shaking her head while covering her mouth]
           ((sign of shyness))
```

This extract demonstrates various scaffolding techniques used by the teacher as OISR. Frequently used question types include designedly incomplete utterances (DIUs) (Koshik, 2002) intended to provide direct prompts to elicit answers from learners. The first question (line 01) asks S to answer using a specific grammatical item along with rising intonation. However, in the following turn the learner responds with a silent reply of 1.3 seconds, while engaged with a gaze, indicating willingness to proceed with the interaction, but offering no clear account. Then, in the following feedback move, the teacher provides more specific instruction ('give us an example') and repeats the question by deploying the sentence formation.

In line 04, there is an even longer silence. However, this time the student shows more concrete embodied action, with body shift and consistent interactional gaze (Stivers et al., 2009), indicating engagement in the interaction. This turn is followed by a teacher's further simplified and focused direct prompts ('for instance?') in line 05. Then, after these continuous attempts at teacher initiation, along with wait time, the learner finally utters part of her intended sentence but softly, indicating lack of confidence in her output. However, in line 07, the teacher's clarification request (=↑dancing?(.) what?) as OISR is partially answered by S with repetition of the words uttered in line 06, but this time more loudly. Then, the teacher's genuine reactive token (↑o::::h), provided as content feedback, finally leads the learner to produce a whole sentence as L2 output.

These exchanges indicate that despite initial lengthy silences, that is, through the teacher's use of wait time by line 06, the learner initiates a sense of her answer which had only been partially expressed. Nevertheless, the sequence of the teacher's feedback moves as precise scaffolding, initiated as OISR, facilitated interaction at subsequent stages by giving the learner opportunities to develop her answers step by step, finally enabling her to accomplish her interactional goal. This also shows that the first question asked by the teacher (line 01), as the first part (question) of an adjacency pair (Sacks et al., 1974), was finally answered by the student in line 10, as the second part (answer), accomplishing the interactional goal. Large stretches of multiple turn exchanges were required to reach alignment and mutual understanding by the participants (Jarvis & Robinson, 1997; McHoul, 1990; van Lier, 1984). This demonstrates that wait time at the initial stage of interaction and subsequent teacher talk gave the learner space to develop her utterances over successive turns.

2. Use of reformulations of questions and contextualisation

Extract 3.2 shows an interaction which started smoothly, talking about the types of music a student likes. However, the second question, initiated by the teacher to develop the topic, was difficult for the student to comprehend.

Extract 3.2
```
01    T:  which music do you like?=
02    S:  =i like classical music=
03→  T:  i like classical music, too(.) what is your favourite classical
          music?
04    S:  (0.5)<i like>
                   + looking away
05        (5.2)
06→  T:  <which one>?(.) which(.)piece(.) is your ↑favourite?
07    S:  (0.9) i think so.
08→  T:  you like music(.) but which(.) piece?(.) which piece of music?(.)
          which composer?
          when you say a classical music, you must give me an example.
09▶  S:  (3.4) beethoven.
```

Despite smooth interactional exchanges at the beginning, a further question was initiated by the teacher in line 03, but it was met with silence. Despite uttering the beginning of a sentence after a short pause of 0.5 seconds, the student began to shift his gaze and a long silence of 5.2 seconds ensued. Following this, in line 06, the teacher tried to reformulate the question by adjusting his tempo, articulating with accentuated emphasis intended to make it easier for the student to comprehend the question's meaning. However, the student's reply at line 07 shows his comprehension is incorrect, as the utterance (i think so) is an inappropriate response to the question asked. Despite this incorrect answer, the teacher attempts to initiate a further turn as OISR by contextualising the question he originally asked at line 03, providing another chance for the student to self-repair his answer. At line 09, mutual alignment is finally attained as the learner appropriately answers the question.

Various types of reformulation were used by the teacher and his fourth OISR turn move made this possible. This extract shows that the teacher's final move gave the learner the opportunity to complete the second part of the delayed adjacency pair.

3. Use of reformulations as DIUs and learners' non-verbal cues as self-initiation

Extract 3.3 is from a class which reached the stage of discussing weekend activities. After one student initiated a question to another, the teacher joined the interaction, asking for clarification, which proved difficult for the student.

Extract 3.3
```
01    S1: ken, what(.) did you do at the weekend?
02    S2: (0.9) i went to fukuoka* (.) and (.) i watched a baseball game.
              ((*name of the city))
03    S1: what(.) did you watch? [↑](.) the game.
04    S2: (0.7) Hiroshima carp* and softbank*=
              ((*name of the teams))
05→T:  = who was playing against softbank?=
06    S2: (4.1)
          =+immediately looked at the teacher but without any
           vocalisation
07→T:  who (.) is the ↑other team?
08    S2: (2.2)
          +briefly shifts his gaze to other students sitting next to him
09    S3: (0.9)
          + leaning his head towards left
10    S2: yes.
11→T:  you told that there are two teams. (.) who is the other team?↑
       hiroshima carp and?↑
12►S:  (1.3) softbank.
```

After the topic was initiated by S1, student S2 smoothly replied to the question. However, in line 05, when the teacher requested clarification, S2 responded with a long silence of 4.1 seconds. Although this was followed by the teacher's simplified questions in line 07, a further longer silence followed, this time with more embodied action by S2 as SIOR, shifted the turn to S3, a third student sitting next to him, to seek immediate peer support. However, this attempted repair work through SIOR generated another problem with no productive peer support. This turn exchange finally led S2 to choose a monosyllabic answer ('yes'), addressed to the teacher as acknowledgement of his engagement with his question in line 05. In response, the teacher-initiated reformulation through contextualisation was followed by repetition of the question ('who is the other team?') and DIUs as direct prompts. This finally enabled the students to answer the question, as the second part of a delayed adjacency pair and to reach alignment in collaborative work.

This extract illustrates an instance of a learner's use of lengthy silence along with clear embodied action towards another student in a learner-initiated repair. Although his self-initiated repair led to misalignment with his immediate peer, this series of silences, accompanied by embodied action and self-initiated turn shifts, made the teacher aware of a residual problem of comprehension deficiency, which he supported through extended wait time. This silent engagement took place without any vocalisation, which can be frustrating for the teacher due to lack of verbal account, which was also not directly addressed to the teacher. However, it can also be regarded as a learner's endeavour, a step to proceed with interaction by holding the floor, seeking mutual alignment with the teacher. This is a good example of non-verbal cues creating 'space for learning' (Walsh, 2011), employed by students and contributing to and shaping their learning space, thus functioning as 'a dialogic and pedagogical role' (Park, 2017: 124) for silence alongside embodied action as an interactional resource. This was further supported by the teacher's scaffolding to lead learners' L2 output.

4. Alternative use of questions and content feedback

In this extract, the teacher initiated a discussion about a person the student met regularly and the question was met with repeated silent replies or monosyllabic answers. However, the alternate use of questions, particularly yes/no questions, in subsequent turns contributed to alignment.

Extract 3.4
```
01   T:  the person you meet regularly, (.) for instance,
02       give me an example of the person you meet regularly
         + teacher gets closer to the student while walking
03   S:  (1.5)
04       yes
         +gaze is still secured, but without vocalisation
05       (2.6)
06   T:  give me one example(.) for instance, i meet a doctor regularly.
07→      do you meet a doctor regularly?
08   S:  (0.8) no=
09→T:    =no (.) i am healthy(.) so, who do you meet regularly?
10   S:  (3.5)
         + leaning her head towards her shoulder
11→T:    do you meet her regularly?
         + teacher points out her classmate sitting next to her
12   S:  (0.6) yes=
         [+nod and smile simultaneously
13→T:    =yes(.) your classmate, of course(.) do you meet the emperor
         regularly?
14   S:  (0.8)
15       no=
16→T:    = do you meet your mother regularly?
17   S:  (0.4)
18       yes.
         +smiling
19→T:    do you meet me regularly?
20   S:  (0.7)
         Yes.
21   T:  <how regularly do we meet?>(.) monthly?↑
22   S:  (3.1)
23►      °four times a month°
24   T:  weekly
```

In this extract, the teacher initiated the turn by asking a question, but this was met by a silent response of 1.5 seconds followed by a monosyllabic answer ('yes') as acknowledgement, then another longer silence. After a wait time, in line 06 the teacher reformulated the question, citing his own experience. At the following turn (line 07), as a natural transition, the teacher initiated a yes/no question. Then, the learner answered immediately. In line 09, this is followed by the teacher's content feedback and then immediate alternation of questions to a wh- question by the teacher, seeking to return to his original question in line 01. However, this wh- question led to another lengthy silence of 3.5 seconds, with the student's change in body posture indicating her engagement in thinking. Following this, the teacher re-alternates the question to a yes/no format, referring to the student's classmate and prompting her immediate reply.

The use of yes/no questions at turns 11, 13, 16 and 19, together with content feedback, shifted the interactional flow and recovered its coherence. Four continuous uses of yes/no questions all receive clear responses from the student. Then, in line 21, the teacher tries to elicit the learner's answer again with another interrogative question (<how regularly do we meet?>(.) monthly?), slowing down the speed of interaction. This time, the learner is able to provide her own answer ('four times a month'). Although her utterance is very soft, indicating lack of confidence, it attains mutual alignment as a reply.

Alternation between wh- question and yes/no questions in this context was an effective means to manipulate the length of silence or wait time, as Smith and King's (2017) study claims and as the shift of the interactional flow in turn exchanges illustrates. The shorter wait time is clearly associated with the use of a low cognitive level of yes/no questions in this extract. At the same time, yes/no questions function as 'interpretive resources' (Lee, 2008: 237) to determine what the learner can or cannot do within the sequences leading up to that point. In this sense, as Nakamura (2010: 13) claims, 'the sequential timing or positioning of the yes/no question' is important within this extract and the teacher successfully creates space for the learner to participate through a series of exchanges, enabling the learner to answer the initial question. This interactional trajectory demonstrates how the teacher facilitates a collective thinking process for students and makes it possible for the teacher to determine how to steer the next course of action, turn by turn.

5. Reformulations and discontinued interaction

The last extract shows an interaction which starts smoothly, then deteriorates when the second wh- question is initiated by the teacher.

Extract 3.5
01   T: where does she live now?
02   S: (0.4)

03   she is in tokyo.(.) she is working at a company now.
          + mutual gaze
04   T: what kind of company?
05   S: (1.2)
06   subway.
07→T: a::::::h, so(.) when will you see her again?=
08   S: =eh?
          pardon?
          + student looks puzzled, looking at the teacher
09→T: when(.) <will you see your friend again?>
10   S: (6.2)
          + looking down
11→T: when(.) *itsu* (.) <will you see your friend again?>
          when
12   S: (10.2)
          + still looking down, at 7.2 seconds, started looking away
13→T: when (.) will you [see her again?]
14▶ S: [↑a::::h, da↑me:::::, wakara↑na:::::i]
                             o::::h, no:::,   (I) don't know

The initial smooth transition of turns encounters trouble after the teacher initiates a second wh- question in line 07. In line 08, the learner immediately code-switches to L1, a Japanese token or interjection to indicate that clarification is required for the question asked. His facial expression also indicates comprehension difficulty. Then, in the following turn (line 09), the teacher reformulates the question with the use of paralinguistic cues such as increased volume and slower tempo. However, in line 10, the student remains silent while looking down, indicating continued uncertainty about the meaning of the question, while the teacher waits a relatively long time (6.2 seconds).

Then the teacher uses intra-sentential code-switching, with more distinctive articulation of individual words and simultaneous attempts to emphasise their meaning, followed by another slow-paced repetition of the original utterance in the previous turns at lines 07 and 09. However, this is followed by the learner's much longer silent response, lasting 10.2 seconds. When the learner starts shifting his gaze direction, the teacher asks the question a fourth time. However, his utterance is overlapped by the student's code-switched utterance in Japanese, meaning (o::::h, no:::, (I) don't know) in English. The student's reaction indicates he has given up proceeding with the interaction as a reactive token, (o::::h, no:::) highlighting his difficulty as he expresses his despair at failing to comprehend. This is emphasised by vowel elongation and his utterance's overlap with the teacher's fourth question. In this case, the way the student responds to the question shows his increasing anxiety at his lack of comprehension.

Although this extract suggests multiple reformulations attempted by teachers, involving the use of paralinguistic cues as well as code-switching, it was not possible to reach alignment because the learner's readiness to comprehend the question did not meet the teacher's expectations. The shift in the learners' gaze as he pauses also indicates psychological change. Although it is beyond the scope of this study to determine the exact cause of this student's highly anxious psychological state and his lack of readiness, which even leads to overlaps with the teacher's utterance, the unreadiness to re-engage in interaction appears to contribute to this. This extract shows that the teacher's awareness of the learner's (un)willingness to communicate (Sert, 2015) associated with high anxiety can also influence the effectiveness of wait time, as it shows how the learner voluntarily shortened the thinking time, indicating comprehension deficiency and terminating the interactional sequence.

Findings

The results of the questionnaire, along with the analysis of L2 classroom interactional discourse and the relationship between the use of wait time by the teacher and teacher talk as CIC, illustrates emerging interactional patterns in L2 output and focal points whose relationships warrant further exploration. First, the questionnaire results indicated that the teachers surveyed did not necessarily have negative perceptions of the 'silent learner'. Instead, learners' silence and associated teachers' frustration are conditional, situated phenomena, depending on the teachers' contextual understanding. In fact, teachers considered wait time an important teaching strategy, along with other elicitation strategies. Teachers referred to three other principal pedagogical approaches to harnessing learner silence as a means to L2 output: (1) linguistic support through reformulations, including the alternation of question types; (2) support with turn-taking organisation through changes to discourse dynamics involving the encouragement of peer interaction or shifting attention to another student; and (3) affective support to encourage L2 output or avoid putting students on the spot, taking account of groupism in the classroom. These three focal points raised by the teachers can be considered important pedagogical perspectives in this specific context.

Second, the data from CA demonstrates the existence of elicitation strategies frequently used by teachers as scaffolding when encountering learner silence. In most cases, its use had dual or multiple functions or was combined with varied elicitation strategies for linguistic support, also contributing to the coherence of interactional flow and providing interactional space for learners to develop answers within a discourse.

In this study, three frequently used representative elicitation strategies emerged: (1) formulations, content feedback, contextualisation and direct prompts as DIUs; (2) interaction with learners' non-verbal cues while reading embodied and paralinguistic messages sent by learners, such as interactional gaze, body posture, repetition and self-selected turn shifts to immediate peers (this is joined by teachers' own use of paralinguistic cues, such as intonation, accentuating emphasis, and volume and speed contributing to collaborative interaction); and (3) alternation of question type, especially between wh- questions and yes/no questions, in response to learners' replies. While the study by Smith and King (2017) showed that extended wait time is associated with longer utterances by advanced learners, signalling self-initiation, in the present study, learners of limited proficiency responded better to questions which led to final L2 output with the alternation of question types. This indicates that effective use of questions with precision timing relative to wait time can be largely context specific and varies according to learners' proficiency levels.

Further, in feedback turns in turn-taking organisation, the initiation of OISR by teachers to provide opportunities for learners to carry out self-repair was dominant. Self-repair was therefore mainly promoted as a reply to a teacher's attempted OISR through very subtle and implicit use of interactional resources such as silence accompanied by embodied action, softly uttered monosyllabic words and the use of repetition. However, with the use of these interactional resources, learners succeeded in maintaining interaction by replying to a teacher's attempted OISR and could also develop answers gradually within the interactional space created as the second part of adjacency pairs as an accomplishment of L2 output.

This study therefore finds that, from an interactional perspective, recurrent use of attempted OISR through wait time and elicitation strategies used by teachers significantly contributes to maintenance of the interactional processes and facilitates learners' verbal output, fostering collaborative interaction to reach alignment, mainly through the construction of extended turns. Although these instances of collaborative interaction did not primarily involve immediate juxtaposition or frequent verbal responses as SISR by learners, teachers' attempted use of OISR led to mutual alignment. That is, with this scaffolded help, learners succeeded in shaping their own learning space through this process and produced L2 output. These processes resulted in frequent delayed adjacency pairs (van Lier, 1984), but as accomplishments of interactional goals, evident through learners' L2 output as appropriate responses to questions asked several turns previously. In this sense, the way teachers interact with learners' silence can make learners' L2 output possible through appropriate elicitation techniques used as strategies for making moment-by-moment decisions. With this kind of scaffolded support, learners could further respond to each question, despite initial vocally unfilled silences, indicating initial difficulties they encountered or inner reflection they needed to undertake. Students chose to remain silent as a way to make tacit requests for teacher support or as part of their personal learning process. Although there were cases when learners' unreadiness prevented them from accomplishing their goals, there were also instances where learner silence interacted with teacher talk, fostering alignment through an extended collaborative process.

Conclusion and Pedagogical Implications

This study has highlighted the implicit role of classroom silence as an interactional resource functioning in various ways as a medium, which acts as a space for learning, thinking, reflecting, requesting teacher or peer support, registering comprehension difficulties or problems with L2 output or displaying partial understanding of pedagogical activity as epistemic status (Sert, 2015). Japanese students' use of silence is mostly non-vocal, or vocally unfilled silence (Saville-Troike, 1985), which can make it difficult for teachers to interpret silence or determine appropriate length of wait times and elicitation strategies. However, the co-presence of non-linguistic cues can also contribute to collaborative interaction.

The current study has also illustrated some interactional patterns showing how engagement with classroom silence is possible through varied scaffolded support from the teacher, usually manifest in the form of multiple extended turns used to accomplish interactional goals through delayed replies which the teacher needs to be mindful of, adopting a step-by-step approach.

Thus, the research presented here reveals specific interactional patterns which lead to L2 learner output towards specific pedagogical goals. Although it focuses on the analysis of dyadic interaction within teacher-fronted classes, varied orientations of activity types or topics at different stages of classroom learning may provide alternative opportunities for learners to self-initiate turns or self-repair their utterances. This can facilitate oral interaction in different ways according to specific group dynamics. This could be investigated further in future studies. However, in the case of the interactional decisions teachers need to make in any context, van Lier (2004: 37) claims that 'amplifying students' access to the linguistic and extralinguistic context means providing students with more than a single opportunity to come to terms with the language and concepts involved'.

Interacting with learners' situated and subtle responses to help them articulate meaning through wait time, and harnessing this interactional process by adjusting and fostering the dynamics of turn organisation along with varied elicitation strategies, not only raise awareness of learners' readiness but also potentially represent a pedagogical approach that is able to accomplish collaborative interaction through the medium of classroom silences.

Appendix. Transcript notations

[ ]	simultaneous talk, overlap
Yea::h	lengthening of sound
(.)	a very short pause or micro-pause
(1.5)	the length of the silence in relation to the surrounding talk
↑↓	sharply rising and falling intonations
< >	slower speech
> <	faster speech
[...]	omitted speech
italics	English translation
° °	soft voice
+	description of action
?	slightly rising intonation
.	slightly falling intonation
<u>line</u>	higher volume
=	no time lapse
(( ))	analyst's notes
→	teacher's move
▶	second part of adjacency pair

Self-reflection/Discussion Questions

(1) Reflect on occasions when you have encountered learner silences in L2 classrooms and discuss the different ways you interacted with students in these situations.

(2) Reflect on the turn exchanges in Extract 3.3 and consider whether you have come across similar tacit silent responses (from line 08) in L2 classrooms in your learning or teaching experience. Also consider whether there were any sociocultural differences between these responses.

(3) Reflect on and discuss silent moments in learning situations which ended in communication breakdown despite mutual efforts to maintain and progress interaction towards L2 output. What are the possible explanations for these silent moments?

(4) Using video-recorded L2 classroom discourse, explore the use of learner silences lasting for more than one second in question–answer sequences involving a teacher and a student. Examine how the third turn in an initiation–response–feedback (IRF) sequence was taken by the teacher or by the student and how initial learner silence was bridged to L2 output through collaborative interaction.

Recommended Reading

Nakane, I. (2005) Negotiating silence and speech in the classroom. *Multilingua – Journal of Cross-cultural and Interlanguage Communication* 24 (1–2), 75–100.

This paper explores interactive situations involving the use of learner silence in mainstream Australian university courses through analysis of classroom exchanges and follow-up interviews. Although this study identifies varied use of silence, the teachers and peers in these situations considered East Asian learners to be reticent. Nakane considers the role of contextual factors influential, especially perceptions of other participants. This study suggests an alternative perspective on the silence of Japanese students.

Harumi, S. (2011) Classroom silence: Voices from Japanese EFL learners. *ELT Journal* 65 (3), 260–269.

Harumi examines the voices of Japanese EFL learners, reflecting on their use of silence in the L2 classroom alongside those of English teachers. While this study identifies differences in their views on the use of silence, it also demonstrates how their perspectives fall into four distinct categories: linguistic, cultural, interactional and a fourth type involving affective factors. Harumi's study also illustrates what learners expect from pedagogy and, specifically, the role of teacher responsiveness in its various forms.

Wong, J. and Waring, H.A. (2012) *Conversation Analysis and Second Language Pedagogy: A Guide for ESL/EFL Teachers.* New York: Routledge.

This book raises awareness of learners' and teachers' spoken discourse in the L2 classroom and uses conversation analysis (CA) to examine different types of interaction. In Chapter 2, 'Turn-taking practices and language teaching', there are some insightful perspectives illustrating the use of silence in a range of sociocultural contexts. This book also suggests pedagogical approaches that can be adopted to enhance learners' L2 interactional skills, including the use of silence.

Gray, P. and Leather, S. (1999) *Safety and Challenge.* London: Delta Publishing.

This book presents a range of creative practical classroom activities, tailored to the needs of Japanese EFL learners in both monolingual and bilingual classrooms. The types of classroom methodology and pedagogical approaches presented illustrate what Japanese learners expect from these environments and ways in which the teacher can enhance oral communication and interact with student silence through these language activities. Gray and Leather also provide opportunities for teachers to reflect on Japanese students' interactional styles in L2 learning.

References

Anderson, F. (1993) The enigma of the college classroom: Nails that don't stick up. In P. Wadden (ed.) *A Handbook for Teaching English in Japanese Colleges and Universities* (pp. 101–110). New York: Oxford University Press.

Bao, D. (2014) *Understanding Silence and Reticence*. London: Bloomsbury.

Carroll, D. (2000) Precision timing in novice-to-novice L2 conversations. *Issues in Applied Linguistics* 11, 67–110.

Chavez, M. (2016) The first language in the foreign language classroom: Teacher model and student language use – an exploratory study. *Classroom Discourse* 7 (2), 131–163.

Gardner, R. (2007) Broken starts: Bricolage in turn starts in second language talk. In Z. Hua and P. Seedhouse (eds) *Language Teaching as Social Interaction* (pp. 58–71). London: Palgrave Macmillan.

Hall, J.K. (2007) Redressing the roles of correction and repair in research on second and foreign language learning. *Modern Language Journal* 91 (4), 511–526.

Hall, J.K., Hellermann, J. and Doehler, S.P. (eds) (2011) *L2 Interactional Competence and Development*. Bristol: Multilingual Matters.

Harumi, S. (2011) Classroom silence: Voices from Japanese EFL learners. *ELT Journal* 65 (3), 260–269.

Hashemi, M.R. (2013) Reflections on mixing methods in applied linguistics research, *Applied Linguistics* 33 (2), 206–212.

Hauser, E. (2010) Sophisticated interaction with limited linguistic resources. In *Language Learning and Social Interaction Through Conversation* (pp. 17–26). Osaka: Kansai University Centre for the Human Activity Theory.

Hawkins, S.J. (2015) Guilt, missed opportunities, and false role models: A look at perceptions and use of the first language in English teaching in Japan. *JALT Journal* 37 (1), 29–42.

Hosoda, Y. (2014) Missing response after teacher question in primary school English as a foreign language classes. *Linguistics and Education* 28, 1–16.

Hutchby, I. and Wooffitt, R. (1998) *Conversation Analysis: Principles, Practices and Applications*. New York: Wiley.

Ingram, J. and Elliott, V. (2015) A critical analysis of the role of wait time in classroom interactions and the effects on student and teacher interactional behaviours. *Cambridge Journal of Education* 46 (1), 37–53. doi: 10.1080/0305764X.2015.1009365.

Jarvis, J. and Robinson, M. (1997) Analysing educational discourse: An exploratory study of teacher response and support to pupils' learning. *Applied Linguistics* 18 (2), 212–228.

King, J. (2013) *Silence in the Second Language Classroom*. Basingstoke: Palgrave Macmillan.

Koshik, I. (2002) Designedly incomplete utterances: A pedagogical practice for eliciting knowledge displays in error correction sequences. *Research on Language and Social Interaction* 35 (3), 277–309.

Kozar, O. (2016) Teachers' reaction to silence and teachers' wait time in video and audio-conferencing English lessons: Do webcams make a difference? *System* 62, 53–62.

Lee, Y. (2007) Third turn position in teacher talk: Contingency and the work of teaching. *Journal of Pragmatics* 39, 180–206.

Lee, Y. (2008) Yes–no questions in the third turn position: Pedagogical discourse processes. *Discourse Processes* 45 (3), 237–262.

Liu, J. (2002) Negotiating silence in American classrooms. *Language and Intercultural Communication* 2 (1), 35–54.

Maroni, B. (2011) Pauses, gaps and wait time in classroom interaction in primary schools. *Journal of Pragmatics* 39, 190–206.

McHoul, A.W. (1990) The organization of repair in classroom talk. *Language in Society* 19, 349–377.

McPake, J. and Powney, J. (1998) A mirror to ourselves? The educational experience of Japanese children at school in the UK. *Educational Research* 402, 169–179.

Morris, S and King, J. (2018) Teachers' frustration in Japanese universities and emotion regulation in university language teaching. *Chinese Journal of Applied Linguistics* 41 (4), 433–452.

Nakamura, I. (2010) Yes/no questions as conversational expanders: Their effects on discourse and identity in interaction. *JALT Journal* 23 (3) (special issue on discourse and identity), 9–13.

Nakane, I. (2005) Negotiating silence and speech in the classroom. *Multilingua* 24 (1–2), 75–100.

Park, J. (2017) Multimodality as an interactional resource for classroom interactional competence (CIC). *Eurasian Journal of Applied Linguistics* 3 (2), 121–138.

Rowe, M.B. (1986) Wait time: Slowing down may be a way of speeding up! *Journal of Teacher Education* 37, 43–50.

Sacks, E., Shegloff, A. and Jefferson, G. (1974) A simplest systematics for the organization of turn-taking in conversation. *Language* 50 (4), 696–735.

Saville-Troike, M. (1995) The place of silence in an integrated theory of communication. In D. Tannen and M. Saville-Troike (eds) *Perspectives on Silence* (pp. 3–18). Norwood, NJ: Ablex.

Schegloff, A. (1968) Sequencing in conversational openings. *American Anthropologist* 70 (6), 1075–1095.

Schegloff, A. (2000) When 'others' initiate repair. *Applied Linguistics* 21 (2), 205–243.

Schegloff, A., Jefferson, G. and Sacks, H. (1977) The preference for self-correction in the organisation of repair. *Language* 53 (2), 361–382.

Seedhouse, P. (2011) Conversation analytic research into language teaching and learning. In E. Hinkel (ed.) *Handbook of Research in Second Language Teaching and Learning, Volume II* (pp. 345–363). New York: Routledge.

Sert, O. (2015) *Social Interaction and L2 Classroom Discourse*. Edinburgh: Edinburgh University Press.

Sert, O. (2017) Creating opportunities for L2 learning in a prediction activity. *System* 70, 14–25.

Sinclair, J. and Coulthard, M. (1975) *Towards an Analysis of Discourse*. Oxford: Oxford University Press.

Smith, L. and King, J. (2017) A dynamic systems approach to wait time in the second language classrooms. *System* 68, 1–14.

Stivers, T., Enfield, N., Brown, P., Englert, C., Hayashi, M., Heinemann, T. *et al.* (2009) Universals and cultural variation in turn-taking in conversation. *Proceedings of the National Academy of Sciences* 106 (26), 10587–10592.

ten Have, P. (2007) *Doing Conversation Analysis: A Practical Guide*. London: Sage Publications.

Tsui, A.B.M. (1996) Reticence and second language anxiety. In K. Bailey and D. Nunan (eds) *Voices from the Language Classroom* (pp. 145–167). New York: Cambridge University Press.

van Compernolle, R. (2011) Responding to questions and L2 learner interactional competence during language proficiency interviews: A microanalytic study with pedagogical implications. In J.K. Hall, J. Hellerman and S. Pekarek Doehler (eds) *L2 Interactional Competence and Development* (pp. 117–136). Bristol: Multilingual Matters.

van Lier, L. (1984) Analysing interaction in second language classrooms. *ELT Journal* 38 (3), 160–169.
van Lier, L. (2004) *The Ecology and Semiotics of Language Learning: A Sociocultural Perspective*. Boston: Kluwer Academic.
Walsh, S. (2011) *Exploring Classroom Discourse: Language in Action*. New York: Routledge.
Walsh, S. and Li, L. (2013) Conversations as space for learning. *International Journal of Applied Linguistics* 23 (2), 247–266.
Young, R. (2008) *Language and Interaction*. New York: Routledge.
Zarrinabadi, N. (2014) Communicating in a second language: Investigating the effect of teacher on learners' willingness to communicate. *System* 42 (1), 288–295.

4 Silence and Anxiety in the English-Medium Classroom of Japanese Universities: A Longitudinal Intervention Study

Jim King, Tomoko Yashima, Simon Humphries, Scott Aubrey and Maiko Ikeda

Introduction

This chapter reports on a longitudinal intervention study which focused on the anxiety, social inhibition and silent behaviour of foreign language learners studying English within three Japanese university English-medium classrooms. It comes in part as a response to King's (2013a, 2013b) large-scale, multi-site enquiry into the prevalence and causes of silence across Japan's varied tertiary L2 sector. Using a mixed-methods approach to data collection (structured observations, semi-structured interviews and stimulated recall), King investigated the oral participation, or lack of it, of over 900 learners within 30 classes at nine universities across Japan. After 48 hours of minute-by-minute structured observation, he found compelling quantitative evidence of 'a robust nation-wide trend, with minimal variation, towards silence within Japanese university foreign language classrooms' (King, 2013a: 95). Such a powerful pattern of silence across a diverse sample of learners suggests that single-cause explanations for student reticence are unlikely. And this was indeed found to be the case, as qualitative phases of the project revealed that the silent behaviour of individual learners emerged for a multiplicity of reasons stemming from the dynamic interplay between learner-internal variables and contextual factors operating at both an immediate classroom level and a higher sociocultural level (for a more in-depth and wide-ranging discussion of the dynamic interplay between context and language learners, see King, 2015). An individual-level analysis of learner silence suggested that in among these various factors, there appeared a strong connection between learners' anxious feelings of social inhibition in the classroom and their avoidance of L2 talk.

The research outlined above was essentially cross-sectional and did not provide any research-backed solutions to non-participatory learner silence, and hence the current longitudinal intervention study described in this chapter. Yashima *et al.* (2016) responded to King's study by designing an innovative small-scale intervention project which sought to answer the question: if silence has become such a strong norm in the Japanese university classroom for English as a foreign language (EFL), how can we encourage learners to break their silence and actively communicate in English? After observing a first-year group's weekly 20-minute discussion tasks over the course of an academic semester, they found dynamically fluctuating levels of oral participation, with an inverted relationship between silence and talk. Among various reasons for not participating in discussions, participants most frequently reported topic difficulty as being behind their silences, with anxiety being the reason mentioned second most often. Based on their findings the researchers suggest that to encourage participation, discussion topics should be selected which have a direct relevance for students and on which they can elaborate, while at the same time more attention should be paid to preparing learners for target language discussions through the use of rehearsal tasks, vocabulary priming and so on.

While silence is an inherently complex and ambiguous phenomenon which can be devilishly difficult to interpret and which defies easy generalisations, in the current study we do take an unapologetically negative view of silence when it is characterised by learner unresponsiveness and a withdrawal from oral participation in the target language. This view is informed by a broad and persuasive body of research on L2 output and interaction (e.g. de Bot, 1996; Ellis, 1999; Gass, 1997; Izumi, 2003; Long, 1996; Swain, 2005) which suggests that meaningful oral communication in the target language aids acquisition. Even so, it would be foolish to deem *all* instances of non-talk as undesirable: some silent episodes, usually involving the micro-silences of extended pausing, can be helpful to learners. For example, echoing Jaworski and Sachdev's (1998) findings within UK mainstream education, Bao (2014) makes the distinction between low-quality inhibitive silence and high-quality facilitative silence for L2 learners, suggesting the latter works to benefit learners' cognitions. Correspondingly, Harumi (2015: 128) suggests that some Japanese learners of English see silence as 'a "desirable space" for learning' which allows them time for comprehension and the formulation of ideas. Smith and King (2017) build upon this notion in their complexity-oriented study of L2 teachers' silent wait time. Defining wait time as 'the duration between a teacher elicitation and student response or second teacher utterance' (Smith & King, 2017: 1), they found this type of micro-silence played an intricate role in influencing patterns of talk in the classroom, with extended wait times (defined as over two seconds) helping shift discourse out of rigid initiation–response–feedback (IRF) patterns and into more student-driven phases. Care should be taken, though, not to overextend wait time, as unusually long inter-turn silences can lead to communication breakdown, are prone to misinterpretation and have the potential to be anxiety-inducing for some interlocutors (see King & Aono, 2017).

Over the last couple of decades, foreign language anxiety has attracted much attention from applied linguistics scholars conducting research within Japan's L2 education system (e.g. Kimura, 2017; Kitano, 2001; Matsuda & Gobel, 2004) and the general consensus of their endeavours is that anxiety works to hinder language learners both performatively and psychologically and is related to poor academic achievement, reduced self-confidence and problems with cognition. Although there exists some debate about the potentially beneficial effects that low levels of anxiety may have on stimulating student performance in certain situations (for a critical account of facilitative anxiety in L2 education, see Horwitz, 2017), the overwhelming evidence is that high levels of anxiety interfere with students' L2 speaking skills in particular, making it more difficult for them to orally interact in the target language and being linked to increased levels of reticence (see Liu & Jackson, 2011; Tsui, 1996). King's (2014) study contributes to this evidence by suggesting the Japanese university L2 classroom resembles an emotional danger zone which has rich potential for triggering anxiety among hypersensitive learners concerned about social evaluation. Adopting the idea that social anxiety is a key element of foreign language anxiety in a context which places great importance on maintaining face, that study found that many Japanese learners of English remained silent in the public arena of the classroom in order to protect their self-image and avoid both embarrassment and the negative judgements of their peers. King and Smith (2017) propose that a potentially effective approach for reducing social aspects of language anxiety and increasing learners' oral participation is for educators to carefully manipulate the group dynamics of their classrooms (see Dörnyei & Murphey, 2003). Among a number of other group-oriented strategies, they advise that:

> anything instructors can do at the start of courses to promote acceptance (a term from Humanistic Psychology meaning non-judgmental, positive regard) amongst class members will be of benefit in reducing the likelihood of negative evaluations occurring within the group. Interpersonal relationships based on acceptance acknowledge that human beings are complex and flawed but that they can still be regarded in a non-evaluative, positive manner. Classrooms characterized by a general feeling of acceptance represent learning contexts in which social fear beliefs are downplayed and the benefits of this for socially anxious silent learners are obvious. (King & Smith, 2017: 104)

Hence in the current study, while we acknowledge that an individual L2 learner's non-participatory silent behaviour may have multiple, interconnected sources (King, 2013a, 2013b), our intervention focuses primarily on strategies which aim to improve classroom dynamics and interpersonal relationships among students, to mitigate their feelings of anxiety and inhibition in L2 learning situations, with the overall goal of encouraging increased oral participation in the target language. If viewed from a complexity perspective (Larsen-Freeman & Cameron, 2008), our study's aim is to add perturbations to the discourse systems of the classrooms under investigation and the individuals within those classrooms with the objective of better understanding system behaviour in relation to oral participation and anxiety.

The Research Setting and Participants

The research was conducted at a large, private university located in a metropolitan area on Japan's main island of Honshu. The institution has a good reputation for its EFL education courses and runs a popular study-abroad programme, which sends large numbers of undergraduates on long-term sojourns to English-speaking countries. Access was gained to three intact first-year classes (Groups A, B and C) whose focus was on improving learners' English language communication skills and in which English was the medium for instruction. The overall student population totalled 71 (31 males, 40 females). Students taking part in the study were aged from their late teens through to their early twenties and their English proficiency levels were assessed to be above average in comparison with mainstream first-year undergraduates studying at other tertiary institutions in Japan. The three teachers were all highly experienced EFL educators who had gained tenured positions at the research site. One teacher was a Japanese woman, while the other two were male expatriates who had lived and worked in Japan for a number of years.

The Intervention Activities

Intervention activities were instigated in each of the three classes around the mid-point of the observation phase of the study (i.e. after the third observation had been completed) and, where appropriate, continued thereafter. In line with King's (2013a, 2013b) complexity-based notion that, rather than there being one single causative factor, student silence is actually governed by multiple, intervening learner-internal and contextual variables, the intervention adopted a multi-strategy approach which acknowledged the key role that factors relating to anxiety and social inhibition can play in the reticence of language learners in Japanese universities (see King, 2014; King & Smith, 2017). Thus, the intervention focused on three interrelated areas: raising awareness of how anxiety can impact upon students' in-class behaviours and classroom discourse patterns; the improvement of group/interpersonal dynamics and social collaboration among students; and encouragement to engage in target language interaction. Students were presented with a fictional case study of a highly anxious language learner and encouraged to reflect upon the case's relevance to their own experiences of learning English. After being introduced to typical cognitive and somatic symptoms that might be experienced by anxious L2 learners (e.g. raised heartbeat, difficulty concentrating), students were provided with an opportunity to discuss what they thought were the situations or activities they faced in lessons that were most likely to provoke anxiety, particularly when called upon to speak in the target language. Students were also encouraged to discuss potential strategies that they could use to deal with anxiety when learning English in order to reduce any feelings of inhibition and increase levels of oral participation in class.

The three groups were taught by highly experienced English language instructors familiar with the tenets and pedagogical techniques associated with a contextually sensitive approach to communicative language teaching in Japan (see Littlewood, 2007; Sato & Kleinsasser, 1999). Their classes typically provide opportunities for learners to engage in meaningful target language dialogue through staff–student and student–student interactions, and could be characterised by what Kramsch (1987) terms *convivial discourse* (i.e. talk that is somewhere between instructional and natural discourse on an interaction continuum). Learners displaying silent behaviour in the observed classes would not be doing so because of a complete lack of opportunity to speak English during lessons and therefore our intervention focused on improving group and interpersonal dynamics among class members, with the aim of encouraging a low-anxiety, cooperative classroom atmosphere in which learners could feel comfortable enough to seize these opportunities to speak in front of their peers when they arose.

To this end, each class group was asked to organise an out-of-class activity to take place as near to the in-class intervention as the students' schedules would allow. To encourage ownership of the task, they were given full autonomy in choosing the type of activity, its timing and venue. Instructors did not attend. Group A played ten-pin bowling together and then went out for dinner at a local restaurant, Group B also went out for dinner together and afterwards visited a karaoke parlour, while Group C had a picnic on the campus grounds. Our aim was to provide an opportunity for participants to freely interact and engage with each other in a situation that did not require English to be spoken and which would likely be less inhibiting than the public realm of the university foreign language classroom, with all its various social performance expectations (see Dörnyei, 2009). Thus, the out-of-class activity was instigated to promote group cohesiveness so that it could subsequently act as a foundation for building a cooperative learning atmosphere within classes. Teachers wishing to increase oral participation in their lessons and improve students' speaking performance ignore social-psychological dynamics at their peril. As Dörnyei and Murphey (2003: 65) rightly state, 'A cohesive group has a more pleasant atmosphere than a non-cohesive group, but cohesiveness is not just about feeling good. Past research has consistently revealed a positive relationship between group cohesiveness and performance.'

Methodology

The project employed a mixed-methods research design that drew its data from four sources: (1) structured classroom observations provided information about changing levels of oral participation and the incidence of silence over the course of six lessons; (2) self-report reflection sheets enabled learners at the end of each class to write down their thoughts about why they did or did not speak; (3) stimulated recall interviews allowed individual students to discuss their thoughts and feelings about specific silent episodes they had encountered in the classroom; and (4) teachers wrote reflection memos after each observed lesson had concluded.

Instruments and Procedures

Structured observations

To track any changes in oral participation patterns and the amount of silence occurring during lessons taking place pre- and post-intervention, a modified version of the Classroom Oral Participations Scheme (COPS) (King, 2013a, 2013b; see also Peng in Chapter 8 of the present volume) was employed. The COPS consists of nine low-inference categories of student/teacher talk and allows for data to be recorded directly onto the scheme using an exclusive focus coding approach (Spada & Fröhlich, 1995). As the observer is required to tally rather than infer classroom events, the COPS provides a highly reliable method of real-time coding that can be performed by a single researcher. The nine COPS categories of participant organisation of oral participation are: teacher-initiated talk; teacher response; student-initiated talk; student response; students speaking in a single pair/group; students speaking in multiple pairs/groups; choral drilling; off-task melee; and silence above the level of pauses and hesitations. These illustrate who is talking during the course of a lesson and how the talk is arranged, and conversely tell us much about who does not talk and remains silent. Structured observation inevitably involves restricted coding categories and so to offset this, space is provided on the COPS for the observer to make freehand notes about classroom events in parallel to in-time coding. On the original COPS, this in-time coding was performed minute by minute. In the current study, we wanted to achieve an even greater level of accuracy than this. Through a process of careful piloting we were able to reduce the observation segment down to 30 seconds, by removing the individual student modality sections of the scheme. An inter-rater reliability score of 84.06% was achieved among three observers following more than two hours of observations in two lessons.

Each of the study's three classes was observed six times over the course of the 2017 spring term (the start of the academic year in Japan), three times before the intervention class and three times after. This resulted in a total of over 21 hours of data built up from more than 2500 observation segments, each of 30 seconds. For each class, the observer took up a non-intrusive position at the front of the classroom so that staff–student/student–student interactions were easily visible and refrained from engaging students in any conversation. By adopting a non-intrusive, passive role during lessons and by audio-recording rather than video-recording the classes, the observer was able to keep participant reactivity (see Allwright & Bailey, 1991) to a minimum.

Self-report reflection sheets, stimulated recall interviews and teacher reflection memos

Complementing the study's observation data, students completed self-report reflection sheets (see Yashima *et al.*, 2016b) at the end of each class. Open-ended questions on the sheets asked learners to reflect upon their oral participation during the preceding lesson and to think about possible reasons that might have contributed to why they either did or did not speak. To help provide rich data, learners were able to choose whether to complete the sheets in English, Japanese or a mixture of both languages. By and large, the vast majority of these retrospective accounts were written in Japanese. The study's three instructors were also asked to reflect upon the classroom events they had encountered during the observed classes and to write down at the end of each lesson a short memo providing their perspectives on students' oral participation patterns, any silence incidents which occurred and, later on, how they perceived the intervention activities and their effects.

Further complementing observation data and providing another more fine-grained source of individual-level analysis as to why some learners in the study refrained from speech, 13 stimulated recall interviews (see Gass & Mackey, 2000) were conducted over the course of the project. Using the completed COPS instrument as the main stimulus, along with learning materials and a digital audio-recording of the lesson when necessary, these interviews elicited retrospective testimony from learners who were either responsible for specific silence incidents (e.g. providing a silent response to a question/solicit) or directly involved in such incidents (e.g. being a member of a group in which one or more participants did not speak). Our aim was to elicit testimony about how individual learners perceived their own silent behaviour, the silences of their co-learners and also the classroom activities they were being asked to perform. Deliberately, the recall sessions were relatively unstructured and so in addition to focusing on students' concurrent thoughts, feelings and emotions, we allowed discussion to take place that was not cognitively oriented but was still relevant to the research topic. To avoid memory decay, all recall interviews took place within 24 hours of the observed lesson. As with the self-report reflection sheets, stimulated recall participants were able to choose whether to use their L1, L2 or a mixture of both languages in order to help them give a fuller account. These accounts were audio-recorded with the participants' consent and later transcribed verbatim. Where translation from Japanese to English was necessary, sections of the data were back-translated (Brislin, 1970) to ensure accuracy.

Results and Discussion

Structured observations: Patterns of talk and silence

Tally marks were counted for each of the nine variables columns of the modified version of the COPS, with the totals indicating how much time was taken up during each observed lesson by the various categories of whole-class oral participation. This then enabled us to work out the average time taken up by each observed data variable over the course of more than 21 hours of structured classroom observation performed

Table 4.1 Observation results across the three groups

	Pre-intervention				Post-intervention					
	Total	M	SD	%	Total	M	SD	%	t	p
T initiated	668	222.67	72.13	48.94	748	249.33	16.26	60.91	0.57	0.63
T response	24	8	11.36	1.76	2	0.67	0.58	0.16	1.15	0.37
S initiated	6	2	1	0.44	2	0.67	1.15	0.16	1.51	0.27
S response	120	40	40.85	8.79	95	31.67	2.52	7.74	0.36	0.76
Ss pair/grp single	0	0	0	0	0	0	0	0	N/A	N/A
Ss pair/grp multi	398	132.67	54.93	29.16	240	80.00	34.18	19.54	2.24	0.15
Choral	0	0	0	0	0	0	0	0	N/A	N/A
Off-task melee	26	8.67	11.72	1.90	102	34.00	6.56	8.31	5.02	0.04*
Silence	123	41	12.12	9.01	39	13.00	5.57	0.73	6.73	0.02*

M, mean; SD, standard deviation; T, teacher; S, student; Ss, students; grp, group; multi, multiple.
*Statistically significant at $p < 0.05$.
1296.5 minutes of observation (21 hours 36.5 minutes).

during the study. Table 4.1 shows the number of 30-second tally marks and means coded for each oral participation category during pre- and post-intervention observations for the three groups combined, along with the percentage changes. The table further shows frequency data for each category of oral participation that was observed across the whole study. Paired *t*-tests were carried out for each type of classroom talk, in order to investigate whether post-intervention changes were statistically significant. With $p < 0.05$, significant differences were found in two categories: off-task melee and silence. This increase in off-task melees and decrease in the amount of silence could indicate an improvement in group dynamics as the learners became more familiar with their peers and comfortable in each other's company.

The results presented in Table 4.1 illustrate well the asymmetrical nature of classroom discourse, with the study's three teachers being responsible for the majority of the talk that was observed both pre- and post-intervention. The study's overall findings on participation patterns are broadly comparable to those uncovered in King's (2013a, 2013b) Japan-wide investigation, with there being a similarly marked contrast in occurrences of near non-existent student-initiated talk in comparison with much more ubiquitous teacher-initiated talk. That said, it should be noted that the apparent decrease in the amount of student-response talk appears to be due primarily to a large amount of student-response talk in one class during the pre-intervention observations (87 coded instances). In fact, two out of three classes increased their talk in this category from pre- to post-intervention. Over the whole study, just over half of all lesson time was taken up by teachers talking (cf. Chaudron, 1988; Tsui, 1985) as they presented information, posed questions, gave task instructions, provided feedback and so on, while a mere four minutes of the study's observation time was taken up by students initiating discourse. The vast majority of teacher-talk was teacher-initiated (e.g. teacher-fronted explanations), with two out of the three observed classes increasing teacher-initiated talk from pre- to post-intervention. The complete absence of any instances of choral drilling or the use of a single pair or group of students to model interactions reflects a movement away from behaviourist approaches to L2 pedagogy.

In spite of the fact that teachers still dominated talk in their classrooms, numerous opportunities were provided for students to speak with each other using the target language in pairs and groups, and this accounted for nearly a quarter of the study's observation time. Even when the majority of the class were actively engaged in this type of activity and it was recorded on the COPS, pockets of silence could still persist within a classroom and instances of this were documented in the instrument's notes column when particular students were observed to be either unable or unwilling to engage in pair-based or group-based speaking tasks. Stimulated recalls and the self-report reflection sheets enabled us to look more closely at why individual learners remained silent either during these speaking tasks or in response to teachers' questions, and so it is to these contributory factors that the discussion now turns.

Pre-intervention student self-reflection reports on the sources of their silent behaviour

Results from the first three observations for each class show that silence was the third most commonly observed data variable, accounting for just under 10% of class time. In the same period, students responding to teachers' solicitations also accounted for just under 10% of lesson time. Although representing a form of student talk, it should be remembered that this category of oral participation tended to involve just a single learner speaking while the rest of his or her classmates remained silent and many participants were observed to be either unwilling or unable to volunteer answers during open-class exchanges with their teacher. Indeed, Group C's instructor reflected that there was 'Almost no response when I (i) greet at the beginning of the class, (ii) ask questions relating to the class topic, (iii) ask for answers to comprehension questions'.

Self-report reflection data from these initial classes point towards a degree of anxiety and inhibition among some participants as they struggled to become accustomed to their new L2 learning situation, with its unfamiliar instructor and peers. As participant B08F put it, 'I wasn't able to speak much because I didn't know anybody. I get tense when I speak up or talk to the teacher.' This learner and others from all three groups used the Japanese term *kinchou suru* on their reflection sheets to indicate they had experienced feelings of tension, nervousness or mental strain which they believed had contributed to them not speaking in English at certain points during the class.

Other learners revealed concerns about their perceived lack of L2 communicative competence and how this affected their participation (for more on the relationship between anxiety, perceived competence and willingness to communicate, see Yashima, 2002). For example, after Group C's first lesson, participant C19M wrote, 'I don't have confidence with my English ability and even when I had some ideas in Japanese, I couldn't put them into English', while C04M revealed, 'I was very nervous as it was the first class. I'm not good at listening and comprehending English.' At the conclusion of Group A's initial class, A10F noted 'I was ashamed of my terrible pronunciation. I couldn't find the right English vocabulary straight away and I was anxious because I wasn't sure the words I was going to use were correct.' Participant A14F disclosed, 'I felt overwhelmed because people around me spoke better English than me. I can't be confident.' Foreign language anxiety strongly correlates with perceived communication competence (see e.g. MacIntyre & Charos, 1996) and anxious students tend to make negative comparisons of their own performance with that of other learners. It is indeed unfortunate that anxious individuals are prone to make negatively skewed assessments of their own performance. In part, this is because their cognitive resources are directed inwards, monitoring internal reactions and perceived self-generated image, thus diverting attention away from an objective assessment of external information (e.g. their interlocutor's responses) relating to how they are actually performing and appearing to others (King, 2014).

Pre-intervention student accounts of specific in-class silence incidents

Stimulated recall interviews conducted immediately after observed lessons allowed us to investigate in more detail specific silence episodes, and provided student participants with an opportunity to volunteer a rich account of their thoughts, feelings and perceptions surrounding their own and others' classroom silences. Findings from recall sessions conducted before the intervention back up the study's self-report reflection data, with almost all of the 13 interviewees revealing they had to some extent experienced feelings of anxiety, worry or embarrassment related to speaking in the target language and concerns were expressed by some participants about the possibility of being negatively evaluated by their peers. For example, Chika (all names are pseudonyms), an 18-year-old member of Group A, was consistently silent in response to open-class solicits posed by her instructor. Preparing for study abroad, with a relatively high TOEIC exam score of 765 (the second highest band achievable) and choosing to do the interview entirely in English, it would be reasonable to assume that Chika did not remain silent because of any lack of language ability. Even so, when asked about her failure to respond to one particular question posed by her teacher, Chika revealed that she was desperately waiting for someone else to answer and that 'I don't want to make mistakes in front of many people. I know that is not a good thing for studying English but I'm Japanese so I'm not good at English.' Apart from her concern about being negatively evaluated by others, it is interesting that Chika saw her nationality as a plausible excuse for her supposed lack of L2 competence. For some time now, scholars employing a nationalism discourse have been debating the threat posed to Japanese identity by English language education (see Aspinall, 2003; Tsuda, 2000). Key to this debate is the idea adopted by Chika and expressed so succinctly by the communication scholar Haru Yamada (1997: 140) that 'You are Japanese because you speak Japanese, and if you speak Japanese, you do not – indeed you cannot speak a foreign language fluently.'

Echoing Chika's testimony, Rie, an 18-year-old languages major from Group C who had been learning English since the age of two, shared her concerns about her classroom self-image and how feelings of inhibition contributed to her silent behaviour. In the class that formed the basis for a subsequent stimulated recall interview with Rie, her instructor posed an open-class question about the level of difficulty of a homework task. After reframing the question twice and waiting for a total of around 10 seconds, the instructor pleaded 'Respond to me!', but was again met by silence from the whole class. When Rie was asked about this incident she related how at high school her excellent pronunciation and willingness to speak had marked her out as being different from her classmates and that her high school English teacher had told her, in no uncertain terms, 'I know you can speak English but it's everyone's class. Don't speak too much.' This negative experience seems to have stayed with Rie, feeding her self-consciousness and helping to shape her current beliefs about what is appropriate classroom discourse and what is not. Hence, in front of the audience of her university classmates Rie avoided volunteering any answers or comments but was happy to respond when directly nominated. This pattern of behaviour reflects the fact that learners' subjective memories of their past learning experiences can strongly connect to present behaviours (Falout, 2016).

For Japanese learners of English, the foreign language classroom represents a highly public social performance situation in which an absence of good interpersonal dynamics between members can contribute to feelings of inhibition, hypersensitivity to others' judgements and the avoidance of talk (King, 2013a, 2014). This is especially true during the initial lessons of a course, when students are on guard and 'observe each other suspiciously, sizing up one another and trying to find a place in an unestablished and unstable hierarchy' (Dörnyei & Murphey, 2003: 14). Rie certainly was sizing up her classmates and making comparisons between their English abilities and her own. In her recall interview she recounted how she had heard one particular classmate, Natsuki, speaking relatively fluently during group-work tasks and that this student's better-than-average English pronunciation had been commented upon by other class members. It turned out that Natsuki was actually a third-year student who was repeating the course after having failed it initially as a freshman. Believing Natsuki had been staring at her, Rie confided she was unsure whether the third year was friendly or not and that Natsuki's presence in the class had made her quieter than would otherwise have been the case. Although seemingly inconsequential, Rie's testimony does illustrate well the tendency of Japanese students to observe quite rigid *senpai/kōhai* (junior/senior) distinctions which impact upon both their language and behaviour. Indeed, in her own stimulated recall interview, Natsuki related how class members had started talking to her using *keigo* (honorific expressions) after they had found out she was a third-year student. Silence and power are inexorably linked and status inequalities do play a role in influencing whether a person decides to refrain from speech within a particular situation (Braithwaite, 1990; Saville-Troike, 1985). Usually, the less power/status a person has, the more likely it is that he or she will remain silent. In contrast to this, Natsuki reported that she held back from giving verbal responses to the instructor's questions because she 'knew all the answers' and wanted to give other students the opportunity to speak. Even so, Natsuki's supposedly higher status did not save her from feelings of apprehension about communicating in the target language and she confided how she felt her younger classmates' expectations were too high: 'I think my English is not perfect but they expect it to be…. I worry about if I'll make a mistake. If I make a mistake, I'll be embarrassed so I don't want other students to expect my English is perfect.'

Post-intervention structured observation results: Changing patterns of talk and silence

With their emphasis on anxiety, inhibition and social discomfort, it is clear from qualitative results garnered from the first half of the study's student reflection reports and stimulated recall interviews that an intervention targeting negative affect among learners and the improvement of group and interpersonal dynamics as a means of combating non-participatory silence was indeed justified. However, how did oral participation patterns change, if at all, after the intervention activities were implemented? Table 4.1 reveals some interesting changes. The first thing to note is that the frequency of whole-class silence recorded on the COPS in the second half of the study dropped by just over 8 percentage points. However, this decrease was accompanied by a significant rise in the proportion of lesson time taken up by teacher-initiated talk (an increase of nearly 12 percentage points averaged out across the three groups), along with a surprising drop in students talking in multiple pairs/groups (down nearly 10 percentage points). Upon closer inspection, the observation results for individual classes tell a slightly more nuanced story. Teacher-initiated talk in Group C actually reduced by just over 6 percentage points during the second phase of observations, while in Groups A and B it increased, with the former group seeing a significant rise of over 31 percentage points, from 37.59% of lesson time to 69.35%. Reflecting upon events of a lesson after the intervention, Group A's instructor wrote: 'I think that I spoke for too long (about 30 minutes). I tried to ask questions, but the students were very quiet today. I had to nominate them…. They were sat at individual desks rather than in groups, so this might have deadened the dynamic.' Of course, the more a teacher talks, the more silent learners may become, and the more silent they become, the likelihood is that the teacher will talk more. Certainly, results for individual groups show that increases in teachers' talking time appeared to correspond to a decrease in opportunities for learners to engage in small-group speaking tasks. While Group C saw a slight rise in the proportion of students speaking in multiple pairs/groups, Groups A and B experienced declines of around 15 percentage points in the second half of the study.

Post-intervention reductions in the proportion of observed whole-class silence were relatively stable across the three groups. Other categories of oral participation saw either negligible changes or no change at all, apart from the variable 'off-task melee'. In the second half of the study, the mean average class time taken up by learners being off-task and engaged in laughter and raucous chatting in Japanese with peers rose by more than 6 percentage points. This finding is significant and is particularly intriguing when we consider that a key aim of the intervention's out-of-class activity was to improve interpersonal dynamics within the classes and make students feel more comfortable with each other in order to facilitate cooperation and interaction. Even though in this case the interaction was not in the target language, an increase in the frequency of off-task melees would suggest improving socio-psychological dynamics between learners as they become more familiar with each other and establish functioning social structures (see Forsyth, 2009). This process could well have occurred anyway as the courses progressed, even without the helping hand of the extracurricular activities. Structured observation data can only paint part of the picture of what is happening in classrooms and so it is to participants' individual-based qualitative data that the discussion now turns, in order to find out more about how participants perceived the intervention activities.

Participants' perceptions of the intervention activities and their effects

Akari, an 18-year-old member of Group C, was observed to be consistently silent during lessons, avoiding giving any answers to questions posed by the teacher and participating only minimally in speaking tasks. Like many others in the study, Akari reported that she was afraid of making mistakes and that she felt speaking out in English was potentially embarrassing. She also described her class as having a 'heavy atmosphere'. In her stimulated recall interview following Group C's fifth observed lesson, Akari revealed that she believed the out-of-class social activity had made little difference in helping class members get to know and feel more comfortable with each other. In comparison with the other groups, Group C's activity of an on-campus picnic appears to have been the most superficial and Akari seems not to have affectively engaged with the event: 'It would've been okay if it'd been one-to-one but we all got together and didn't know what to talk about ... it ended up just being a photo opportunity.' Other students were much more positive about having the opportunity to interact with peers outside of class, particularly interviewees from Group A. For example, Chika believed that the 'social activity might have helped us. Since then, everyone definitely opened up. Before it, we knew each other's faces but nothing more.... I think the social activity has made us more positive'. Naota described having 'talked to people who I don't talk to normally and we became good friends.... It used to be difficult to talk to others because they were strangers but now I know who's who. There used to be a distance but now I know who they are and it's better.'

The instructors' reflection memos revealed that their reactions to the social activity were mixed. Group A's teacher deemed the initiative to have been a great success and related that, in their subsequent class, students very much enjoyed watching a video and looking at photos of the event. This lively atmosphere contrasts sharply with the one perceived by Group B's instructor, who believed his students' event had had some unexpected consequences for the level of oral participation in the subsequent class. He wrote:

> This was the day after the out-of-class activity. There were five students absent (the most all semester) and students seemed very tired. They went out for dinner the night before, maybe some of them drank some alcohol, so the atmosphere wasn't very conducive for lots of interaction. Additionally, the discussion topic was very challenging. In terms of speaking English, I would say this was probably the worst discussion of the semester.

Qualitative data related to the in-class intervention activities focusing on students' feelings of anxiety and inhibition when speaking English were, on the whole, more positive. During the intervention, learners were taught to recognise typical cognitive and somatic reactions to anxiety and discussed what type of activities in the foreign language classroom typically made them feel anxious. Possible strategies for overcoming negative affect and actively participating in the target language were also discussed. In two of his post-intervention self-reflection reports, C24M used the expression *haji o suteru* (literally 'throw away the shame') when explaining why he had spoken up in classes subsequent to the anxiety intervention, noting 'I tried to look into the person's eyes while talking. I threw away the shame.' Also commenting on how she felt better able to deal with negative affect, participant A75F disclosed, 'I think I was more confident than usual because we discussed as a class how to get rid of the tension before group discussions.' The comments of these students and others point towards the effectiveness of the intervention and an improving atmosphere in their classrooms which could encourage them to increase their target language participation. That said, it would be misleading to give the impression that some students did not continue to struggle with feelings of embarrassment and inhibition impacting upon their participation in post-intervention lessons. Also, it should be remembered that the causes of learner silence are multiple and dynamic, and relate not only to individual and group psychological processes (King, 2013a). Data from self-reflection reports show that, for a number of learners, task complexity and the difficulty of the topic for discussion (cf. Yashima *et al.*, 2016a) in particular continued to play a role in this regard during the second half of the study.

Conclusion

By employing a series of structured classroom observations of three English-medium classes over the course of a semester, this study tracked the oral participation levels of 71 undergraduates studying English as a foreign language in lessons designed to improve their speaking and listening skills. Despite making some tentative claims, there are some limitations to this study that need to be highlighted in order to direct future studies. Firstly, our research design lacked a control group, therefore making it difficult to attribute the reduction in non-participatory silence exclusively to the intervention. Secondly, while the sample was of a respectable size and contained participants from a very specific context (i.e. first-year students of good proficiency), a future study with a larger sample size could, for example, investigate proficiency as a mediating variable.

Despite accomplished instructors using a context-sensitive form of communicative language teaching and the relatively high L2 proficiency levels of students, the research presented in this chapter provides further quantitative evidence of the lack of student-initiated discourse and the continued existence of non-participatory silence that can be found among some learners within the Japanese university EFL classroom. Qualitative data collected prior to the intervention from students' written self-report reflections and a series of stimulated recall interviews pointed towards individuals' feelings of anxiety about using English and learners' social inhibition and discomfort as key factors connected to the avoidance of target language talk during lessons. These findings would appear to justify the project's intervention activities, which were designed to mitigate student anxiety, improve classroom dynamics and build group cohesiveness, with the overall aim being a reduction in the frequency of non-participatory silences. While the proportion of silence across the classes did reduce in the second half of the study, that is, after the intervention, this drop was accompanied by a reduction in students talking in pairs/groups and a significant increase in teacher-initiated talk. These findings serve to underline the key role teachers play in shaping discourse participation patterns within classrooms as their institutional status allows them to determine learning tasks, topics for discussion and who has access to the floor. While it is difficult to assign the drop in observed instances of whole-class silence conclusively to the intervention activities, noticeable increases in off-task melees would suggest that interpersonal relationships between class members had improved by the second half of the study. Although the intervention activities were by no means a panacea for all participants, qualitative data from this phase of the study suggest that many students perceived the out-of-class group-building events and in-class anxiety-related learning activities to be useful in encouraging them to deal with feelings of social embarrassment, to break free from inhibitive silence and to actively participate in their English classes.

Self-reflection/Discussion Questions

(1) Think about the last time you had to speak in a public situation in front of people you did not know very well. For example, it might have been in a meeting, at a social gathering or perhaps within a classroom. How did you feel before, during and after speaking? Did you feel comfortable or uncomfortable at any time? Why?
(2) Citing Smith and King (2017), this chapter argues that promoting *acceptance* (non-critical, positive regard) among learners is a key part of manipulating group dynamics in order to reduce anxiety and encourage target language interaction. What are some possible ways that language teachers can promote acceptance at the start of courses?
(3) The three classes in this study undertook an extracurricular activity in order to try to improve social relationships among group members. To what extent do you think teachers in universities should be involved in or should encourage this type of initiative? What are the possible pros and cons?
(4) It would seem that the nature of the learning task is a key factor (among many) in whether someone experiences anxiety and remains silent in the L2 classroom. Do you think it is possible to design learning tasks that are so interesting and stimulating that learners become fully engaged during the task and their anxious feelings about speaking just fall away? If so, what might be some characteristics of these tasks and how might they be presented to learners in a classroom context you are familiar with?

Recommended Reading

Dörnyei, Z. and Murphey, T. (2003) *Group Dynamics in the Language Classroom*. Cambridge: Cambridge University Press.

This is an excellent introductory text for educators wanting to find out more about how group dynamics can affect student behaviour and discourse within language classrooms. Written in an accessible style with lots of practical pedagogical tips, the book considers why some groups of learners develop the ability to cooperate and communicate with each other well and why others do not.

Smith, L. and King, J. (2018) Silence in the foreign language classroom: The emotional challenges for L2 teachers. In J.D. Martinez Agudo (ed.) *Emotions in Second Language Teaching* (pp. 323–340). Dordrecht: Springer.

This chapter considers the emotional effects that silence can have on teachers and their identity development within the foreign language classroom. Smith and King draw attention to three types of affective silence (related to embarrassment, anger and disengagement) that teachers might encounter in their work and suggest a series of emotion-regulation strategies for mitigating the negative effects of these silences.

King, J. and Aono, A. (2017) Talk, silence and anxiety during one-to-one tutorials: A cross-cultural comparative study of Japan and UK undergraduates' tolerance of silence. *Asia Pacific Education Review* 18 (4), 489–499.

Like the current chapter, this open-access paper explores the issues of silence and anxiety in an educational setting but does so from a cross-cultural, comparative perspective and focuses on one-to-one tutorials. Comparing Japanese English majors with their UK counterparts in a quasi-experimental study, the research questions the notion of a 'silent East' versus a 'talkative West', with some surprising results about how tolerant to silence students actually are when faced with an interlocutor who refuses to speak.

Acknowledgements

This project was funded in part by the Kansai University Visiting Scholar scheme. The lead author would like to express his thanks to Kansai University's Faculty of Foreign Language Studies and to Professor Tomoko Yashima in particular for helping to make this project of international collaboration possible. Thank you also to Professor Glenn Fulcher for his invaluable advice on statistical matters.

References

Allwright, D. and Bailey, K.M. (1991) *Focus on the Language Classroom: An Introduction to Classroom Research for Language Teachers*. Cambridge: Cambridge University Press.
Aspinall, R.W. (2003) Japanese nationalism and the reform of English language teaching. In R. Goodman and D. Phillips (eds) *Can the Japanese Change Their Education System?* (pp. 103–117). Oxford: Symposium.
Bao, D. (2014) *Understanding Silence and Reticence: Ways of Participating in Second Language Acquisition*. London: Bloomsbury.
Braithwaite, C.A. (1990) Communicative silence: A cross-cultural study of Basso's

hypothesis. In D. Carbaugh (ed.) *Cultural Communication and Intercultural Contact* (pp. 321–327). Hillsdale, NJ: Lawrence Erlbaum Associates.

Brislin, R.W. (1970) Back-translation for cross-cultural research. *Journal of Cross-cultural Psychology* 1 (3), 185–216.

Chaudron, C. (1988) *Second Language Classrooms: Research on Teaching and Learning*. Cambridge: Cambridge University Press.

de Bot, K. (1996) The psycholinguistics of the output hypothesis. *Language Learning* 46 (3), 529–555.

Dörnyei, Z. (2009) Individual differences: Interplay of learner characteristics and learning environment. *Language Learning* 59 (issue supplement 1), 230–248.

Dörnyei, Z. and Murphey, T. (2003) *Group Dynamics in the Language Classroom*. Cambridge: Cambridge University Press.

Ellis, R. (1999) *Learning a Second Language Through Interaction*. Amsterdam: John Benjamins.

Falout, J. (2016) Past selves: Emerging motivational guides across temporal contexts. In J. King (ed.) *The Dynamic Interplay Between Context and the Language Learner* (pp. 47–65). Basingstoke: Palgrave Macmillan.

Forsyth, D.R. (2009) *Group Dynamics* (5th edn). Belmont, CA: Wadsworth, Cengage Learning.

Gass, S.M. (1997) *Input, Interaction, and the Second Language Learner*. Mahwah, NJ: Lawrence Erlbaum Associates.

Gass, S.M. and Mackey, A. (2000) *Stimulated Recall Methodology in Second Language Research*. Mahwah, NJ: Lawrence Erlbaum.

Harumi, S. (2015) The implicit role of classroom silence in Japanese EFL contexts. In T. Harrison, U. Lanvers and M. Edwardes (eds) *Breaking Theory: New Directions in Applied Linguistics. Proceedings of the 48th Annual Meeting of the British Association for Applied Linguistics* (pp. 121–130). London: Scitsiugnil Press.

Horwitz, E.K. (2017) On the misreading of Horwitz, Horwitz, and Cope (1986) and the need to balance anxiety research and the experiences of anxious language learners. In C. Gkonou, M. Daubney and J.-M. Dewaele (eds) *New Insights into Language Anxiety: Theory, Research and Educational Implications* (pp. 31–47). Bristol: Multilingual Matters.

Izumi, S. (2003) Comprehension and production processes in second language learning: In search of the psycholinguistic rationale of the output hypothesis. *Applied Linguistics* 24 (2), 168–196.

Jaworski, A. and Sachdev, I. (1998) Beliefs about silence in the classroom. *Language and Education* 12 (4), 273–292.

Kimura, H. (2017) Foreign language listening anxiety: A self-presentational view. *International Journal of Listening* 31 (3), 142–162.

King, J. (2013a) *Silence in the Second Language Classroom*. Basingstoke: Palgrave Macmillan.

King, J. (2013b) Silence in the second language classrooms of Japanese universities. *Applied Linguistics* 34 (3), 325–343.

King, J. (2014) Fear of the true self: Social anxiety and the silent behaviour of Japanese learners of English. In K. Csizér and M. Magid (eds) *The Impact of Self-concept on Language Learning* (pp. 232–249). Bristol: Multilingual Matters.

King, J. (ed.) (2015) *The Dynamic Interplay Between Context and the Language Learner*. Basingstoke: Palgrave Macmillan.

King, J. and Aono, A. (2017) Talk, silence and anxiety during one-to-one tutorials: A cross-cultural comparative study of Japan and UK undergraduates' tolerance of silence. *Asia Pacific Education Review* 18 (4), 489–499.

King, J. and Smith, L. (2017) Social anxiety and silence in Japan's tertiary foreign language classrooms. In C. Gkonou, M. Daubney and J.-M. Dewaele (eds) *New Insights into*

Language Anxiety: Theory, Research and Educational Implications (pp. 92–110). Bristol: Multilingual Matters.

Kitano, K. (2001) Anxiety in the college Japanese language classroom. *Modern Language Journal* 85 (4), 549–566.

Kramsch, C. (1987) Interactive discourse in small and large groups. In W. Rivers (ed.) *Interactive Language Teaching* (pp. 17–30). Cambridge: Cambridge University Press.

Larsen-Freeman, D. and Cameron, L. (2008) *Complex Systems and Applied Linguistics.* Oxford: Oxford University Press.

Littlewood, W. (2007) Communicative and task-based language teaching in East Asian classrooms. *Language Teaching* 40 (3), 243–249.

Liu, M. and Jackson J. (2011) Reticence and anxiety in oral English lessons: A case study in China. In L. Jin and M. Cortazzi (eds) *Researching Chinese Learners* (pp. 119–137). Basingstoke: Palgrave Macmillan.

Long, M.H. (1996) The role of the linguistic environment in second language acquisition. In W.C. Ritchie and T.K. Bhatia (eds) *Handbook of Language Acquisition. Vol. 2: Second Language Acquisition* (pp. 413–468). New York: Academic Press.

MacIntyre, P.D. and Charos, C. (1996) Personality, attitudes, and affect as predictors of second language communication. *Journal of Language and Social Psychology* 15 (1), 3–26.

Matsuda, S. and Gobel, P. (2004) Anxiety and predictors of performance in the foreign language classroom. *System* 32 (1), 21–36.

Sato, K. and Kleinsasser, R.C. (1999) Communicative language teaching (CLT): Practical understandings. *Modern Language Journal* 83 (4), 494–517.

Saville-Troike, M. (1985) The place of silence in an integrated theory of communication. In D. Tannen and M. Saville-Troike (eds) *Perspectives on Silence* (pp. 3–18). Norwood, NJ: Ablex.

Smith, L. and King, J. (2017) A dynamic systems approach to wait time in the second language classroom. *System* 68, 1–14.

Spada, N. and Fröhlich, M. (1995) *COLT Communicative Orientation of Language Teaching Observation Scheme: Coding Conventions and Applications.* Sydney: National Centre for English Language Teaching and Research, Macquarie University.

Swain, M. (2005) The output hypothesis: Theory and research. In E. Hinkel (ed.) *Handbook of Research in Second Language Teaching and Learning* (pp. 471–483). Mahwah, NJ: Lawrence Erlbaum.

Tsuda, Y. (2000) *Eigo beta no susume: Eigo shinkō wa mō suteyō [A Recommendation for Bad English: Let's Get Rid of English Worship].* Tokyo: Wani no NEW Shinsho.

Tsui, A.B.M. (1985) Analyzing input and interaction in second language classrooms. *RELC Journal* 16 (1), 8–32.

Tsui, A.B.M. (1996) Reticence and anxiety in second language learning. In K.M. Bailey and D. Nunan (eds) *Voices from the Language Classroom: Qualitative Research in Second Language Education* (pp. 145–167). Cambridge: Cambridge University Press.

Yamada, H. (1997) *Different Games, Different Rules: Why Americans and Japanese Misunderstand Each Other.* New York: Oxford University Press.

Yashima, T. (2002) Willingness to communicate in a second language: The Japanese EFL context. *Modern Language Journal* 86 (1), 54–66.

Yashima, T., Ikeda, M. and Nakahira, S. (2016a) Talk and silence in an EFL classroom: Interplay of learners and context. In J. King (ed.) *The Dynamic Interplay Between Context and the Language Learner* (pp. 104–126). Basingstoke: Palgrave Macmillan.

Yashima, T., MacIntyre, P.D. and Ikeda, M. (2016b) Situated willingness to communicate in an L2: Interplay of individual characteristics and context. *Language Teaching Research* 22 (1) 115–137.

5 Examining L2 Learners' Silent Behaviour and Anxiety in the Classroom Using an Approach Based on Cognitive-Behavioural Theory

Kate Maher

Introduction

At some point during a foreign language teacher's career, they have probably felt some unease about why students do not speak in the classroom as much as they expected them to. For some teachers, silent displays can make them feel concerned about how much the students are learning, especially if they hold beliefs about the importance of participation for developing language skills (Tsui, 1996). However, what about students' unease about their in-class behaviour and how they perceive the effect it is having on their language skills development? In the following excerpt, Mari, a second-year English major, is recounting one of her silent episodes in her English class, and the frustration, disappointment, fear and anxiety she felt about her in-class oral behaviour.

> I stayed up until 2 a.m. practising what I wanted to say, but when I went to class and sat with my group, I looked at their faces and imagined what they were thinking about me. Then it was gone. I didn't speak. (Mari)

Using King's (2014) model of silent L2 learners' social anxiety, based on cognitive-behavioural theory (CBT), this chapter examines the relationship between Mari's anxiety and observed in-class silent behaviour in the context of a Japanese university foreign language classroom. It also reports on the insights gained by the author and Mari through a series of CBT-style interviews and an activity. This approach revealed how her thoughts, emotions and physical sensations from being in the social context of the classroom were related to her silent behaviour by keeping her in a cycle of negative thoughts and anxiety that affected her oral participation. I will suggest how using CBT-style interviews and activities with anxious learners can help to improve confidence to participate in speaking tasks by increasing their awareness of the influence of negative cycles and how to break them.

A Review of Language Anxiety and Silence in the Japanese Context

Language anxiety can affect even proficient language learners – those who do not feel inhibited by content-specific factors such as linguistic knowledge or pronunciation (Horwitz, 2010; MacIntyre & Dewaele, 2014). This finding suggests that the context of the classroom can also play a significant role in the anxiety of some students. Young (1991) described context-specific triggers as relating to personal and interpersonal anxieties, instructor–student interactions and classroom procedures such as speaking in front of a group. Studies centred around the context-specific aspects by King (2014, 2016), King and Smith (2017) and Gkonou (2017) have led to new insights that show the foreign language classroom as a unique social and learning context. King (2014) defines the foreign language classroom as a social situation that can trigger social anxiety, which can lead to silent behaviour due to the social performances of speaking in the target language. King and Smith explain that social anxiety is 'not an entirely separate phenomenon to foreign language anxiety, rather it represents a deep seam running through the latter construct' (King & Smith, 2017: 91). This argument is supported by Kitano (2001), who stated that although the anxiety in a language classroom is not solely social anxiety, the extent of the influence of interpersonal relationships means that social anxiety is an important aspect to consider among other affective factors. Despite the integral nature of context-specific factors, they have received less attention in the literature on language anxiety (Horwitz, 2010; Young, 1991). This review of the literature focuses on the social aspects of the classroom, where silence and anxiety formed a negative cycle of language learning behaviour for Mari.

In the Japanese university foreign language classroom, some students are hesitant to speak in the target language (Shea, 2017), and studies by King (2013, 2016) have highlighted the issue of low levels of oral participation and anxiety. Tsui (1996) found similar connections between reticence and anxiety in the Hong Kong context. The reality is that the classroom is often not used as a space for developing speaking skills by students (Curry, 2014; Harumi, 2011; King, 2013; Kurihara, 2006). King's (2013) investigation into the amount of oral participation found silent behaviour to be prevalent in this context, existing in multiple forms, and with less than 1% of talk initiated by students. Although jumping to conclusions about silence should be avoided – as King states, there is a multitude of reasons for students' silent displays – speaking is often at the heart of the foreign language anxiety of Japanese students (Williams & Andrade, 2008), suggesting that there is a connection between silence and anxiety in this context. So, considering Williams and Andrade's (2008) finding that almost 50% of the Japanese students they asked expected to feel anxious in the foreign language classroom, the influence of the context for these students requires further examination.

Both the purpose of English in this context and how it is presented to students are influenced by its role as a core subject for high-stakes exams for entering high school and university. Although changes are being made to incorporate speaking tests (Teeter, 2017), these exams have predominantly tested reading and listening skills. The washback effect of this style of testing has meant that English classes are used for exam preparation and therefore most of the time is dedicated to studying grammar and vocabulary, with little time allowed for developing speaking skills (Gorsuch, 1998; Hino, 1988; Nishino & Watanabe, 2008; Osterman, 2014). So, aside from private English conversation school lessons or study-abroad programmes, in the context of the formal school English class, Japanese students do not get much experience of speaking in the target language and are not familiar with communicative pedagogical methods (Nishino & Watanabe, 2008; Shachter, 2018).

In addition to pedagogical factors, sociocultural norms and expected behaviour in the classroom have also been found to influence speaking-related anxiety more generally in Japan. From when Japanese students join their first classroom in kindergarten, they learn that expected social and academic behaviour emphasises listening over speaking. Social norms require individuals to listen and be sensitive to their environment to prioritise the needs of the group over their own (Peak, 1989). Academic expected behaviour centres around the teacher talking and students listening (Aspinall, 2006). These defined roles and behaviours are not unique to the Japanese classroom; however, silent behaviour in the classroom is more likely to receive a favourable evaluation than verbal participation by teachers and peers in the Japanese context (Nozaki, 1993; Wadden, 1993).

As well as student silence being expected behaviour by teachers, perceptions of peer attitudes towards speaking in class can also affect anxiety (Effiong, 2016; Lee-Cunin, 2004). Studies show that peer evaluation can lead to students feeling uneasy about speaking in class due to fear of negative evaluation. In further examination of the functions of student silence, King found that socio-psychological factors inhibited students from speaking in the social context of the classroom (King, 2014; King & Smith, 2017). These sociocultural norms are at odds with expected participatory behaviours in the foreign language classroom, where communicative activities are used to develop speaking skills. The interaction that these activities demand may conflict with the sociocultural beliefs held by some students about appropriate behaviour. Studies have found that Japanese students feel concerned about speaking in class for this reason. They do not want to disturb other students by speaking 'loudly', saying something uninteresting, or putting peers in an awkward position should they not understand what they said (Bao, 2014; Greer, 2000; King, 2013; Nakane, 2007). Some studies have found that students use silent behaviour to monitor and assess the atmosphere of the room before they speak, known as *kūki o yomu* (reading the air). For some students, this preoccupation with peers and consideration of their needs before speaking means that spontaneous talk or responding in class could result in a long pause in preparation to speak or complete withdrawal from the interaction (Okano & Tsuchiya, 1999; Yoneyama, 1999). Japanese students may feel that they can fulfil their academic and social roles effectively through silent behaviour. Considering the pedagogical and sociocultural factors that create the learning space where English is taught and previous experiences of using it, it is understandable that students, like Mari, might feel apprehensive about speaking the target language in the classroom.

A CBT-Based Approach

Cognitive-behavioural theory (CBT) is a well established psychotherapy for treating anxieties (Heimberg, 2002; Kennerley *et al.*, 2017; Strongman, 1995; Thurston *et al.*, 2017). The principle of CBT is to develop individual's ability to deal with their anxiety in the situations they face by focusing on finding solutions that build on their existing strengths (Corrie *et al.*, 2016; Kennerley *et al.*, 2017). A CBT formulation uses insights gathered from the individual's perceptions of their anxiety. By collecting evidence of their thoughts, emotions, behaviours and bodily sensations related to the problem, the individual becomes aware of the influence of their thoughts over their emotions and behaviours and the negative cycles that can emerge (Figure 5.1) (Beck, 1979; Kennerley *et al.*,

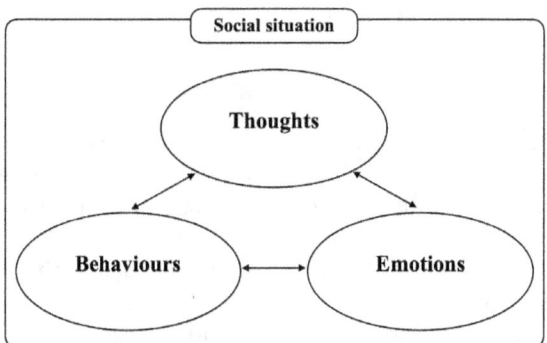

Figure 5.1 Cognitive-behavioural cycle (based on Kennerley *et al.*, 2017)

2017). CBT interventions look to break the cycle and promote positive thoughts to create a better balance. CBT formulations also incorporate the person's core beliefs to gain a deeper understanding of unique contextual factors – the environment where the problem occurs.

Identifying a student's core beliefs about the foreign language classroom could be significant for approaching the intervention in the Japanese context. Silent behaviour may not be perceived as something they can change or have control over, considering the sociocultural norms and expected behaviours they have learnt.

Cognitive theory has shaped the current understanding of student silence and anxiety related to the foreign language classroom (Gkonou et al., 2017; King, 2014). Moreover, it has advanced the idea of how these phenomena can feed into one another and sustain a cycle of thoughts, emotions and behaviours that can affect some students' language learning. While the pedagogical and sociocultural factors described may not be unique to the Japanese context (Bao, 2014; Gilmore, 1985; Reda, 2009), the sociocultural norms and expected behaviours that form part of the socialisation process for Japanese students could result in some students finding it harder to engage in oral participation in the foreign language classroom. Consideration of how the social aspects of the environment are interlinked with thoughts, emotions and behaviours could lead to a better understanding – and, therefore, more effective interventions – than applying to Japan frameworks or concepts devised in a different cultural context.

Two previous studies have used similar psychological approaches for dealing with anxiety in the Japanese context: Toyama and Yamazaki's (2019) rational emotive therapy-based class activities for anxiety reduction, and Curry's (2014) cognitive-behavioural therapy-based activities in a learner advisor capacity. In the present study, King's (2014) cognitive-behavioural model was used to provide a construct for examining silence and anxiety related to the social aspects of the foreign language classroom in the Japanese context. This section will outline the elements of King's model (Figure 5.2) which I used to understand Mari's unease.

Feared predictions

Feared predictions related to the social aspects of the foreign language classroom include negative emotions about competence in the target language and identity-based fears that spring from these doubts. Gregersen and Horwitz (2002) found that the fear of making mistakes in front of others can lead to silence. Some students decide that it is safer for them to remain silent rather than to produce a less than perfect performance (Kitano, 2001). Conversely, some students may not want to appear over-competent. Their silent behaviour is motivated by trying to fit in with their peers. In this situation, students who are fearful of showing

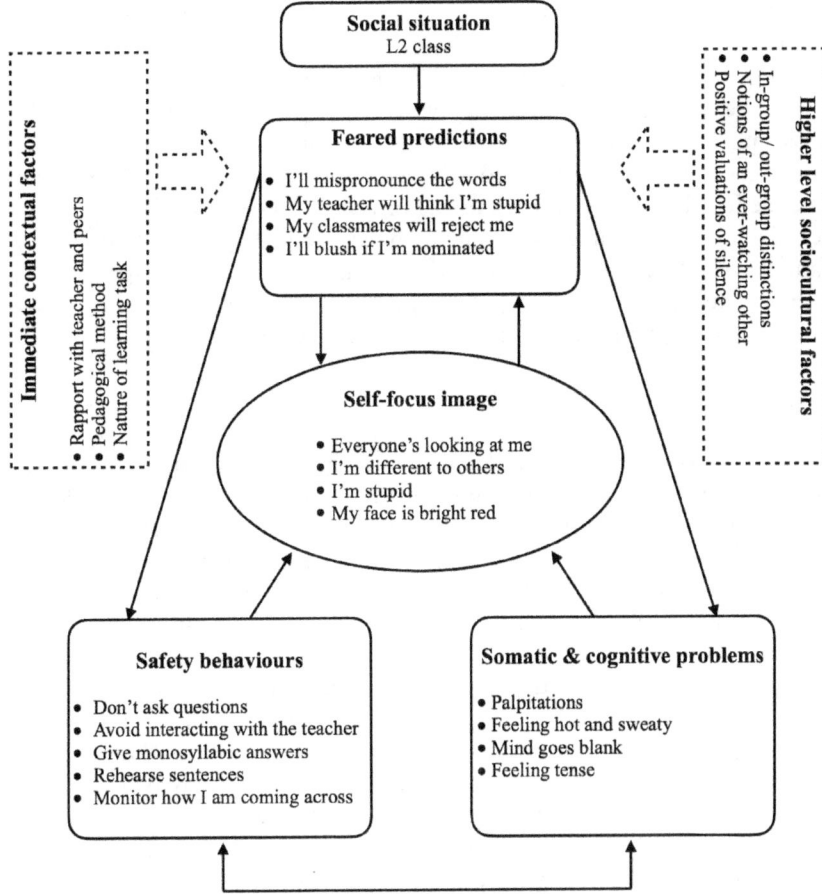

Figure 5.2 A cognitive-behavioural model of a silent L2 learner's social anxiety (King & Smith, 2017, adapted from King, 2014)

their language ability prioritise evaluation by their peers over academic evaluation by the teacher (Bao, 2014; Greer, 2000; Harumi, 2015; King, 2013, 2014; King & Smith, 2017; Kitano, 2001; Kondo & Ying-Ling, 2004; Liu, 2002; McVeigh, 2002; Nakane, 2007).

Self-focus image

Anxious students can become overly aware of themselves as a social object in the classroom. Their attention becomes almost entirely focused on their performance in the target language and how others are evaluating them. In a foreign language classroom, this may involve comparison of their performance with their peers' performances, as well as with native speakers of the target language (often the teacher) (Gregersen & Horwitz, 2002; Kitano, 2001). After their performance, some anxious students may evaluate themselves, which Leary and Kowalski (1995) refer to as the 'post-mortem' in their theory of impression management. The post-mortem idea is comparable to the custom of *hansei*, where Japanese students conduct self-evaluations in front of others regarding their performance in school activities. Elements of *hansei* were evident in interviews carried out with students in studies by Greer (2000), King (2013, 2014) and McVeigh (2002). If an anxious student has negative thoughts after a performance, this could trigger further feelings of anxiety and maintain the cycle of negative thoughts, emotions and behaviours.

Safety behaviours

The safety behaviours in King's model are forms of silent behaviour. Using silence can be an effective way of reducing anxiety, as the student is less likely to experience negative evaluations about their performance. In the short term, avoidance of speaking and negative evaluations positively reinforces their silent behaviour, making them feel more able to deal with their anxiety. In the long term, however, this reliance could sustain a cycle of negative thoughts, emotions and behaviours which the student will struggle to break if they do not test their fears about speaking (Kennerley et al., 2017; King, 2014). As King (2013) suggests, silence in the foreign language classroom can become an attractor state that can have negative repercussions for language learning. When silence is used as a safety behaviour, it is likely to sustain feelings of anxiety. The more a student uses silence to avoid their feared predictions and to safely negotiate the participatory patterns in the social context of the foreign language classroom, the harder it is for them to recognise that their silent behaviour is contributing to the negative cycle of their language anxiety and limiting their language learning (Clark & Wells, 1995; King, 2014; LeDoux, 2015; Strongman, 1995).

Method

This study took place in a medium-sized private institution with a university and junior college on campus, located in a metropolitan area in Honshu, the main island of Japan. The university has a foreign studies faculty with several specialised language departments. Of these departments, English is the largest, accounting for 45% of the undergraduate student cohort. During the second term of the academic year, I carried out 11 observations of English classes. The purpose of the observations was to find students who displayed forms of silent behaviour and conduct interviews with them to examine their perceptions of their behaviour and what factors influence it.

The first observation was unstructured, to acclimatise to the class dynamics, followed by three structured observations, to look at the individual modality of students who displayed recurring silent behaviour and anxious body language (on non-verbal cues of anxious language learners, see Gregersen, 2005, 2009). For the structured observations, I used the Classroom Oral Participation Scheme (COPS) (King, 2013), which has been used for examining student silence in the foreign language classroom. The COPS gave a quantitative perspective to the higher inferential unstructured observation data. By quantifying behaviours, I could see the degree and frequency with which they occurred and highlight any patterns.

Mari

Mari was one of the students whom I focused on during the observations. A 19-year-old first-year English major with no study-abroad experience, she attended on-campus mixer events with international students and took part in international student conferences in Japan. Her instructor described her as a 'panicky' student in class, but a hard worker. From her observable body language during speaking activities with peers, Mari appeared to be experiencing some discomfort. The activities included speaking with a partner or a small group, a speaking test, as well as talking one to one with the teacher. Her face was red, and she often fanned her face. I also noticed her wringing her hands when speaking. Other anxious non-verbal cues included keeping her head down, looking at the desk and sitting back in her chair, away from her group. Her silent behaviour included non-talk; she also used Japanese when the teacher expected the target language. Further, she cut short her speaking turn on several occasions; for example, in five-minute free-talk tasks with a partner she tended to talk a little before taking the listener role for three and a half to four minutes. During timed speaking tasks where students were given a question and expected to respond for 90 seconds, she often stopped after 50–60 seconds and was silent until the time ran out.

I also noticed her preparing to speak by making notes or reading notes before it was her turn to speak. She often appeared to be distracted, preparing and rehearsing rather than listening to her partner or group members speak. During the fourth observation of Mari's class, there was a speaking test in which students were supposed to give a 90-second speech in front of five classmates. When she was in the audience, Mari spent most of the time writing notes, even though the topic was randomly chosen. When it was her turn, she smiled a lot, closed her eyes or looked down. Her voice was soft, demonstrated by her audience leaning forward to listen. After she ended her turn 20 seconds before the timer rang, she laughed, said 'Oh well, I guess you have the same evaluation of me … a small voice', and followed this with a sigh. The combination of her body language and silent displays suggested she felt anxious about speaking English.

Interviews

After the last observation, I conducted a follow-up interview to get her perceptions about her silent behaviour. Then, in the first term of her second year, Mari agreed to participate in further interviews. Over two months, we had three meetings of about 90 minutes each. I followed a CBT-style interview format for these four interviews: assessment, formulation and an intervention activity (see Corrie et al., 2016; Kennerley et al., 2017: ch. 4; Persons & Tompkins, 2010).

Assessment interview

In the first interview, and follow-up to the observations, I wanted to investigate whether Mari's in-class oral behaviours were related to her feeling anxious about speaking in the foreign language classroom, and to what extent she felt that her anxiety was affecting her speaking skills and whether she wanted to improve her confidence to speak in class. I designed an interview guide that contained adapted items from existing instruments (Table 5.1) that are used for diagnosing social anxiety in clinical settings and assessing foreign language anxiety. The first section of items contained nine scenarios about speaking English in the classroom, for example speaking with peers who are friends, speaking with peers she does not know well, speaking in front of the class, and speaking to the teacher. Items that ask respondents to consider a series of scenario items feature in diagnostic instruments for social anxiety. I adapted some scenarios from these instruments for the context of this study by using items from the Foreign Language Classroom Anxiety Scale and the Managing Your Emotions for Language Learning questionnaire (see Table 5.1). Scenario-style items allowed me to focus the interview by asking about situations in the classroom that were of interest to me, having observed some classes. Scenario items were also to help focus Mari's thoughts, by providing a clear context for her to refer to, and by

Table 5.1 Instruments from which interview items were drawn

Application	Instrument	Reference
Context specific	Foreign Language Classroom Anxiety Scale (FLCAS)	Horwitz et al. (1986)
	Managing your Emotions for Language Learning (MYE)	Gkonou and Oxford (2016)
General anxiety	State-Trait Anxiety Inventory (STAI)	Spielberger et al. (1983)
Social anxiety, avoidance and fear	Liebowitz Social Anxiety Scale (LSAS)	Liebowitz (1987)
	Social Phobia Inventory (SPIN)	Connor et al. (2000)
	Fear of Negative Evaluation (FNE)	Leary (1983)

reducing the ambiguity that might arise due to language differences. A further benefit of the scenarios was being able to make the questions less or more direct about Mari and her participatory behaviours. If she appeared reluctant to talk about herself, the scenarios made it possible to adapt the questions into hypothetical situations rather than pushing her to discuss herself.

At the end of the interview, I recapped what Mari had told me, and asked her whether she had any speaking goals that she felt her anxiety was preventing her from achieving. Through discussing the scenarios, it became clear that Mari was aware of how her silent behaviour was hindering her chances to practise speaking in class and her frustration with not being able to overcome her nerves despite all the work she was doing before class to prepare herself for speaking tasks. She was able to decide two specific speaking goals and explained why they were necessary for her to make progress. At the time of the interview, Mari was planning to study abroad at a university in Indonesia, followed by an internship, so she wanted to be able to use class time more for speaking practice to prepare for going abroad. Also, she expressed a keen interest in overcoming her anxiety and discussing it further. Her awareness, goals and intentions to change indicated that she could benefit from a CBT-based approach. These factors must be evaluated when determining whether someone is likely to gain from a CBT intervention (Kennerley et al., 2017).

Formulation interviews

The purpose of the second and third interviews was to review Mari's goals and gather further evidence of her silence and anxious feelings by talking about recent examples to elicit her thoughts, emotions, behaviours, bodily sensations and beliefs. The aim was to get a detailed understanding of the factors that were maintaining her anxiety and silence. To capture the various elements of the example problem, I used a CBT model (Figure 5.3) and visual tool for use in CBT sessions. As we discussed the examples, Mari and I co-created a personalised model of her silence and anxiety. As well as asking what was happening during the moment when the behaviour or emotion was evident, I also asked her to think about each element of the model leading up to the moment and afterwards to look for triggers and maintaining processes (Kennerley et al., 2017).

Intervention: Balanced thinking activity

In the final interview, we reviewed her goals again, what she had previously told me about her situation, and discussed other recent examples. Using one of these examples, we did an activity to challenge her negative thoughts about what she perceived to be happening at the time (see

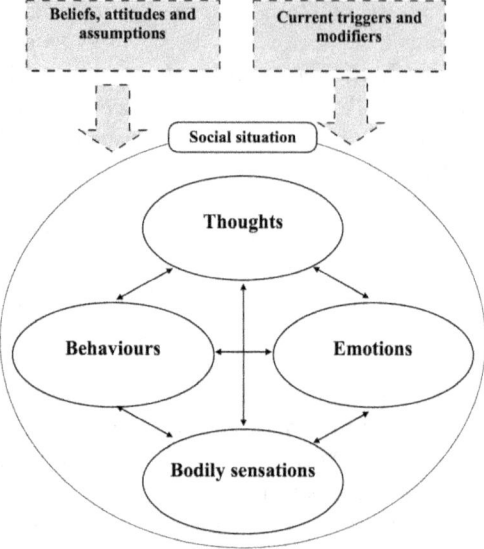

Figure 5.3 The CBT model (based on Kennerley et al., 2017)

Stallard, 2002: 84). Firstly, she listed the negative thoughts she had had at the time, followed by any evidence she could think of that supported these thoughts. For example, one of her negative thoughts was 'My classmates don't want to listen to me'. Mari recounted how she had seen some of her classmates whispering and yawning when she tried to speak, which she perceived as their response to her speaking and was evidence to support her negative thoughts. The next part of the activity asked her to think of any evidence that could challenge those negative thoughts, for example 'It was a morning class, so they could have been sleepy'. Finally, it asked her to think of advice or words of encouragement that she would give to a friend who was experiencing the same worries about speaking in class.

Analysis

Mari decided to do the interviews in English; she occasionally spoke Japanese in a self-talk capacity to prepare before she responded in English. However, considering issues that can arise in cross-cultural interviews related to language barriers (Squires, 2009), I used ideas from Kato and Mynard (2016), who have developed techniques in Japanese and English for use in advising on language learning. Their reflective dialogue techniques include active listening to provide non-verbal feedback, giving sufficient wait time, as well as repeating and restating in English and Japanese (in my case to make sure Mari knew that I had understood her) to reduce any language anxiety about being misunderstood.

After each interview, I reflected on the session, and then transcribed and analysed it before the next interview. The interviews were transcribed in full to review all utterances and paralinguistic behaviour such as laughter, sighs and silence (King, 2013; Richards, 2003). This allowed me to review what was said and how she said it. I transcribed Japanese parts into Japanese before having them translated them into English. Having lived in Japan for more than 12 years, I felt my level of sociocultural competence and language knowledge was sufficient for me to act as one of the translators. I was also aware, though, how language barriers might have affected my understanding and interpretations, so I used an independent translator to check the transcription before making a technically accurate translation to compare with my translation and interpretative notes (Squires, 2009).

To analyse the interviews, I used a qualitative data analysis programme with a detailed code book for consistency. In the first round of coding, I used interpretative codes, prompting me to maintain an ongoing process of voicing my assumptions and generating alternative interpretations in preparation for the next round of analysis (Senior, 2006). In further rounds, I used codes from King's model. As Mari had expressed multiple times during the first interview how her peers negatively affected her, the model was a suitable construct to apply. After coding the interviews, I used iterative categorisation (Neale, 2016), summarising the data for each code to consider the best fit through constant comparison.

Cognitive-Behavioural Model of Mari's Silence and Anxiety in the Foreign Language Classroom

Assessment interview

In the first interview, it became clear that Mari was anxious about speaking and that this negative emotion was related to the social aspects of the classroom. She expressed positive intentions to speak in class but described how her mind often felt 'full of worries'. Her participatory behaviour was influenced by negative thoughts about her ability. These thoughts were connected to her peers in two ways: the impact of their oral participatory behaviour and seeking assurance about her speaking skills.

Inhibited by her speaking partner

A recurrent theme was how she followed the lead of her speaking partner. If they used Japanese, she would use it too, instead of speaking English. Even though she often spent time outside of class preparing for speaking tasks and felt motivated, she would suppress her desire to practise speaking English. She worried about what her partner's reaction would be if she spoke in English: 'They would accuse me or think "Why are you speaking English?"', as if she was acting strangely or would annoy them. When I asked her if she had tried to change the conversation back into English, she spoke of her hopelessness in feeling compelled to use Japanese while looking down at the notes she prepared but not being able to use them. In this type of situation, she often remained in a state of quiet frustration. She described similar experiences when attempting to initiate talk or ask the teacher a question. Even when she felt that she had something to contribute, Mari did not put up her hand and stayed silent, fearing that her classmates would think 'Why did she ask that question?' Mari explained how she was losing many opportunities to practise speaking due to her mind being taken over with worries about her peers' reactions, so, rather than speaking, she chose to avoid 'annoying' them.

Need for reassurance

When possible, Mari asked her friends to check the notes she had made to prepare for speaking tasks in class. While she was positive about receiving feedback and having mistakes corrected, her reliance on having her notes checked suggested there was a degree of self-doubt underlying this need for reassurance. Once her notes had been checked, and there were 'no mistakes', she could feel more relaxed about reading them out in class. This self-doubt was not only related to her linguistic knowledge; rather, she worried that her topic would be boring or annoy her peers. These negative thoughts had led to Mari cutting her speaking turn short; she found it particularly stressful to start conversations before she had had a chance to gauge the topics raised by her partner.

The speaking test I observed was an episode which brought together both ways that her peers influenced her. Mari explained that she did her best to prepare for it even though the topics were chosen randomly; she tried to guess the topics and wrote notes for each one, which she had checked by a friend. In the end, the topic she received was not what she had prepared for, and when she realised this, Mari worried so much about whether her response contained linguistic mistakes and whether it was boring that her mind went blank, and she stopped before the timer went off.

Goals

At the end of the interview, I asked Mari to think of any speaking goals she had and what types of speaking situations in class that she would like to feel more confident about. She decided on putting up her hand to initiate talk in front of peers, which she said she wanted to be able to do without worrying what others were thinking, in preparation for studying abroad. She also chose not silencing herself and having more confidence to keep talking.

Formulation interviews

In the second and third interviews, we looked at recent examples of when Mari had tried to achieve her goals but her anxiety had prevented her from doing so. Figures 5.4 and 5.5 are two of the CBT models that we made during the interviews: when she could not put up her hand to initiate speaking in class (Figure 5.4) and when she rushed to finish speaking (Figure 5.5). Figure 5.6 is King's (2014) cognitive-behavioural model applied to the data from Mari's interviews to summarise her formulation.

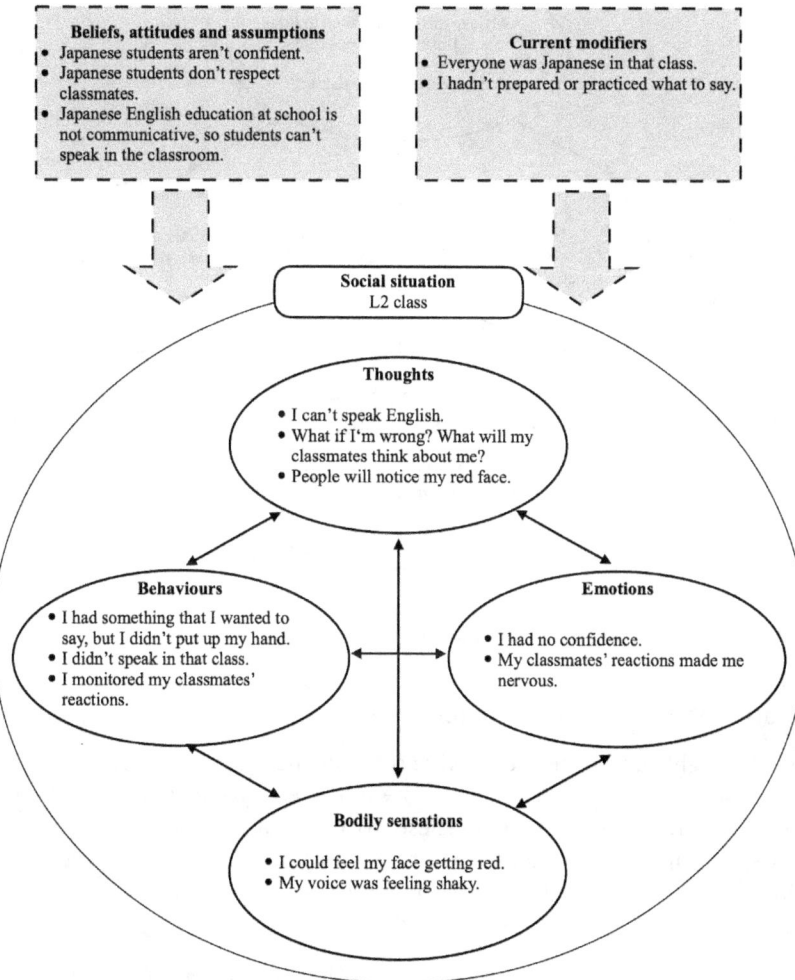

Figure 5.4 CBT model of not initiating talk

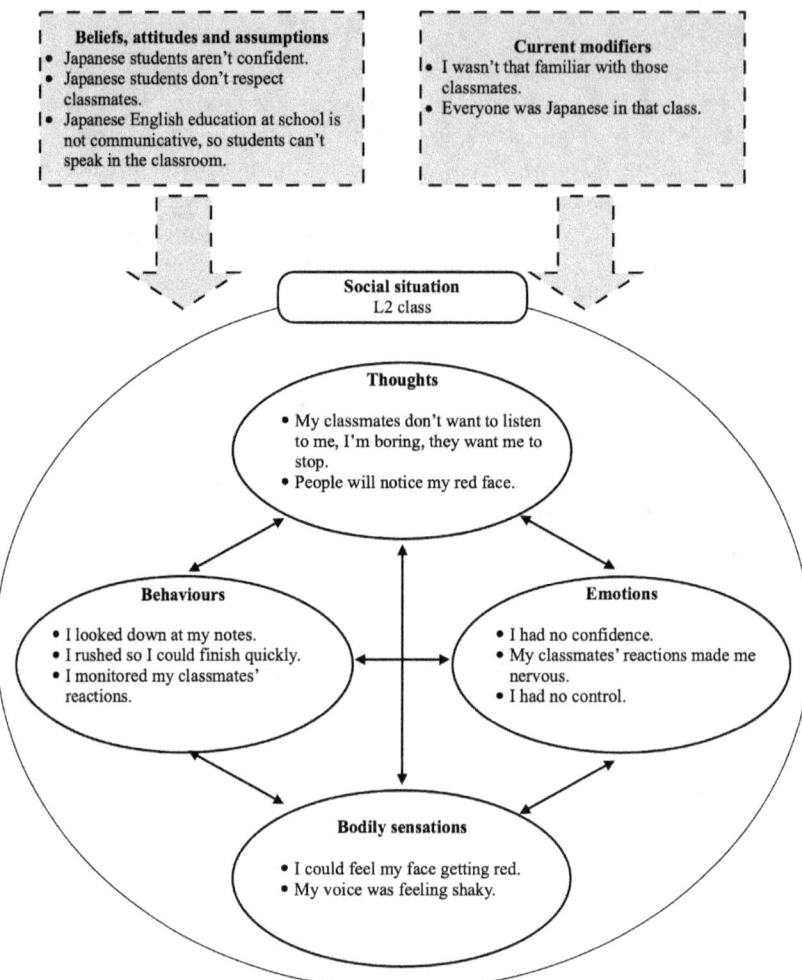

Figure 5.5 CBT model of ending speaking turn

Feared predictions and self-focus

Thoughts about her peers were often at the forefront of Mari's mind when she tried to speak. She became inhibited by her worries that they were negatively evaluating her. These worries took over, leading her to end her speaking turn in order to avoid these negative feelings. She expressed this eloquently, as quoted in the Introduction to this chapter and worth repeating:

> I stayed up until 2 a.m. practising what I wanted to say, but when I went to class and sat with my group, I looked at their faces and imagined what they were thinking about me. Then it was gone. I didn't speak.

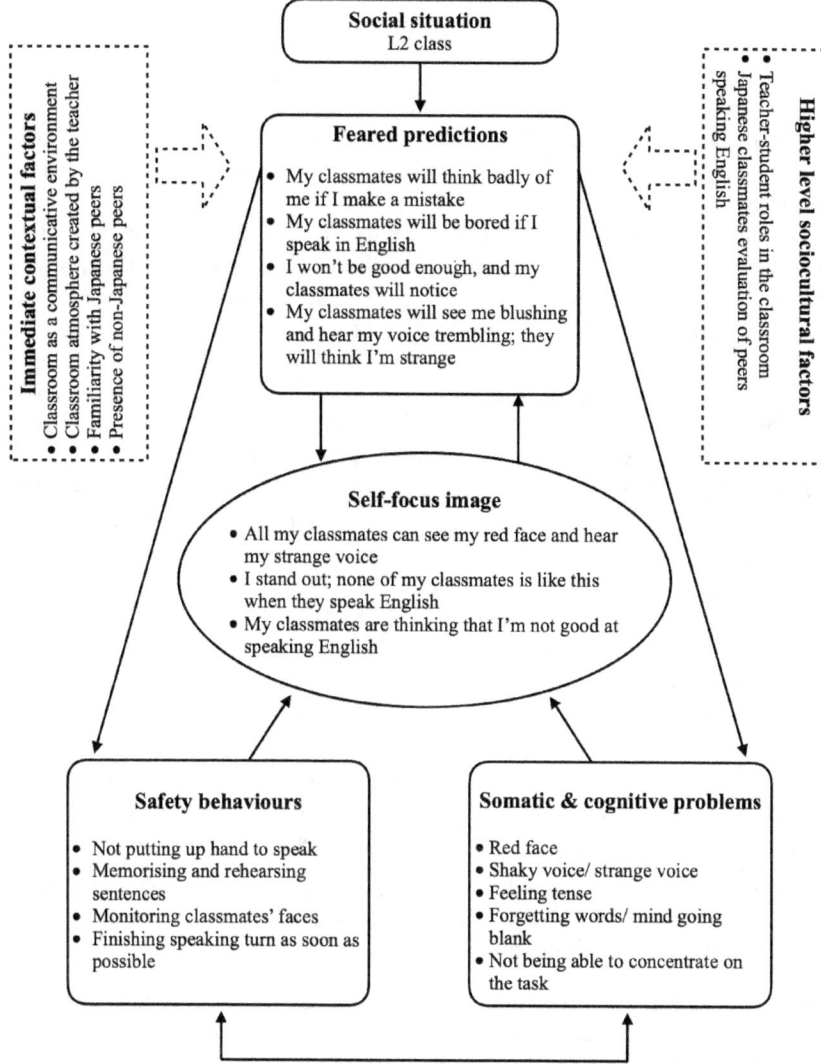

Figure 5.6 Cognitive-behavioural model of Mari's silence and anxiety in the foreign language classroom (based on King, 2014)

Previous studies have found similar findings to Mari's fears, where some people would rather not speak than produce a less than perfect performance (Kitano, 2001; Leary & Kowalski, 1995) as well as students who prioritise their peers' evaluations over academic evaluation by the teacher (Bao, 2014; Greer, 2000; Harumi, 2015; King, 2013, 2014; King & Smith, 2017; Kitano, 2001; Kondo & Ying-Ling, 2004; Liu, 2002; McVeigh, 2002; Nakane, 2007). Even though Mari admitted that when others were speaking she did not evaluate their speaking and that this could be true for others when she spoke, her dominant and most frequent worry was that her peers were finding her faults when she spoke. This is an example of how negative thoughts can become automatic, making them hard to dismiss (Stallard, 2002). The strength and automatic nature of Mari's negative thoughts might have been connected to her fear of revealing that she was not good enough at English in the classroom, which would confirm her self-doubts about her ability. Mari reported thinking 'The teacher will not enjoy my speech. He will not praise me like he will praise the others, and then I will stand out, and my classmates will notice.'

A further example was regarding her elective speaking class. She explained that she had to persuade the teacher to allow her to take it because it was oversubscribed, and it took courage for her to ask the teacher. Since that moment she had feared that her classmates would realise that she was too low level and think 'Why is she in this class?' Despite her recognition that she was motivated and tried to challenge herself to speak in class, she still doubted herself. Her self-doubts could be why she needed reassurance in the form of having her notes checked before she could feel relaxed enough to speak, and why she avoided unprepared speech such as initiating talk in class.

One belief that modified Mari's fears was her perception that Japanese peers were more critical of her than international students. In previous experiences, she had received support and positive reactions from classmates who were international students, even when she made a mistake and they could not understand her. However, she described Japanese students as being harsh about imperfections and showing their lack of interest in their facial expressions. She said:

> Japanese classmates won't be respectful when I speak. They won't show any response, and this will make me scared because maybe they are thinking negative things about me.

When I asked her to explain this further, she talked about the influence of the Japanese education system. Mari described how from primary school onwards, Japanese students are not encouraged to put up their hand to speak and their oral participation is limited to answering teachers' questions with one-word answers that are correct or not. She had never been asked her opinion in class until she entered university. Therefore, she felt that Japanese students have no confidence to speak in class because they are not used to it, which Shachter (2018) argued, saying that Japanese students are not familiar with communicative activities in the classroom, making it hard for them to participate orally. Mari described the communication patterns in the classroom by comparing such communication to bowling, where the teacher talks and the students listen. She went on to say that university classes are more like catch-ball, but reflected that 'it is too late to start at university because we've already lost our voice'.

From these beliefs, a specific factor about her fear of negative evaluation became clear. For Mari, her peers' non-verbal cues were part of her negative cycle. Her opinion that Japanese students showed less expression in their faces has been endorsed in studies about cultural differences in emotion display rules (Matsumoto & Ekman, 1989; Yuki *et al.*, 2007); however, it was Mari's perception of what the lack of facial expression means that affected her anxiety about speaking. Stopa and Clark (2000) suggest that people with social anxiety are more likely to be biased towards negative evaluations about social situations and their performances. Their negative appraisals can arise from various sources, including interpretations, attention to cues in the environment and existing memories. In the classroom context, she was not able to gain feedback about her speaking performance from peers' vague non-verbal reactions, which might have triggered or modified her anxiety.

Safety behaviours

Although the term 'safety behaviour' was not used in our interviews, Mari was aware that she at times avoided speaking to reduce her anxiety, either by not initiating talk or by finishing her speaking turn as soon as possible, both of which are variations of silent behaviour. These behaviours were causing her to feel frustration and were affecting her confidence to speak English and were adding to her self-doubt about her ability. Her frustration and lack of confidence were why she decided that she wanted to stop using these safety behaviours as her goals to help her prepare for studying abroad and became central in the intervention activity in our final interview. These types of specific goals that relate to the current problems faced by the person are essential for interventions, as, if they do not test an alternative hypothesis where her fears do not come true, the person will continue to use safety behaviours to avoid their fears, sustaining a negative cycle of thoughts, emotions and behaviours (Clark & Wells, 1995; Kennerley *et al.*, 2017; King, 2014).

Intervention: Balanced thoughts activity

I selected an intervention activity aimed at showing Mari how to have a more balanced perception of her situation due to the apparent strength and automatic nature of her negative thoughts. Also, I thought this activity would be meaningful for Mari, as she had revealed in her interviews how she often relied on her friends for support, and the last part of the activity asked the person to imagine what advice they would give to a friend who was experiencing the same problems. Although Mari was able to think of evidence that challenged her negative thoughts, when we worked on the last task, about advising a friend, the strength of her negative thoughts and fears became evident again. She initially thought of some encouraging words, such as 'At least you tried'; however, by thinking about her friends, she started thinking about them giving her feedback, which led her back to her peers' negative evaluations. At this point, we returned to the CBT models of her example situation to review her negative cycle. This visual reminder of how powerful her negative thoughts were seemed to reinforce the importance of balanced thinking.

Suggestions for Using a CBT-Based Approach

In this section, I suggest some ways to use a CBT-based approach. I will also share some of the strengths of using this approach, which I have discovered as a researcher and as a teacher when supporting anxious learners.

- Using scenario items in the assessment interview allows the interviewer to create a list of situations that affect the learner's anxiety. Having a list of scenarios can help to keep the interview focused on language learning issues to ensure that the learner understands that you are not expecting them to reveal sensitive information related to other areas of their life. As a researcher, scenarios can become a useful way of collecting data when examining what elements of a class trigger certain emotions. When working with an anxious learner, scenarios can be a good starting place to support goal-setting. Also, going through the scenarios with the learner can boost their confidence as they realise that their anxiety is dynamic and (usually) not related to every aspect of language learning. This can be an opportune moment to remind them of what they enjoy about it.
- In the formulation interviews, I used a CBT model to elicit elements of the learner's anxiety by looking at recent examples (Figures 5.4 and 5.5). In this chapter, I have reported on Mari's negative examples; however, I recommend asking the learner to tell you about positive examples as well. This can build the learner's confidence by reminding them of their successful moments, and that they can repeat their success in the future. Also, having visuals of negative and positive examples helps the learner to compare the situations and consider what factors modify their cycles, which can help the learner to realise what factors affect them the most.
- CBT uses a lot of visual guides during sessions and for independent homework tasks. In this chapter, I have used the CBT model for examples. I also produced a confidence graph (Figure 5.7) to help Mari explain how her feelings changed before, during and after her anxiety episode. These visual guides are especially useful for providing linguistic support during interviews. Furthermore, as you create the visuals with the learner, they become more aware of how their negative thoughts are affecting them, as Mari did in the intervention activity.

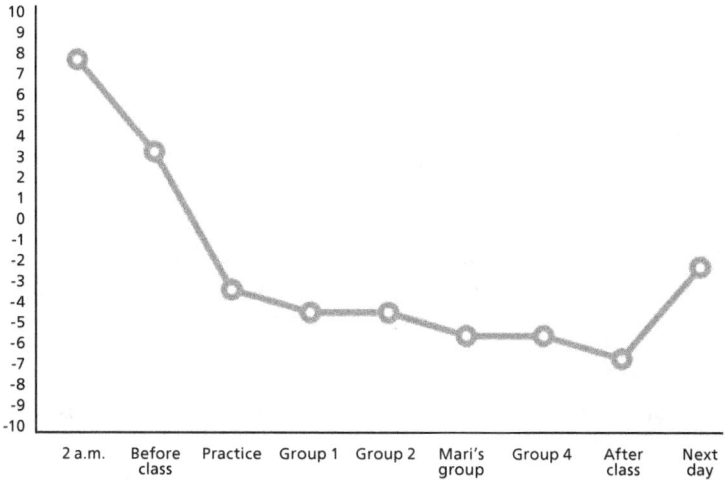

Figure 5.7 Confidence graph

- The intervention activity I used with Mari can be adapted for use in class with a group of students. I recommend modelling the process first, then asking the students to try an example as a group, before asking them to try it individually about their negative thoughts. Talking to peers and sharing coping strategies can be a good source of support for some anxious learners as they realise they are not the only nervous speakers in their class (Toyama & Yamazaki, 2019).

I will end this section with some words about sensitivity and ethical responsibilities when using this approach. Care needs to be taken when talking to the learners as some of the terminologies – anxiety, CBT and emotions – are sensitive and may alarm them due to their mental health implications. I recommend planning ahead of interviews how you intend to explain the purpose of the questions you are asking and what terms you will use. I think it is better to use terms that are less intimidating, such as 'confidence-boosting' and 'controlling your nervous feelings'. Finally, it is vital to be prepared for learners to misunderstand the purpose of the interviews or your role as a researcher/teacher and ask for support with personal problems that are not related to language anxiety or the foreign language classroom. I have encountered this while working as a language advisor in a self-access learning centre, where students wanted advice about family or health issues rather than their studies. In these situations, I followed the centre's guidelines that instructed advisors how to acknowledge the topic raised by the student before reminding them of the purpose of the centre and gently return the topic to language learning. If necessary, I would recommend services available on campus for them to use for advice about personal problems.

Conclusion

Through using a CBT-based approach to examine the relationship between silence and anxiety, I gained a greater understanding of the influences of the social aspects of the foreign language classroom on learners by looking at how multiple elements are complexly interrelated. Although this study looked only at an individual student, Mari's situation revealed further insights into unique factors within the Japanese context. Also, this approach helped Mari to become more aware of what was affecting her speaking confidence. Reflecting on the interviews, I noticed moments that demonstrated the effectiveness of this approach for Mari, what Kato and Mynard (2016) call 'aha moments':

- at the start of the third interview, Mari came in ready with examples that she wanted to discuss;
- silent moments of reflection followed by Mari summarising the factors that influenced her anxious feelings;
- when, after a long pause, she said 'Oh, I have never noticed that before!' about her automatic negative thoughts when I reminded her of the CBT model during the intervention activity.

A limitation of this study and something that needs to be addressed in future studies is the lack of follow-up to monitor the effects of this approach. After the last interview, Mari was getting ready to leave for her study-abroad programme. However, she was able to give her feedback in an email. Although she was still worried about making mistakes due to the negative impression it might give her peers, she was feeling more confident to try rather than remaining silent. Regarding the CBT-based approach, she said that it helped her to notice things about language learning which she had not been aware of before and that she could 'recognise myself'. Finally, she commented that probably a lot of Japanese students do not consider the importance of balanced thinking when speaking a foreign language, yet it is something that could help them to improve if anxiety is leading them into silence.

Self-reflection/Discussion Questions

(1) Imagine yourself in the role of a language learner in the context where you teach. Can you think of any social aspects of the classroom that might make you feel anxious about speaking? Now imagine yourself in the teacher's role, or the researcher's. Make a list of scenarios that you could use to make an assessment interview schedule.
(2) Figures 5.4 and 5.5 show the CBT cycle models for Mari's episodes of anxiety and silent behaviour in the classroom. Think of a time when you felt nervous about speaking in a foreign language. Use the model to outline your cognitive-behavioural cycle.

(3) What can you learn about your language anxiety from the cycle? Figures 5.2 and 5.6 show the cognitive-behavioural model of a silent L2 learner's social anxiety (King & Smith, 2017, adapted from King, 2014). What might the higher-level sociocultural factors in your context be where you teach or plan to teach?
(4) Thinking of your own experiences in the classroom, what forms of language learner silence have you observed? What reasons can you think of to explain this behaviour? If you suspected that it was anxiety-related and wanted to offer support, how would you go about approaching the student?

Recommended Reading

King, J. and Smith, L. (2017) Social anxiety and silence in Japan's tertiary foreign language classrooms. In C. Gkonou, M. Daubney and J.-M. Dewaele (eds) *New Insights into Language Anxiety: Theory, Research and Educational Implications* (pp. 92–110). Bristol: Multilingual Matters.

Following King's (2014) chapter on social anxiety and the silent behaviour of Japanese learners of English, King and Smith's chapter uses the cognitive-behavioural model of a silent L2 learner's social anxiety to examine the relationships between an anxious learner's thoughts, behaviours and environment. They provide a complete explanation of the model, as well as an in-depth explanation of the contextual factors that can facilitate the silent behaviour of socially inhibited learners.

Kennerley, H., Kirk, J. and Westbrook, D. (2017) *An Introduction to Cognitive Behaviour Therapy: Skills and Applications*. Singapore: Sage.

Although this guide is aimed at people who are training to become mental health professionals or to work in a clinical setting, it provides an approachable and comprehensive overview of cognitive behavioural therapy that would be useful for gaining an understanding of the theory and skills used in assessment and formulation. In addition to the text, there is also a companion website that contains videos that illustrate the skills and that uses example cases to demonstrate interview techniques.

Stallard, P. (2002) *Think Good – Feel Good: A Cognitive Behavioural Therapy Workbook for Children and Young People*. Chichester: Wiley.

This book also gives an approachable overview of CBT and ideas for practical application but focuses on working with children and young people. For those who are interested in using a CBT-based approach with these age groups, Stallard explains how the theory and skills can be applied and presented. Also, this book has a series of activities, attractive visuals and worksheets, with guides on how to use them.

References

Aspinall, R.W. (2006) Using the paradigm of 'small cultures' to explain policy failure in the case of foreign language education in Japan. *Japan Forum,* 18 (2), 255–274.
Bao, D. (2014) *Understanding Silence and Reticence: Ways of Participating in Second Language Acquisition.* London: Bloomsbury.
Beck, A.T. (1979) *Cognitive Therapy and the Emotional Disorders.* London: Penguin.
Clark, D.M. and Wells, A. (1995) A cognitive model of social phobia. In R.G. Heimberg, M.R. Liebowitz, D.A. Hope and F.R. Schneier (eds) *Social Phobia: Diagnosis, Assessment and Treatment* (pp. 69–93). New York: Guilford Press.
Connor, K.M., Davidson, J.R., Churchill, L.E., Sherwood, A., Foa, E. and Weisler, R.H. (2000) Psychometric properties of the Social Phobia Inventory (SPIN): New self-rating scale. *British Journal of Psychiatry* 176 (4), 379–386.
Corrie, S., Townend, M. and Cockx, A. (2016) *Assessment and Case Formulation in Cognitive Behavioural Therapy* (2nd edn). London: Sage Publications.
Curry, N. (2014) Using CBT with anxious language learners: The potential role of the learning advisor. *Studies in Self-access Learning Journal* 5 (1), 29–41.
Effiong, O. (2016) Getting them speaking: Classroom social factors and foreign language anxiety. *Tesol Journal* 7 (1), 132–161.
Gilmore, P. (1985) Silence and sulking: Emotional displays in the classroom. In D. Tannen and M. Saville-Troike (eds) *Perspectives on Silence* (pp. 139–162). Norwood, NJ: Ablex Publishing.
Gkonou, C. (2017) Towards an ecological understanding of language anxiety. In C. Gkonou, M. Daubney and J.M. Dewaele (eds) *New Insights into Language Anxiety: Theory, Research and Educational Implications* (pp. 135–155). Bristol: Multilingual Matters.
Gkonou, C. and Oxford, R.L. (2016) *Questionnaire: Managing Your Emotions for Language Learning.* Colchester: University of Essex.
Gkonou, C., Daubney, M. and Dewaele, J.M. (eds) (2017) *New Insights into Language Anxiety: Theory, Research and Educational Implications.* Bristol: Multilingual Matters.
Gorsuch, G.J. (1998) Yakudoku EFL instruction in two Japanese high school classrooms. *JALT Journal* 20 (1), 6–32.
Greer, D.L. (2000) 'The Eyes of Hito': A Japanese cultural monitor of behavior in the communicative language classroom. *JALT Journal* 22 (1), 183–195.
Gregersen, T. (2005) Nonverbal cues: Clues to the detection of foreign language anxiety. *Foreign Language Annals* 38 (3), 388–400.
Gregersen, T. (2009) Recognizing visual and auditory cues in the detection of foreign-language anxiety. *TESL Canada Journal* 26 (2), 46–64.
Gregersen, T. and Horwitz, E.K. (2002) Language learning and perfectionism: Anxious and non-anxious language learners' reactions to their own oral performance. *Modern Language Journal* 86 (4), 562–570.
Harumi, S. (2011) Classroom silence: Voices from Japanese EFL learners. *ELT Journal* 65 (3), 260–269.
Harumi, S. (2015) The implicit role of classroom silence in Japanese EFL contexts. In T. Harrison, U. Lanvers and M. Edwardes (eds) *Breaking Theory: New Directions in Applied Linguistics. Proceedings of the 48th Annual Meeting of the British Association for Applied Linguistics, Aston University, Birmingham* (pp. 121–130). London: Scitsiugnil Press.
Heimberg, R.G. (2002) Cognitive-behavioral therapy for social anxiety disorder: Current status and future directions. *Biological Psychiatry* 51 (1), 101–108.
Hino, N. (1988) Yakudoku: Japan's dominant tradition in foreign language learning. *JALT Journal* 10 (1), 45–53.
Horwitz, E.K. (2010) Foreign and second language anxiety. *Language Teaching* 43, 154–167.

Horwitz, E.K., Horwitz, M.B. and Cope, J. (1986) Foreign language classroom anxiety. *Modern Language Journal* 70 (2), 125–132.

Kato, S. and Mynard, J. (2016) *Reflective Dialogue: Advising in Language Learning*. New York: Routledge.

Kennerley, H., Kirk, J. and Westbrook, D. (2017) *An Introduction to Cognitive Behaviour Therapy: Skills and Applications*. Singapore: Sage.

King, J. (2013) *Silence in the Second Language Classroom*. Basingstoke: Palgrave Macmillan.

King, J. (2014) Fear of the true self: Social anxiety and the silent behaviour of Japanese learners of English. In K. Csizér and M. Magid (eds) *The Impact of Self-concept on Language Learning* (pp. 232–249). Bristol: Multilingual Matters.

King, J. (2016) Classroom silence and the dynamic interplay between context and the language learner: A stimulated recall study. In J. King (ed.) *The Dynamic Interplay Between Context and the Language Learner* (pp. 127–150). Basingstoke: Palgrave Macmillan.

King, J. and Smith, L. (2017) Social anxiety and silence in Japan's tertiary foreign language classrooms. In C. Gkonou, M. Daubney and J.M. Dewaele (eds) *New Insights into Language Anxiety: Theory, Research and Educational Implications* (pp. 91–109). Bristol: Multilingual Matters.

Kitano, K. (2001) Anxiety in the college Japanese language classroom. *Modern Language Journal* 85 (4), 549–566.

Kondo, D.S. and Ying-Ling, Y. (2004) Strategies for coping with language anxiety: The case of students of English in Japan. *ELT Journal* 58 (3), 258–265.

Kurihara, N. (2006) Classroom anxiety: How does student attitude change in English oral communication class in a Japanese senior high school? *Accents Asia* 1 (1), 34–68 [online].

Leary, M.R. (1983) A brief version of the Fear of Negative Evaluation Scale. *Personality and Social Psychology Bulletin* 9 (3), 371–375.

Leary, M.R. and Kowalski, R.M. (1995) The self-presentation model of social phobia. In R.G. Heimberg, M.R. Liebowitz, D.A. Hope and F.R. Schneier (eds) *Social Phobia: Diagnosis, Assessment and Treatment* (pp. 94–112). New York: Guilford Press.

LeDoux, J. (2015) *Anxious: The Modern Mind in the Age of Anxiety*. London: Oneworld Publications.

Lee-Cunin, M. (2004) *Student Views in Japan: A Study of Japanese Students' Perceptions of Their First Years at University*. Lancaster: Fieldwork Publications.

Liebowitz, M.R. (1987) Social phobia. *Modern Problems in Pharmacopsychiatry* 22, 141–173.

Liu, J. (2002) Negotiating silence in American classrooms: Three Chinese cases. *Language and Intercultural Communication* 2 (1), 37–54.

MacIntyre, P.D. and Dewaele, J.M. (2014) The two faces of Janus? Anxiety and enjoyment in the foreign language classroom. *Studies in Second Language Learning and Teaching* 4 (2), 237–274.

Matsumoto, D. and Ekman, P. (1989) American–Japanese cultural differences in intensity ratings of facial expressions of emotion. *Motivation and Emotion* 13 (2), 143–157.

McVeigh, B.J. (2002) *Japanese Higher Education as Myth*. New York: M.E. Sharpe.

Nakane, I. (2007) *Silence in Intercultural Communication: Perceptions and Performance*. Philadelphia, PA: John Benjamins.

Neale, J. (2016) Iterative categorization (IC): A systematic technique for analysing qualitative data. *Addiction* 111 (6), 1096–1106.

Nishino, T. and Watanabe, M. (2008) Communication-oriented policies versus classroom realities in Japan. *TESOL Quarterly* 42 (1), 133–138.

Nozaki, K.N. (1993) The Japanese student and the foreign teacher. In P. Wadden (ed.) *A Handbook for Teaching English at Japanese Colleges and Universities* (pp. 27–33). New York: Oxford University Press.

Okano, K. and Tsuchiya, M. (1999) *Education in Contemporary Japan: Inequality and Diversity*. Cambridge: Cambridge University Press.

Osterman, G.L. (2014) Experiences of Japanese university students' willingness to speak English in class: A multiple case study. *SAGE Open* 4 (3), 1–13.

Peak, L. (1989) Learning to become part of the group: The Japanese child's transition to preschool life. *Journal of Japanese Studies* 15 (1), 93–123.

Persons, J.B. and Tompkins, M.A. (2010) Cognitive-behavioral case formulation. In T.D. Eells (ed.) *Handbook of Psychotherapy Case Formulation* (pp. 314–339). New York: Guilford Press.

Reda, M.M. (2009) *Between Speaking and Silence: A Study of Quiet Students*. Albany, NY: State University of New York Press.

Richards, K. (2003) *Qualitative Inquiry in TESOL*. Basingstoke: Palgrave Macmillan.

Senior, R.M. (2006) *The Experience of Language Teaching*. Cambridge: Cambridge University Press.

Shachter, J.M. (2018) Tracking and quantifying Japanese English language learner speaking anxiety. *The Language Teacher* 42 (4), 3–7.

Shea, D.P. (2017) Compelled to speak: Addressing student reticence in a university EFL classroom. *Asian Journal of Applied Linguistics* 4 (2), 173–184.

Spielberger, C.D., Gorsuch, R.L., Lushene, R., Vagg, P.R. and Jacobs, G.A. (1983) *Manual for the State-Trait Anxiety Inventory*. Palo Alto, CA: Consulting Psychologists Press.

Squires, A. (2009) Methodological challenges in cross-language qualitative research: A research review. *International Journal of Nursing Studies* 46 (2), 277–287.

Stallard, P. (2002) *Think Good – Feel Good: A Cognitive Behavioural Therapy Workbook for Children and Young People*. Chichester: Wiley.

Stopa, L. and Clark, D.M. (2000) Social phobia and interpretation of social events. *Behaviour Research and Therapy* 38 (3), 273–283.

Strongman, K.T. (1995) Theories of anxiety. *New Zealand Journal of Psychology* 24 (2), 4–10.

Teeter, J.L. (2017) Improving motivation to learn English in Japan with a self-study shadowing application. *Languages* 2 (9), 1–27.

Thurston, M.D., Goldin, P., Heimberg, R. and Gross, J.J. (2017) Self-views in social anxiety disorder: The impact of CBT versus MBSR. *Journal of Anxiety Disorders* 47, 83–90.

Toyama, M. and Yamazaki, Y. (2019) Anxiety reduction sessions in foreign language classrooms. *Language Learning Journal*, 1–13. doi: 10.1080/09571736.2019.1598474.

Tsui, A.B. (1996) Reticence and anxiety in second language learning. In K.M. Bailey and D. Nunan (eds) *Voices from the Language Classroom* (pp. 145–167). Cambridge: Cambridge University Press.

Wadden, P. (ed.) (1993) *A Handbook for Teaching English at Japanese Colleges and Universities*. New York: Oxford University Press.

Williams, K.E. and Andrade, M.R. (2008) Foreign language learning anxiety in Japanese EFL university classes: Causes, coping, and locus of control. *Electronic Journal of Foreign Language Teaching* 5 (2), 181–191.

Yoneyama, S. (1999) *The Japanese High School: Silence and Resistance*. London: Routledge.

Young, D.J. (1991) Creating a low-anxiety classroom environment: What does language anxiety research suggest? *Modern Language Journal* 75 (4), 426–437.

Yuki, M., Maddux, W.W. and Masuda, T. (2007) Are the windows to the soul the same in the East and West? Cultural differences in using the eyes and mouth as cues to recognise emotions in Japan and the United States. *Journal of Experimental Social Psychology* 43 (2), 303–311.

6 Communicative Language Teaching and Silence: Chinese (Pre-service) Teachers' Perspectives

Michael Karas and Farahnaz Faez

Communicative language teaching (CLT) remains a popular approach in English language teaching (ELT). With its focus on interaction and communication, CLT has served as a response to 'traditional' methods such as grammar-translation and the audio-lingual method. It emphasises the importance of communicative competence and learning to communicate for learners. While it still has its critics, and it can at times be an ambiguous concept, CLT seems to pervade many contexts and, despite its ambiguity, most teachers in the West would describe their teaching as 'communicative' (Larsen-Freeman & Anderson, 2011). However, when discussing CLT, the role of silence is not clear. Communication cannot happen if everyone speaks at the same time. Good communication is not only talking but listening as well. In the student-centred CLT classroom, students must engage in interaction which includes both silence and talking. However, silence as a communicative function is rarely considered (Bao, 2014). Rather, students' non-verbal behaviour is often viewed negatively and as a sign of disengagement (Granger, 2013). At times, this may be the case, but it is important for teachers to consider the complexity of student silence and how it functions in the talk-heavy CLT environment. Silence can mean different things across cultures and contexts, and students and teachers may have different interpretations of silent behaviour (King, 2013b). This complicates any implementation of CLT.

English language teaching is a border-crossing profession and industry (Selvi, 2012); teachers travel across borders to earn teaching qualifications and also teach in foreign contexts, while students also venture to new contexts to learn English. The same can be said about ELT methods. ELT methods and resources, and especially CLT, traverse borders and contexts. Because of this, the suitability of CLT for other contexts must be considered, a notion that has been discussed previously (e.g. Chowdhury & Phan, 2008; Hong & Pawan, 2014). Specific to CLT, it is important to consider the vocal nature of CLT in the classroom, but also to recognise that students and teachers may not be accustomed to student-centred classrooms and may have difficulty navigating this new domain. This is especially important for teachers who study overseas in Western-based TESOL programmes with the intention of returning to their home contexts to teach. While many Western-based TESOL programmes broadly support the notion of CLT as an ELT approach, its implementation in other contexts is not always straightforward.

Focusing on China, there is a push to implement CLT in more classrooms. In 1992, the Chinese government introduced a new syllabus for English that stated the need for English to be used communicatively, and this gave CLT some importance for the first time in China (Hong & Pawan, 2014). However, this top-down initiative has met with resistance, and implementation on the ground level has been far from smooth (Hu & McKay, 2012). Despite top-down orders and new materials that advocate CLT, it is teachers who must implement communicative lessons in the classroom. Thus, understanding Chinese teachers' perspectives on CLT, and specifically teachers who study in a Western context that emphasises CLT in the classroom, is valuable. This study seeks to partially address this issue. Focusing on CLT and silence, this study investigates the perspectives of Chinese (pre-service) teachers studying in a Master of TESOL programme in Ontario, Canada. Data consist of focus group discussions and reflective writing pieces on the role of silence in the CLT classroom, the utility of CLT for the Chinese context, and how teachers can address the needs of students who may prefer to learn silently in the CLT classroom.

CLT, Silence and the Chinese Context

CLT is an approach that emphasises interaction and communication as its goal for language teaching. The purpose of CLT is to foster the development of 'communicative competence', a term coined by Dell Hymes (1966, 1972) in reaction to Chomsky's distinction between linguistic competence and performance. There are different views on what constitutes communicative competence and hence different models have been proposed. The first and most widely adopted framework of communicative competence was proposed by Canale and Swain (1980); it includes grammatical, sociolinguistic, discourse and strategic competencies. While grammatical competence in this model aligns with Chomsky's notion of linguistic competence in emphasising the accurate use of features of language, the other competencies emphasise the appropriate use of language in social contexts. Later, in reaction to Krashen's (1981) input hypothesis, 'the hypothesis that the *cause* of second language acquisition is input that is understood by the learner' (Swain, 2000: 98),

Swain (1985) proposed the 'output hypothesis', which states that attempts to produce a language provide the necessary conditions for learning it. Swain (2000: 102) later extended the significance of output by proposing that *collaborative dialogue* – which is 'dialogue in which speakers are engaged in problem solving and knowledge building' – is fundamental for mediating language learning. More recently, Swain (2006: 97) has used the notion of *languaging* to refer to the process of using language or 'talking it through- to another, with another, or with the self' as a way to mediate language learning.

The 'social turn' within applied linguistics has continued as researchers emphasise the importance of interaction for language learning (e.g. Swain, 2000, 2006). However, the role of silent non-verbal behaviour in the social learning environment remains unclear (Bao, 2014). There are different types of non-verbal behaviour, and the positive and negative functions of voiceless activity must be considered. One useful distinction that is made is differentiating between silence and reticence. Bao (2014) highlights the differences, noting silence as a voluntary action that can often help L2 acquisition and serve a communicative purpose in the classroom. Oppositely, reticence is involuntary, impedes L2 acquisition and also serves to affect communication negatively. Bao (2014) further notes that both teachers and learners often find it difficult to distinguish between the two, but such a distinction serves an articulatory and pedagogical purpose that can help highlight the complexity of non-verbal behaviour.

Across diverse contexts, researchers have further shown the complexity of silent behaviour in the (communicative) classroom environment. Chinese learners in the United States noted, despite not being involved in classroom discussions, they still found great value in silently listening to their classmates (Liu, 2002). In a large-scale study of Japanese university students, King (2013a) noted numerous types of silent behaviour, including silence of disengagement, silence due to teacher-centred methods and even silence caused by confusion. Also looking at Japanese learners, Harumi (2011) found many causes of student non-verbal behaviour, including linguistic incapability, but also issues with turn-taking. Often stereotyped as passive and silent, Japanese learners in Australia found it difficult to participate in both English for academic purposes (EAP) classrooms and mainstream classrooms as they noted issues with turn-taking, but also, problems with their teachers, as instructors, often contributed to their silent behaviour; teachers assumed they did not want to be called on to speak (Ellwood & Nakane, 2009). Linking L2 learning strategies and classroom turn-taking, the two Chinese students in Karas (2017) were aware that they spoke less often than their classmates, but also emphasised the positive ways they used their silent time in their EAP class to enhance their L2 learning by monitoring others' speech, preparing their own responses, and other useful functions.

However, silence does not always serve a communicative or learning purpose, but rather may negatively affect classroom interactions and the learning process. Part of this can be attributed to different understandings of silence. Different cultures attach different meanings to silence, and classroom interactions can be impacted when students and teachers have conflicting interpretations of silent behaviour (Bao, 2014; King, 2013b). This confusion can lead to dysfunctional reticence. Lee and Ng (2010) highlight conflicting teacher–student interaction patterns as a cause of student reticence in their study, but also emphasise task type, pedagogical goals of the lessons and student proficiency as factors that impact students' (lack of) verbal activity. Proficiency has been noted in other studies, where more proficient students showed more willingness to communicate in classroom discussions in Chinese university classrooms (Liu & Jackson, 2009). With Vietnamese learners, Bao (2007) found numerous causes of reticence, including respect and apprehension for the teacher, fear of poor performance, low self-esteem and others. Anxiety was a major source of reticence in Chen (2003), as a Japanese learner and a Korean learner both feared making mistakes in front of the teacher. Mak (2011) also notes speech anxiety and fear of negative evaluations as major contributors to student reticence. Thus, while there is considerable overlap between the concepts of silence and reticence, the above studies further highlight the need to distinguish between different kinds of non-verbal behaviour, as they can impact students, teachers and the overall classroom in both positive and negative ways.

Despite these nuances, in many ELT contexts, especially those that espouse CLT approaches, speech is often highly privileged while silence is negatively labelled as a lack of engagement and inactivity (Granger, 2013). However, it is important to adopt a more refined approach when discussing CLT and silence. While talk and interaction are certainly valuable, silence is itself a form of communication and often a misunderstood one (Bao, 2014; Granger, 2013). The relationship between CLT and silence becomes more important as CLT is being implemented in various contexts, including China. In China, there is a push to study English at a younger age, with English instruction now beginning in grade 3 (Hong & Pawan, 2014). The government of China encourages teachers to use more communicative methods and promotes CLT as a compliment to traditional methods (Hong & Pawan, 2014). However, Jin and Cortazzi (2006) argue that spontaneous speaking is rare in Chinese classrooms and students are perhaps more accustomed to memorisation activities. They note a gap between a desire to have more student-centred approaches, as purported by the government and education officials, and the reality that exists in Chinese classrooms. Hu (2002) focuses on cultural elements and argues that students in China value knowledge accumulation, not knowledge construction, making CLT practices difficult for some students. The 'learn by using' approach in CLT is often at odds with the traditional philosophy of 'learn to use' recognised by many Chinese students (Hu, 2002: 99).

For many in China, English appears to have very little use outside of the educational domain (Bolton & Graddol, 2012). For most students, English is simply another subject in which they must succeed in order to get into prominent high schools and universities (Hu & McKay, 2012). Partially because of this, English classrooms in China often remain highly teacher-centred, with students engaged in more silent forms of learning. However, others argue for a more complex assessment. Cheng (2000) argues that it is not accurate to over-generalise Chinese students as being reticent, and that many factors must be considered, not just culture. Peng (2012: 211) focused on Chinese EFL learners and found that communicative activities were not 'universally rejected', as students with a high willingness to communicate did embrace CLT activities. Peng (2012) argues that individual, environmental and linguistic factors must all be considered when evaluating students' engagement in classroom discussions. Thus, while CLT's implementation in the Chinese context has been somewhat difficult, based on the studies above, it is perhaps overly simplistic to attribute only one cause to this trouble. In many ways, CLT does not mesh with Chinese learning culture (Hu, 2002), and students react to this often by staying silent in class, but reasons for student silence and/or reticence are numerous and can be overcome with creative pedagogical solutions (Peng, 2014).

This study's main focus is on CLT and silence in the Chinese context, but from the perspectives of Chinese (pre-service) teachers, placing it under the broader subject area of language-teacher cognition. It is now widely accepted that what teachers think, know and believe (i.e. their cognitions) are important and can impact teachers and students (Borg, 2003, 2006; Burns et al., 2015). For this study, the term 'perspectives' is utilised to represent teachers' cognitions. Research into language-teacher cognition has seen many terms used to describe teachers' inner mental workings, but drawing clear distinctions is often difficult, even between terms like 'knowledge' and 'beliefs' (Borg, 2006, 2015). While the term 'perspectives' is used here, it is interchangeable with the more common term 'beliefs', which emphasises teachers' subjective pedagogical thoughts about teaching and learning. What teachers think is at least partially related to what they do in the classroom (Borg, 2015). This acknowledgement has led researchers to consider what types of cognitions teachers may have about teaching and learning in general (e.g. Busch, 2010), their cognitions about specific aspects of teaching (e.g. grammar; Borg, 1998) and, similar to this study, the cognitions of pre-service teachers on LTE programmes (e.g. Graus & Coppen, 2016). In relation to silence, Bao (2014: 18) argues that 'language teachers are not trained to observe silence, let alone to listen to and manage it', highlighting the lack of attention silence seems to receive within LTE programmes.

Conversely, CLT is often placed at the core of LTE programmes, especially in Western contexts, but at times with little regard as to how students may implement CLT at home, and whether it is even appropriate (Chowdhury & Phan, 2008). In light of these concerns, this study investigates the perspectives of Chinese (pre-service) teachers on the role of silence in the CLT classroom, the suitability of CLT for China, and also how they may be able to accommodate silent learners in the talk-heavy CLT classroom.

Methodology

This study followed a qualitative research design. Data were gathered from two sources: reflective writing pieces and focus group discussions. Participants for this study were 91 Chinese international students completing a master of TESOL programme in Ontario, Canada. The majority of participants had no, or less than one year of, formal teaching experience, although many participants had served as teaching assistants and tutors in China. The participants were in the final semester of their course-based master's degree when they participated in the study. The programme provided courses on TESOL methodology and the teaching of language skills and competencies, along with teaching observations of ESL classrooms. The majority of the participants were in their early twenties and most had been in Canada for just less than one year, the duration of the master programme.

As is common in Western TESOL programmes, students were introduced to the CLT approach and its principles. A brief lecture on the tenets of CLT and another on the functions of silence and some potential causes of reticence were provided. As pre-reading for these lectures, students read chapter 1 of Bao (2014) for an overview of silence, and chapter 4 of Hong and Pawan (2014) for an overview of CLT in China. In his chapter, Bao (2014) highlights the various theoretical perspectives on silence, contrasts silence with reticence, and indicates the value of silence for communication and language learning. In their chapter, Hong and Pawan (2014) outline the evolution of CLT in China and some of the main principles of CLT. These chapters served as useful reading on the way to blend the discussion of CLT with silence, and in light of all of the participants being from China. Participants then took part in focus group discussions. Students were divided into groups of four or five and asked to discuss how silence is or can be used in talk-heavy CLT classrooms, how suitable CLT is for China, and what strategies could be used to help students engage in the CLT classroom in the Chinese context. Each group made notes on large board paper and presented the main points of their discussion to the class. These discussions were not audio-recorded, but the summary notes made on the large sheet of paper were used as data for this study, as were the field notes taken by the observing researchers. Also, each participant completed a reflective writing piece of approximately two pages about silent learning strategies and CLT, using reflection prompts, and submitted them a week later.

There were three questions that guided this study.

(1) What is the role of silence in the CLT classroom?
(2) How do participants view the suitability of CLT for the Chinese context? What may be some issues?
(3) How can teachers implement CLT in traditionally teacher-centred contexts and account for students who may prefer to learn more silently?

These were provided to students as prompts for their group discussions and reflective papers, although they were slightly reworded to ask the participants directly what their beliefs were about these issues.

Data analysis comprised systemic qualitative thematic analysis (Creswell, 2008; Patton, 2002). Both of the present authors made reflective notes during and following the focus groups to record issues and ideas 'both *in situ* and away from the situation' (Cohen *et al.*, 2011: 235). Afterwards, both authors reviewed the main points provided by each group on the large chart paper. The reflective writing pieces were reviewed to identify specific perspectives about the role of silence and the suitability of CLT for teacher-centred contexts. Each writing assignment was reviewed and emerging perspectives were noted in the margins. These perspectives were then categorised and compared across different participants and focus group discussions, and common themes were identified. When all the writing pieces had been reviewed once, they were re-read and common themes that occurred across reflections were noted as salient themes. The two authors compared and discussed their coding to reach inter-coder agreement (Nunan & Bailey, 2009). Salient themes were identified, and representative and interesting quotations were noted and are presented in the Results section below.

With such a methodology, there is a high chance that students' responses will overlap, and this limitation is acknowledged. Because students took part in focus group discussions, they potentially influenced the opinions of other students. Furthermore, because these group discussions were not audio-recorded, only the main points drawn from researcher notes and notes made by the participants on their chart paper were used. Thus, fine details could not be garnered from these discussions. The reflective writing pieces provided more in-depth data for analysis, but they also have limitations. Because CLT and silence were both presented in class as part of the course curriculum, participants were potentially influenced by their coursework, the course readings, the presentations on CLT and silence before the focus group discussions, and also their classmates.

Results

Common themes are presented below with quotations from the participants. Given the large number of participants, it did not seem useful to apply pseudonyms to all participants. When analysing data, participants were given a number in order to organise the writing pieces and track quotations. However, for readability, and to maintain the participants' voices, quotes from the reflective writing pieces are intermingled throughout this Results section, but the actual participant numbers utilised during analysis have been left out. To ensure a spread of voices, no participant is quoted more than twice. The quotes are included as they are representative of the broader themes outlined during analysis.

Functions of silence (and causes of reticence) in the CLT classroom

The first research question concerned how Chinese (pre-service) teachers view the role of silence in the CLT classroom. The participants suggested a variety of roles for silence, and highlighted the numerous positive aspects of silence but also the negative aspects that may cause students to be reticent in the classroom. For this analysis, it was useful to distinguish between silence and reticence (Bao, 2014). While it is impossible to draw clear distinctions between the two concepts, it was useful to separate the voluntary aspects of non-verbal behaviour highlighted by participants and those that they viewed as imposed on students in the CLT classroom.

Only 12 of the 91 participants discussed causes of reticence in their reflective writing pieces. However, reticence did feature prominently in the group discussions. Looking across both data sets, lack of language ability, anxiety and the fear of embarrassment were the most commonly mentioned. One participant noted that she often did not speak in class when she 'didn't know the right word'. Another participant remarked: 'There are times I want to speak, but I don't know how to say it, so I stay silent'. A lack of language ability was mentioned across all of the group discussions as a key cause of reticence. Language anxiety and feeling unsafe to speak in class were also commonly mentioned sources of reticence. One participant noted her experience as a tutor and said she found that 'students become reticent due to anxiety and lack of confidence' when asked to speak in front of the class. Another participant related her own experiences of non-participation, noting she often did not talk when feeling 'negative emotions like anxiety and unsafety'. Finally, and connected to the previous two, was a simple fear of embarrassment and losing face. 'I am afraid others cannot understand what I am saying' noted one participant as a justification for why she did not talk in the classroom at times. The notion of 'losing face' was listed as a discussion point for all of the group discussions.

The positive functions of silence were emphasised more by participants, especially silence as a communicative function in the classroom and its role in enhancing learning and L2 acquisition. The communicative function of silence was noted by all participants in their reflective writing pieces and by all of the groups in their discussions. Participants viewed silence as a way to communicate with the teacher by 'showing confusion' with instruction, 'dissatisfaction towards the teacher', as a 'sign of respect' for the teacher or to show that 'students do not understand the question'. While a minority of participants noted silent 'defiance' of the teacher, the majority of participants emphasised silence as a way to communicate respect and admiration for their teachers. Dealing with classmates, participants also noted communicative aspects of their silent behaviour. One participant mentioned the 'confrontational silence' she had used with her classmates in discussions, but more commonly participants emphasised silence as a way to 'give partners a chance to express their different opinions' and its 'communicative role' during conversations, allowing 'other new voices to be heard'. A minority of participants discussed communication through silence as a 'cultural preference' and as a form of 'traditional etiquette', allowing students to show humility, which they argued to be a virtue in Chinese culture. The potential semiotic nature of silent behaviour allowing students to use facial expressions and gestures as means of communication was also mentioned by one participant, while four participants noted silence as a way to express a lack of motivation when they are 'bored' or 'not interested in the topic' in the classroom. However, the most prominent communicative functions of silence were to show respect for the teacher and to allow space for others to speak in the classroom.

Finally, participants also noted numerous functions of student silence related to learning and L2 acquisition. Broadly related to learning, participants discussed silence as a way for them to 'rest and recharge the mind' and to 'find their own pace of learning'. Others noted silence as a time to 'process knowledge', 'reflect and digest knowledge' or to 'internalise knowledge'. More specific to L2 acquisition, silent learning strategies were crucial to some participants: 'I always need some space in the mind to think about how to construct a second language', one noted. Others emphasised the need to 'rehearse the answers in my mind', or the need to 'prepare their thoughts' and the need for time to prepare 'responses in my mind silently', allowing a 'safe space where I can practise my speaking' before producing verbal output. Some even drew on the language of sociocultural theory, relating silence as an opportune time for 'languaging' and 'as a sign of active inner speech'. More broadly, based on both the reflective writing pieces and the group discussions, participants discussed silence as a time for reflection and overall 'cognitive processing' in the language classroom, 'allowing learners to think more creatively, efficiently and critically'.

Suitability of CLT for Chinese classrooms

Research question 2 concerned participants' perceptions of the suitability of CLT for traditionally teacher-centred contexts, specifically China, and what issues may arise when implementing CLT in such a context. Data from the reflective pieces and the focus group discussions did show, at times, an optimistic view of the suitability of CLT for China but, on the whole, more participants argued that CLT would not be suitable for China and offered many reasons why they believed this to be so. While CLT emphasises verbal interaction in the classroom, silence will inevitably play a role, as it does in all social interactions. This question served to partially address this relationship, as participants discussed the suitability of CLT in China and how it may, or may not, suit traditional learning styles in China that often place the learner as silent receivers of knowledge (Hu, 2002).

Beginning with the optimistic responses, only nine of the 91 reflective writing pieces took a positive tone towards CLT and its implementation in Chinese classrooms. For these participants, CLT in China could work, if done appropriately. For example, some noted that CLT could be implemented in China if blended with traditional methods: 'Based on my own experience, CLT is most suitable as a complementary part, rather than a replacement' (of traditional methods). Many participants felt that teachers in China were not properly trained to utilise CLT, but some did feel that, if given such training, teachers could certainly adapt: 'it is difficult for teachers to integrate CLT in the classroom, but it is not unachievable'. Some even mentioned that they had experience with CLT in China, for example in observing other teachers. One participant noted watching 'a teacher successfully engage over 40 students in CLT activities'. Some mentioned their experience as learners, noting that 'teachers start[ed] to implement communication activities' when they were in public school.

A second group of participants (30 of 91) took a more balanced approach and noted the possibilities for CLT in China but with some trepidation and potential limitations. For example, one participant noted CLT as possible 'in some tutoring classes' but also felt 'communicative language teaching is not possible in language education in public schools and institutes'. Another noted her experience in university as being communicative, but emphasised that her 'primary and high school classrooms were teacher-centred'. Interestingly, some in the group discussions noted a divide between larger Chinese cities and more rural areas, arguing that CLT is often experienced only by students in larger cities in China and those in rural areas may have different experiences. One participant aptly noted that teachers 'must keep an open mind' to new ideas. If given strong institutional support, and with consideration to what type of classroom context, CLT can be properly utilised in teacher-centred classrooms within China and 'close the gap between teachers and students', mending what many participants noted as a very 'rigid' relationship. Thus, while this group noted potential impediments to CLT in certain contexts within China, they took a pragmatic perspective and noted its potential utilisation in their country in certain venues.

There was, thus, some general acknowledgement that CLT could be, and indeed has been, applied successfully in Chinese classrooms. However, the majority of participants (52 of 91) emphasised major issues that, in their opinions, would prevent CLT from succeeding in China. The role of silence is intertwined, directly and indirectly, with their responses. Many referenced large classroom sizes as an impediment to CLT implementation. One participant referenced her experience as a student: 'There were over 50 people in my high school class. The teacher talked the whole time.' With classrooms often in excess of 50 students, teachers simply will not be able to control the class if CLT is implemented. Classroom management becomes 'one big headache when implementing CLT in Chinese classrooms' one participant noted and many simply stated that it is 'easier' to control the class if students remain silent. Furthermore, if students were to discuss in class, monitoring the interactions of so many students/groups would be impossible, leaving students with no feedback or assessment of their English use. Related to this was an emphasis on teachers' sharing of school space with other teachers. If a class of over 50 students engages in small-group work with interaction, this likely creates a lot of noise, potentially disturbing other classrooms where only the teacher is speaking. Drawing on their own teaching experiences, even when student–student interactions were attempted by teachers, many struggled, as 'students refused to interact with their peers' when teachers tried more CLT-type activities. Students are 'trained to be passive' in China, as one participant noted, and attempting CLT will result more in confusion than in productive interactions. It was simply 'too time-consuming' another argued. Somewhat discouraging, participants noted that, as students, they rarely had had CLT English classes in public school: 'There was no chance for us to speak and communicate with others using the language we learned'.

Exams were another common theme, as CLT was deemed not useful because students need to prepare for exams. Chinese language policy was consistently emphasised by participants, who argued that exams were the most important element for students, not their ability to communicate. Participants noted that the 'main job of teachers is helping students get high grades for examinations' and that 'teachers just need to finish the teaching tasks and let students get higher scores'. 'Listening and speaking count for very little on the university exam' stressed one participant.

Connected to this was the role of students' parents. If students perform badly in exams and are engaged in communicative tasks deemed not relevant for students' success, teachers are often blamed for poor performance and 'parents may think the teacher is lazy', which could 'damage the teacher's future career'. 'Teachers have great pressure in China', noted one participant, in their roles to prepare students for these important gate-keeping exams. Beyond parents, participants argued that even teaching colleagues might be critical of the CLT approach.

The relationship between teachers and students was also frequently discussed. Participants emphasised the authoritarian role of the teacher in China and also the great respect for the profession. Rather than allowing students to engage in interaction and challenge teachers' perspectives, one argued that it is 'extremely impolite and disrespectful to argue with them' (teachers). One participant discussed the strict relationship between teachers and students as a 'manifestation of China's totalitarian ideology; the power dynamics of traditional classrooms foster obedience and oppose different opinions'. Because of this, many argued that it is simply safer for students to remain silent in the classroom and not potentially challenge teachers' authority. This 'rigid relationship between students and teachers creates an atmosphere that makes students not want to talk', argued one participant.

Another common theme was that teachers simply were not adequately prepared to teach CLT. This was partly related to teachers' perceived lack of English language proficiency, as many participants argued that teachers often have no overseas experience. 'Teachers will need better proficiency' noted one participant. Lack of knowledge about English-speaking cultures was also discussed, even though knowledge of English-speaking nations' cultures is now often deemed not necessary by many academics who now support the idea of English as an international language (e.g. Matsuda, 2017). This lack of proficiency, both linguistic and cultural, was seen as a large impediment to successful implementation of CLT. Beyond proficiency, many simply felt teachers were not adequately trained to use CLT, as they were only prepared to give teacher-centred lectures in the classroom. Bluntly put, one participant noted that teachers just 'can't change their teaching style'. 'CLT requires higher qualifications' and if teachers are forced to use it, this will 'push the teacher into an awkward place' as they may not be ready to implement it. Furthermore, even if teachers did want to implement CLT, they would potentially need to develop their own CLT materials, which many participants felt they lack the training to do.

Accommodating silent learners in the CLT class

The final research question asked participants to consider how teachers could implement CLT in traditionally teacher-centred contexts while accounting for students who prefer to learn silently. This question served as an opportunity for participants to consider pedagogical strategies they could use if they needed to or chose to use CLT when teaching in China. The most common suggestion by participants was simply to create a comfortable atmosphere that would encourage students to speak. Reiterating that students are often not accustomed to speaking out in class, participants emphasised the need to 'maintain a safe atmosphere'. To accomplish this, participants suggested teachers need to 'give enough time for students to prepare to talk'; provide students with discussion questions in advance so they could prepare their answers; refrain from forcing students to speak; and also allow students various options when completing a task, enabling them to do it in whatever mode of communication they thought best.

Another common theme was the need for teachers to 'be creative' when developing CLT activities and 'develop activities that require every learner to take part'. If activities are interesting and engaging, many participants felt that students would be more encouraged to speak. The role of advanced, more proficient students was also mentioned extensively. Participants argued that more 'expert' students could be used strategically, by placing them in different groups and allowing them to support their classmates in discussions. Interestingly, there was little mention of how more productive uses of silence could be implemented in the classroom along with methods to encourage more talk.

Discussion

The results of this study provide insights into the perspectives of Chinese (pre-service) teachers on the functions of silence, the suitability of CLT for Chinese classrooms, and potential strategies to accommodate silent learners in vocal communicative classrooms. Focusing on the first part of this study, teachers' perceptions about the roles of silence, the participants offered a range of functions for student silence in the classroom. Broadly, these fell into two main themes: (1) silence for communicative purposes; and (2) silence for learning and L2 acquisition. The responses provided were not necessarily novel – many of these strategies have been discussed by other researchers (e.g. Bao, 2014; King, 2013a). However, it was encouraging to note that the participants did see the many useful ways silence can be employed in the classroom, even offering ways they have used silence themselves as learners. Somewhat surprisingly, participants made little reference to notions of involuntary silence, often referred to as reticence. While there was some discussion about language anxiety, lack of language ability and fear of embarrassment as common causes of student reticence, the focus was very much on productive elements of silent behaviour, those that can enhance L2 learning and serve as communication tools.

However, these positive functions of silence were not connected to the second research question, which addressed participants' views on CLT implementation in Chinese classrooms. Rather, when discussing the utility of CLT for China, participants often viewed its suitability in terms of speech only, not mentioning communicative functions of silence. A minority of participants acknowledged that CLT could be utilised in Chinese classrooms, but more participants highlighted major issues with CLT in China and how these aspects limited students' talking. Common issues included large class sizes, Chinese learning cultures, the authoritative role of teachers and too much focus on examinations. These issues are also not entirely new, as scholars have noted similar impediments to CLT in China (e.g. Bolton & Graddol, 2012; Hong & Pawan, 2014; Hu & McKay, 2012; Jin & Cortazzi, 2006). However, while these are certainly noteworthy contextual issues, they do not eliminate the possibility of CLT and silent communicative/learning strategies coexisting. King (2013a) cites a successful CLT classroom in Japan with over 100 students, showing that class size can be overcome. The authoritative role of teachers can change, potentially with newer generations of teachers such as these participants entering the teaching force. The ambiguous notion of the Chinese learning culture, cited by the participants, certainly does not preclude the use of CLT, but rather requires its skilful implementation in the Chinese classroom to allow for the aforementioned benefits of silence also to be present. Many focused on the issue of examinations and how English is a key study area for students to move into university. Yet, there was no acknowledgement of the potential for more social learning styles to help students prepare for their exams in tandem with the already present teacher-centred methods that emphasise student silent learning. Thus, while participants noted many benefits of silence, these did not seem present when discussing CLT in China. Rather than discussing possible ways for these silent learning behaviours to coexist with CLT, their causes (class sizes, exams, etc.) were often viewed as insurmountable blocks to CLT and silence coexisting in a harmonious relationship.

However, participants did offer many useful strategies to accommodate more silent learners in the CLT classroom. Despite the majority of participants arguing that CLT is not suitable for Chinese classes, many proposed very useful strategies (e.g. more preparation time for students, selecting engaging topics, etc.) to encourage students who may not be accustomed to speaking in the classroom to participate. However, it was interesting to note that many of their strategies still privileged talk over silence in the classroom. For example, creating a comfortable atmosphere was commonly noted, as was providing students with discussion questions in advance. These were proposed to promote more speaking. Despite acknowledging the communicative benefits of silence and its role in L2 learning, there was more emphasis on getting students to talk in the classroom rather than enhancing valuable silent learning/communication strategies. Furthermore, while they offered many potential solutions, these solutions did not appear to impact their views on CLT and China. These results may be partially affected by the questions posed to students for their discussions and the writing assignment, along with the study's other limitations, especially the likelihood of participants influencing each other's responses. However, it was interesting to find that participants discussed many benefits of silence, and even presented numerous ways silent learning and talk can coexist, but when placed specifically in the context of China, these aspects did not persuade the majority of participants to consider CLT for the Chinese context.

Conclusion

The class readings, lectures, group discussions and reflective assignment all served the purpose of bringing the issue of silence to the forefront for these teachers to consider. As Bao (2014) notes, silence literacy is often lacking for teachers, especially within teacher education. Encouraging participants to consider the role of silence, and its relationship with CLT, served as a useful exercise for these participants as they completed their master of TESOL programme. While their perspectives on the appropriateness of CLT for China were often pessimistic, their consideration of the various productive roles of silence, and how various strategies can be used to assist more silent students in the CLT classroom, allowed teachers to come up with specific pedagogical strategies they can take to their classrooms. Top-down measures to implement CLT in China are noteworthy (Hong & Pawan, 2014), but it is teachers who are responsible for implementing any curriculum. Considering the preponderance of teachers studying in Western-based TESOL programmes, it is important to consider how they view the methods/approaches learned on these programmes for their own contexts. Silence can be a deeply embedded construct in some cultures, often representing highly positive attributes (Bao, 2014). Its cultural importance and its function as a communicative tool and a means to enhance L2 acquisition should be emphasised. CLT will almost certainly be discussed in any TESOL teacher education programme, as it remains a predominant approach in ELT, and connecting these two aspects offers teachers the opportunity to reflect on how speech and silence can, and must, interact.

Self-reflection/Discussion Questions

(1) Large classroom sizes are often noted as an impediment to effective implementation of CLT in certain contexts; however, there are examples of teachers overcoming this (e.g. King, 2013a). What are some strategies teachers can use to implement communicative methodologies in classrooms with more than 50 students?
(2) CLT is gradually being implemented in the Chinese context (see Hong & Pawan, 2014). What is the role of CLT in your teaching/learning context?

(3) What are some ways you have used silence to enhance your own learning in the (English) language classroom?
(4) Many of the solutions offered by participants in this study emphasised speech over silence. What are some activities that can be used in the CLT classroom that can be done either with speech or in silence?

Recommended Reading

Hong, P. and Pawan, F. (2014) *The Pedagogy and Practice of Western-Trained Chinese English Language Teachers: Foreign Education, Chinese Meanings.* New York: Routledge.

Hong and Pawan focus on a growing population: Chinese English language teachers who travel to Western-based contexts for language teacher education. They provide an excellent background on differing motivations for students to go overseas, but also a background on CLT and how it is slowly being implemented in the Chinese context.

Karas, M. (2017) Turn-taking and silent learning during open class discussions. *ELT Journal* 71 (1), 13–23. doi: 10.1093/ELT/ccw051.

Karas looks at the turn-taking habits of an EAP (English for academic purposes) class in Ontario, Canada, and notes disparate turn-taking between the students. Interview data with two Chinese students in the class notes how they used their non-verbal time during class, which included many communicative activities, to enhance their language learning.

References

Bao, D. (2007) Enhancing the language learning process for reticent learners of Vietnamese and of English in Vietnam. In B. Tomlinson (ed.) *Language Acquisition and Development* (pp. 205–224). New York: Continuum.
Bao, D. (2014) *Understanding Silence and Reticence: Ways of Participating in Second Language Acquisition.* London: Bloomsbury.
Bolton, K. and Graddol, D. (2012) English in China today. *English Today* 28 (3), 3–9. doi:10.1017/S0266078412000223.
Borg, S. (1998) Teachers' pedagogical systems and grammar teaching: A qualitative study. *TESOL Quarterly* 32 (1), 9–38.
Borg, S. (2003) Teacher cognition in language teaching: A review of research on what language teachers think, know, believe, and do. *Language Teaching* 35, 81–109.
Borg, S. (2006) *Teacher Cognition and Language Education: Research and Practice.* London: Continuum.
Borg, S. (2015) Researching teacher beliefs. In B. Paltridge and A. Phakiti (eds) *Research Methods in Applied Linguistics: A Practical Resource* (pp. 487–504). London: Bloomsbury.
Burns, A., Freeman, D. and Edwards, E. (2015) Theorizing and studying the language-teaching mind: Mapping research on language teacher cognition. *Modern Language Journal* 99 (3), 585–601.

Busch, D. (2010) Pre-service teacher beliefs about language learning: The second language acquisition course as an agent for change. *Language Teaching Research* 14 (3), 318–337.

Canale, M. and Swain, M. (1980) Theoretical bases of communicative approaches to second language teaching and testing. *Applied Linguistics* 1 (1), 1–47.

Chen, T. (2003) Reticence in class and on-line: Two ESL students' experiences with communicative language teaching. *System* 31, 259–281. doi:10.1016/S0346-251X(03)00024-1.

Cheng, X. (2000) Asian students' reticence revisited. *System* 28, 435–446.

Chowdhury, R and Phan, L.H. (2008) Reflecting on Western TESOL training and communicative language teaching: Bangladeshi teachers' voices. *Asia Pacific Journal of Education* 28 (3), 305–316.

Cohen, L., Manion, L. and Morrison, K. (2011) *Research Methods in Education* (7th edn). London: Routledge.

Creswell, J.W. (2008) *Educational Research: Planning, Conducting, and Evaluating Quantitative and Qualitative Research* (3rd edn). Upper Saddle River, NJ: Pearson Prentice Hall.

Ellwood, C. and Nakane, I. (2009) Privileging of speech in EAP and mainstream university classrooms: A critical evaluation of participation. *TESOL Quarterly* 43 (2), 203–230.

Granger, C.A. (2013) Silence and participation in the language classroom. In *The Encyclopedia of Applied Linguistics* (pp. 1–4). New York: Blackwell Publishing.

Grauss, J. and Coppen, P.A. (2016) Student teacher beliefs on grammar instruction. *Language Teaching Research* 20 (5), 571–599.

Harumi, S. (2011) Classroom silence: Voices from Japanese EFL learners. *ELT Journal* 65 (3), 260–269. doi: 10.1093/elt/ccq046.

Hong, P. and Pawan, F. (2014) *The Pedagogy and Practice of Western-Trained Chinese English Language Teachers: Foreign Education, Chinese Meanings*. New York: Routledge.

Hu, G. (2002) Potential cultural resistance to pedagogical imports: The case of communicative language teaching in China. *Language, Culture and Curriculum* 15 (2), 93–105.

Hu, G. and McKay, S.L. (2012) English language education in East Asia: Some recent developments. *Journal of Multilingual and Multicultural Development* 33 (4), 345–362. doi: 10.1080/01434632.2012.661434.

Hymes, D.H. (1966) Two types of linguistic relativity. In W. Bright (ed.) *Sociolinguistics* (pp. 114–158). The Hague: Mouton.

Hymes, D.H. (1972) On communicative competence. In J.B. Pride and J. Holmes (eds) *Sociolinguistics: Selected Readings* (pp. 269–293). Harmondsworth: Penguin.

Jin, L. and Cortazzi, M. (2006) Changing practices in Chinese cultures of learning. *Language, Culture and Curriculum* 19 (1), 5–20.

Karas, M. (2017) Turn-taking and silent learning during open class discussions. *ELT Journal* 71 (1), 13–23. doi: 10.1093/ELT/ccw051.

King, J. (2013a) Silence in the second language classrooms of Japanese universities. *Applied Linguistics* 34 (3), 325–343. doi: 10.1093/applin/ams043.

King, J. (2013b) *Silence in the Second Language Classroom*. New York: Palgrave Macmillan. doi: 10.1057/9781137301482.

Krashen, S.D. (1981) *Second Language Acquisition and Second Language Learning*. Oxford: Oxford University Press.

Larsen-Freeman, D. and Anderson, M. (2011) *Techniques and Principles in Language Teaching*. Oxford: Oxford University Press.

Lee, W. and Ng, S. (2010) Reducing student reticence through teacher interaction strategy. *ELT Journal* 64 (3), 302–313.

Liu, J. (2002) Negotiating silence in American classrooms. *Language and Intercultural Communication* 2 (1), 35–54.

Liu, M. and Jackson, J. (2009) Reticence in Chinese EFL students at varied proficiency levels. *TESL Canada Journal* 26 (2), 65–81.

Mak, B. (2011) An exploration of speaking-in-class anxiety with Chinese ESL learners. *System* 39, 202–214.

Matsuda, A. (ed.) (2017) *Preparing Teachers to Teach English as an International Language*. Bristol: Multilingual Matters.

Nunan, D. and Bailey, K.M. (2009) *Exploring Second Language Classroom Research: A Comprehensive Guide*. Boston, MA: Heinle, Cengage Learning.

Patton, M.Q. (2002) *Qualitative Research and Evaluation Methods* (3rd edn). Thousand Oaks, CA: Sage Publications.

Peng, J.E. (2012) Towards an ecological understanding of willingness to communicate in EFL classrooms in China. *System* 40, 203–213. doi: 10.1016/j.system.2012.02.002.

Peng, J.E. (2014) *Willingness to Communicate in the Chinese EFL University Classroom: An Ecological Perspective*. Bristol: Multilingual Matters.

Selvi, A.F. (2012) A quest to prepare all English language teachers for diverse settings: If not us, who? If not now, when? PhD thesis, University of Maryland.

Swain, M. (1985) Communicative competence: Some roles of comprehensible input and comprehensible output in its development. In S. Gass and C. Madden (eds) *Input in Second Language Acquisition* (pp. 235–253). Rowley, MA: Newbury House.

Swain, M. (2000) The output hypothesis and beyond: Mediating acquisition through collaborative dialogue. In J.P. Lantolf (ed.) *Sociocultural Theory and Second Language Learning* (pp. 97–114). Oxford: Oxford University Press.

Swain, M. (2006) Languaging, agency and collaboration in advanced second language proficiency. In H. Byrnes (ed.) *Advanced Language Learning: The Contribution of Halliday and Vygotsky* (pp. 95–108). London: Continuum.

7 Silence in Japanese Classrooms: Activities and Factors in Capacities to Speak English

Simon Humphries, Nobuhiko Akamatsu, Takako Tanaka and Anne Burns

Introduction

The Rugby World Cup in 2019 and the Tokyo Summer Olympics have provided incentives for the Japanese government and businesses to boost the population's ability to speak the international lingua franca with overseas visitors. In fact, Japanese companies have pushed for decades for the government to improve the nation's English-speaking education. Therefore, since the 1980s, there have been various policies to this end. For example, since 1987, the Japan Exchange and Teaching (JET) Programme has invited assistant language teachers (ALTs) from various countries to team-teach in secondary schools, according to the Programme's website (http://jetprogramme.org/en/history). More recently, such policies culminated in a directive that, from April 2013, high school English classes should be delivered in the target language in principal (Tahira, 2012).

Although it is true that students need input through listening and reading and some cultures may use silence as a communication strategy (Basso, 1970; Harumi, 2011; Shigemitsu, 2007), there are several benefits to be gained from speaking in class. As noted by Swain (1995), it is uncontroversial that speaking improves fluency through practice, but she also explains that, through the negotiation of meaning with an interlocutor, three benefits can arise for improving accuracy: (1) learners become aware of gaps in their linguistic knowledge; (2) they test hypotheses through modifying their output; and (3) as they reflect upon their language use, learners can control and internalise their linguistic knowledge. In addition to these benefits in relation to second language acquisition (SLA), speaking English can lead to professional and academic opportunities

(Goh & Burns, 2012), whereas silence may give the impression of poor competence (Nakane, 2007).

Despite the advantages of using the target language, classroom observations indicate that secondary school Japanese teachers of English (JTEs) tend to continue using *yakudoku*, which is a teacher-centred grammar-translation approach conducted predominantly in Japanese (Thompson & Yanagita, 2017; Underwood, 2017). From the point of view of teachers, various reasons have been posited for the continuing use of *yakudoku*, such as entrance test preparation, institutional norms, lack of confidence, fear of losing control of the class, lack of training and inadequate materials (Humphries, 2014). However, after extensive observations of university classes, King (2013) noted the prevalence of student silence. Moreover, at the secondary level, teacher attempts at nominating students to speak English have been met with resistance strategies such as: providing responses in Japanese, remaining silent, employing extended pauses or using Japanese *katakana* pronunciation (Humphries & Stroupe, 2014).

When trying to understand silence in the language classroom, studies have primarily focused on the opinions of undergraduates and teachers, and there has been a lack of empirical research into the preferences of secondary school students, which this study aims to address.

Factors That May Influence Capacity to Speak

There has been extensive research into willingness to communicate (WTC), which is defined as 'the tendency of an individual to initiate communication when free to do so' (Yashima, 2002: 55). Therefore, underlying WTC is an assumption that there is the volition to communicate in a second language (L2), which may seem logical in the context of English as a second language (ESL), where students are likely to have an integrative orientation through studying in the target language country (Warden & Lin, 2000). However, in many Asian countries like Japan, where non-majors study English as a foreign language (EFL) as a compulsory subject at the secondary and tertiary levels, it could be argued that many students lack WTC. In particular, they may not want to communicate orally. This claim might sound dramatic but, as King (2013) observed from 48 hours in classes across nine Japanese universities, student-initiated talk accounted for only 0.24% of class time. Therefore, rather than WTC, we measure capacity to speak (CTS). CTS is defined as 'students' perceptions of their abilities to speak under various classroom situations' (Humphries *et al.*, 2015: 165). In other words, CTS focuses directly on classroom situations that can help speech or cause silence.

The following sections discuss the cognitive demands of activities, learner personality traits, and issues in Japan or similar cultural contexts.

Cognitive demands of the activity

Robinson (2005) suggests the Triadic Componential Framework to gauge cognitive learning demands. It consists of: (1) intrinsic complexity, (2) learner perceptions of difficulty (based on their ability and affective responses) and (3) task conditions (such as one-way or two-way participation, or group dynamics). Learner perceptions and group dynamics should influence CTS, but they are discussed later in this chapter, in the sections on psychological and sociocultural factors. Robinson (2005: 4) himself notes that intrinsic complexity 'should be the major basis for proactive pedagogic task sequencing'. He distinguishes between two dimensions of task complexity: resource-directing and resource-dispersing. Resource-directing dimensions 'are those in which the demands on language use made by increases in task complexity and the increased conceptual demands ... can be met by specific aspects of the linguistic system' (Robinson, 2005: 4). Resource-directing dimensions include temporality of reference and reasoning. In contrast, resource-dispersing dimensions, such as prior knowledge and planning time, do 'not direct learners to any aspects of language code' (Robinson, 2005: 7). Robinson argues that increasing the complexity of resource-directing dimensions can push learners to improve the accuracy and complexity of their language, whereas increasing the complexity of resource-dispersing dimensions diverts learners' attention. Therefore, although spontaneous interaction is a desirable communicative goal, such real-time pressure may hinder language production in the EFL classroom.

For Japanese students, there is evidence that time pressure (resource-dispersing complexity) tends to cause silence. In particular, class discussions may prove problematic due to the 'limited time allowed to interpret, think and react to the preceding comment or question' (Nakane, 2007: 171). In contrast, speeches or presentations, which may involve high resource-directing cognition, tend to facilitate CTS due to the mitigation of the resource-dispersing dimension (lack of planning time) (Humphries et al., 2015).

Psychological personality traits

Research into the psychological influences on speaking in an L2 has tended to follow the work of MacIntyre and colleagues into WTC (see for example: MacIntyre, 1994, 2007; MacIntyre & Charos, 1996; MacIntyre et al., 1998). MacIntyre and Charos (1996) used path analysis to demonstrate that the WTC of Canadian students was influenced by motivational orientations such as integrativeness to the target community as well as anxiety and perceived L2 confidence. Integrativeness refers to a learner's interest in a target L2 community; therefore, although it might be strong in a bicultural country such as Canada or the ESL environment,

EFL students may be more likely to have instrumental motivations for learning (Dörnyei, 1990). For example, in Japanese secondary schools, the washback from university entrance examinations that focus on reading comprehension and lexicogrammatical translation has often been blamed for diverting energy from communicative practice (Sakui, 2004). However, in one context where students had no entrance examination pressure, because they could study additional tertiary years on-site, teachers complained that this lack of assessment reduced motivation for *any* language study (Humphries, 2014).

The processes of globalisation and rapid urbanisation in various parts of the world mean that many learners identify English users as the more educated or cosmopolitan members of their societies, making it difficult to maintain the integrative/instrumental motivation distinctions (Lamb, 2012). In Indonesia, 'many learners see proficiency in English as broadening their horizons, bringing a range of social, economic, and cultural options within reach' (Lamb, 2012: 1000). In the Japanese context, Yashima proposed the construct of international posture. She claimed that English symbolises 'the world around Japan, something that connects them to foreign countries and foreigners' (Yashima, 2002: 57). In other words, international posture reflects an openness to other non-specific cultures. In her study, she found a significant correlation between international posture and WTC and L2 learning motivation, but L2 communication confidence had the strongest correlation with WTC and L2 learning motivation. There was no direct path between motivation and WTC (Yashima, 2002).

Perceived proficiency may be more influential than actual proficiency for predicting performance. Yashima (2002) found no significant relationship between L2 proficiency and L2 confidence, which was supported by later qualitative studies (see, for example, Nakane, 2007; Yashima *et al.*, 2018). Interestingly, rather than higher proficiency correlating with greater confidence, it has been shown to lead to higher levels of anxiety (Kitano, 2001). Kitano (2001: 558) explains that advanced classes tend to have 'more authentic and sophisticated communication'; therefore, advanced/experienced learners 'may have more chances of noticing their own errors in speaking'. Underestimating self-competence 'may lead to a self-fulfilling prophecy; with less effort and self-confidence, [learners] will not make good progress' (Liu & Jackson, 2008: 82). It has been found that anxious students tend to underestimate their ability, whereas relaxed students overestimate what they can do (MacIntyre *et al.*, 1997).

Research into language learning anxiety has shown that it is situation specific; in other words, this is a trait that recurs in language learning classrooms for people who may not be anxious in their everyday lives (Horwitz, 2017). Language learning anxiety can have academic effects (for example, lower grades), cognitive effects (for example, it can hinder speakers from trying to retrieve information from their short-term memory) and social effects (anxious learners do not communicate as often as relaxed learners) (MacIntyre, 2017).

Regarding the influence of language learning anxiety on unwillingness to communicate in English in the Chinese context, Liu and Jackson (2008) found a positive correlation. They claim that silence and anxiety feed off each other to make the situation worse: 'As a result of anxiety, [language learners] often choose to remain silent ... then, because of their silence ... they become (more) anxious' (Liu & Jackson, 2008: 72). For ESL students in Australia, Woodrow (2006) had slightly more nuanced results regarding the correlation between anxiety and oral performance. Although she found that anxiety influenced oral communication, the negative correlation was not strong. From her quantitative and qualitative data, activities at the front of the class, such as presentations and role-play performances, developed the highest levels of anxiety; however, it is interesting to note that giving an oral presentation 'was the only anxiety variable that was not significantly correlated with oral performance' (Woodrow, 2006: 322). Other anxiety variables such as discussions, role-play and answering the teacher had significant negative correlations with oral performance. Woodrow also noted that students from China, Japan and South Korea exhibited higher levels of anxiety than European and Vietnamese students. Other studies have also noted reticence among students from Confucian heritage cultures (CHC) (for example, Wen & Clément, 2003); therefore, the sociocultural influence on silence is important.

Sociocultural factors

Sociocultural factors can be viewed from three interrelated perspectives: the underlying values of the society (such as the Confucian heritage), the education system and the types of interaction in classrooms.

Underlying values

Wen and Clément (2003) argue that models for WTC (such as MacIntyre *et al.*, 1998) are based on research conducted principally in Western cultures. They suggest that Confucian values 'with an emphasis on the collective' form barriers to communication in the L2 for Chinese speakers (Wen & Clément, 2003: 24). These barriers include (1) 'face' protection, (2) the insider effect, (3) a submissive way of learning and (4) the rules that should be followed. These cultural values can also be seen among Japanese learners (Nakane, 2007).

Nakane (2007) observes that face-protecting silence can be understood by both teachers and students in Japan as an unmarked phenomenon that does not cause offence. She explains that, when students feel that they cannot answer a teacher's question correctly, they use silence as an 'off-record' face-saving strategy, which seems to be recognised and accepted by Japanese teachers, who therefore tend not to pressurise students to answer. In addition to using silence for self-protection, students may use it to avoid threatening the teacher's (or their peer's) face by disagreeing or showing a lack of understanding. To avoid raising new topics or asking questions, which may threaten the face of a speaker, Japanese listeners can use pauses to create space for clarification (Shigemitsu, 2007). Pausing functions include '1) "ruminating about what the speaker is talking about", 2) "showing that they are listening and encourage [sic] the speaker to continue" and 3) "waiting to be given more information or a turn"' (Shigemitsu, 2007: 11).

The insider effect is strongly connected to face-saving, as people avoid risking disapproval from members of the same group. In the Japanese context, the fear of negative evaluation by peers has been noted as a powerful barrier to speaking (King & Smith, 2017). Group dynamics in Japanese schools mean that bullying often takes place in the classroom rather than in the schoolyard, which makes it understandable for students to stay silent to avoid standing out (Yoneyama & Naito, 2003). Despite these negative influences, qualitative studies in Japan have often indicated that students can find it easier to speak when there is a good atmosphere with classmates (Humphries *et al*., 2015; Yashima *et al*., 2016).

Students from CHCs appear more submissive or passive because they are supposed to defer to the authority of elders (Carless, 2012), which is closely related to the fourth issue raised by Wen and Clément (2003), that there are a set of rules that should be followed. In Japan, a concern to follow one correct way reinforces *yakudoku* in schools. This perfectionist focus on the correct grammar may lead to concern about making mistakes and doubts over action (Dewaele, 2017).

Education system

In the Asia Pacific region, the examination culture is deeply rooted in the education system (Butler, 2011). School and university 'brands' (*gakkōreki*) are more important than a student's academic credentials (*gakureki*) (Amano & Poole, 2005). This creates demand from parents and students for academic high schools and private cramming schools that are ranked by their ability to get students into prestigious universities (Gorsuch, 2000). The falling birthrate means that there is an oversupply of places at all levels of the education system and universities are experimenting with new criteria for admission, such as high school recommendation letters (McCrostie, 2017). However, the prestigious universities continue to use traditional forms of assessment such as reading challenging passages, multiple choice items and translation focusing on grammar and vocabulary (Kikuchi & Browne, 2009). As a result, despite government policies and teacher attempts to encourage communication, students tend to regard grammar-translation examination practice as 'real' study (Sakui, 2007). The Ministry of Education, Culture, Sports,

Science and Technology (MEXT) has outlined a plan of university entrance examination reforms that was due to begin in 2020. The plan proposes the integration of all four language skills 'so that students can assertively make use of their English skills, think independently, and express themselves' (MEXT, 2014: 3). However, at the time of writing, MEXT had given few details on how these aims would be achieved.

In combination with the perceived need to prepare students linguistically for university entrance examinations, other factors combine against speaking English in class. Government-authorised textbooks claim to contain communicative values, but they consist mostly of reading passages and gap-filling activities (Humphries, 2013). A recent survey of nearly 4000 secondary school JTEs across Japan by Negishi et al. (2016) indicated desire from teachers to encourage students to express their thoughts and use all four skills in an integrated manner. However, the study also revealed that the teachers felt that they had not taught in this way. The main difficulties faced by JTEs included: (1) student issues (poor study habits and low motivation), (2) a lack of preparation time due to too many extracurricular responsibilities, (3) difficulty trying to encourage communicative ability while preparing students for entrance examinations and (4) inability to find effective teaching methods.

Teacher training is often insufficient and too theoretical, and fails to address local problems (Kizuka, 2006; Nagasawa, 2004). As a result, there can be a fear of losing face and losing control of the classroom (Sakui, 2007), which leads teachers to fall back on their apprenticeship of observation from their own school days (Lortie, 1975). In other words, they teach in the same way as their high school teachers – they use *yakudoku* – which directly influences classroom interaction.

Classroom interaction

In many parts of the world, language classrooms tend to follow teacher-centred transmission-based practices (Littlewood, 2007; Wedell, 2003). Consequently, interactions tend to follow a teacher-led initiation–response–feedback (or follow-up) (IRF) pattern (Sinclair & Coulthard, 1975). This IRF pattern has received criticism because students cannot initiate communication on areas of interest. Instead, they are responding to the lexicogrammatical items selected by the teacher and teacher talk usually dominates the class time (Nunan, 1987; Thornbury, 1996). Van Lier (1996: 151) notes that student reluctance increases due to the demand to display knowledge and the judgement on competence, which can 'turn every student response into an examination'. The third IRF turn also closes the exchange, preventing any further exploration of student contributions (Van Lier, 1996; Wong & Waring, 2009). This imbalance of power in classroom interactions can involve intolerance of silence, uneven distribution of turns, incomprehensible input and short wait times, which can contribute to the students' reluctance to participate orally (Tsui,

1996). In the Japanese high school context, Nakane (2007) observed that self-selected turns by students were rare and there were no instances of overlapping talk. Her results therefore support quantitative observational data from King (2013) taken from university classes in Japan.

The Study

We explore silence from three perspectives:

(1) What types of activities have students experienced in class?
(2) What activities increased and decreased students' CTS?
(3) What underlying factors strongly influenced students' CTS?

Participants

Students from five high schools (three public high schools, one private high school and one engineering school from the western Kansai region and central Japan) participated in the study. The high schools were selected as a convenience sample through English teachers known to the first author. We received 260 complete responses from the students (83 from grade 10, 61 from grade 11 and 116 from grade 12).

Instrument and data collection

The main instrument for data collection was a questionnaire. English teachers from the participating schools received copies of an access sheet to distribute to their students. The access sheet described the study (in Japanese) and contained a web-link and quick-response (QR) code for students to access anonymously and voluntarily in their free time. The questionnaire contained a section for classifying their school, grade and other general details plus two main sections that addressed the research questions (please contact the first author for the Japanese original or the English translation of the survey). All instructions and items were written in Japanese. This questionnaire was piloted with high school students known to the researchers before dissemination to the schools.

There were 28 items with six-point Likert scale responses that measured attitudes to seven underlying factors (latent variables) that may cause silence: motivation, anxiety, confidence, school context, experience of/with English outside class, classroom support, and use of English by others. The motivation questions were based on Lamb (2012) and comprised two items relating to instrumentality and two relating to international posture (Yashima et al., 2004). There were four situation-specific anxiety questions, based on Horwitz et al. (1986), relating to fears that students may have about making mistakes in front of their peers (King & Smith, 2017). The four confidence items were based on the linguistic self-confidence scale developed by Papi and Abdollahzadeh (2012). The four items for the school context factor explored whether language classes were conducted primarily in Japanese or English, and whether the main purpose was to improve communicative ability or entrance examination performance. Experience of using English outside the classroom measured time spent in a foreign country and the frequency with which the respondent spoke to foreigners, and read and watched movies for pleasure in English. The last two latent variables had items based on categories that arose in a qualitative pilot study, where respondents had referred to the use of English and level of support by/from classmates and the teacher (Humphries *et al.*, 2015).

Secondly, students were asked about seven speaking activities that have different levels of cognitive difficulty and spontaneity of response: (1) answering a simple English question from the teacher (such as a 'how are you?' greeting), (2) repeating after the teacher or compact disk (CD) in English, (3) reading aloud from the textbook, (4) giving a speech (prepared in advance), (5) performing a gap-filling skit with a classmate, (6) discussing a topic given in advance in a group and (7) discussing a topic given in advance in a pair. For each activity, respondents were asked if they had experienced it in class, followed by their perceived CTS for that activity (using a six-point Likert scale).

Data analysis

We analysed the data from three perspectives: (1) types of activities experienced, (2) perceived CTS in different activities and (3) factors underlying CTS. For the 'yes'/'no' results in relation to which types of speaking activities had been experienced, we examined statistical significance using a binomial test. For analysing the perceived CTS for each speaking activity, we converted the six-point scores (from the Likert scale) into two-point scores (high or low) and explored the significance of the results using the chi-square test of independence. Regarding the impact of the factors underlying students' perceived CTS (or, conversely, silence), we conducted a structural equation model (SEM) using AMOS 24 software. We tested the pathways of the seven latent variables that may influence CTS in relation to each other and in relation to the CTS latent variable. As we had no missing data, we could use suggestions from the bootstrapping function in AMOS to delete variables and change pathways until our model had a good fit.

Results

Types of activities experienced

Binomial tests indicated that the proportions of respondents who had experienced the most types of activities were greater than the random

Table 7.1 Descriptive statistics of speaking activities in class and results of binomial tests

Speaking activities in class	Done	Not done	p (2-tailed)
Teacher asks a simple English question	218 (83.8%)	42 (16.2%)	< 0.001
Repeat after the teacher or CD in English	215 (82.7%)	45 (17.3%)	< 0.001
Reading aloud from the textbook	242 (93.1%)	18 (6.9%)	< 0.001
Speech (prepared in advance)	201 (77.3%)	59 (22.7%)	< 0.001
A gap-filling skit with classmate	207 (79.6%)	53 (20.4%)	< 0.001
Group discussion (topic given in advance)	135 (51.9%)	125 (48.1%)	= 0.577
Pair-work discussion (topic given in advance)	152 (58.5%)	108 (41.5%)	= 0.008

Note. The test proportion of responses in each speaking activity is 0.50.

null hypothesis of 50%, with p values less than 0.05. Students had experienced most speaking activities in class, apart from group discussions (Table 7.1).

Perceived CTS in different activities

Regarding students' perceived CTS in these activities, we used the chi-square test of independence to identify significant relationships between CTS and each speaking activity. A p value of less than 0.05 indicates a significant relationship. The chi-square results show that students significantly favoured activities with a lower cognitive load: answering a simple question, repeating after the CD or teacher, reading aloud from the textbook and performing a gap-filling skit with a classmate. It is also a significant result that students had low CTS for group discussion. There were no significant differences in CTS for giving speeches and participating in pair-work discussions (p values greater than 0.05) (Table 7.2).

Table 7.2 Descriptive statistics of students' perceived CTS for speaking activities in class and results of chi-square tests of independence

Speaking activities in class	Low CTS	High CTS	Chi-square	d.f.	p value
Teacher asks a simple English question	72	188	51.754	1	< 0.001
Repeat after the teacher or CD in English	70	190	55.385	1	< 0.001
Reading aloud from the textbook	84	176	32.554	1	< 0.001
Speech (prepared in advance)	138	122	0.985	1	= 0.321
A gap-filling skit with classmate	99	161	14.785	1	< 0.001
Group discussion (topic given in advance)	150	110	6.154	1	= 0.013
Pair-work discussion (topic given in advance)	127	133	0.138	1	= 0.710

Factors underlying CTS

To examine the interrelatedness between students' affective factors, classroom context, experience outside class and CTS, we constructed SEM Model 1 with seven latent variables: motivation, anxiety, confidence, classroom support, use of English by others, experience outside class and CTS (see Table 7.3 for the reliability of internal consistency for each construct). We excluded school context because of its unreliable internal consistency (Cronbach's alpha: –0.503). We hypothesised that the constructs of the affective factors (motivation, anxiety and confidence) and those of classroom context (use of English and classroom support) were correlated with each other in each domain (see Figure 7.1).

Table 7.3 The reliability of internal consistency (Cronbach's alpha) for the latent variables in Models 1 and 2

Model	MOT	ANX	CON	UEO	CS	EOC	CTS	Total scale
Model 1	0.749 (4)	0.701 (4)	0.849 (4)	0.825 (4)	0.717 (4)	0.711 (4)	0.851 (7)	0.905 (31)
Model 2			0.849 (4)	0.825 (4)	0.717 (4)	0.711 (4)	0.851 (7)	0.920 (23)

Note. The numbers in parentheses represent quantity of questionnaire items.
MOT: Motivation; ANX: Anxiety; CON: Confidence; UEO: Use of English by others; CS: Classroom support; EOC: Experience outside class; CTS: Capacity to speak.

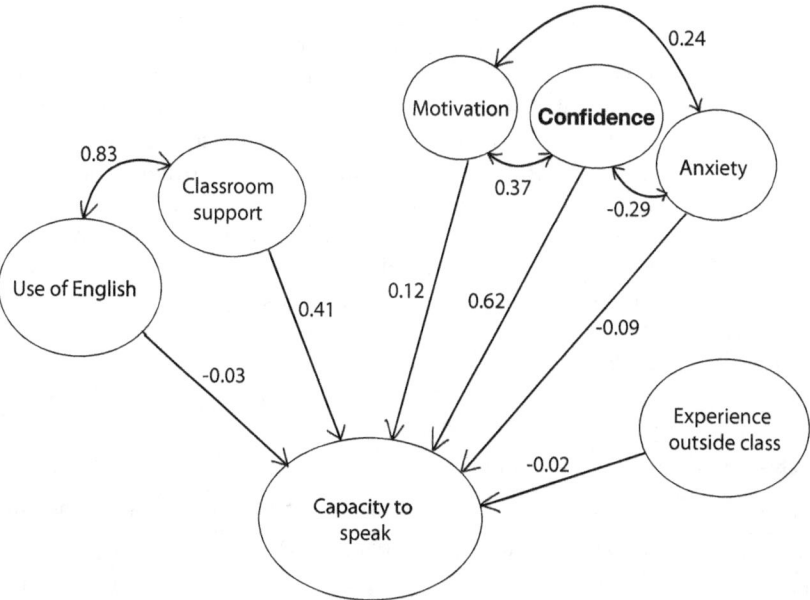

Figure 7.1 Model 1: Standardised estimates of factors influencing capacity to speak (CTS)

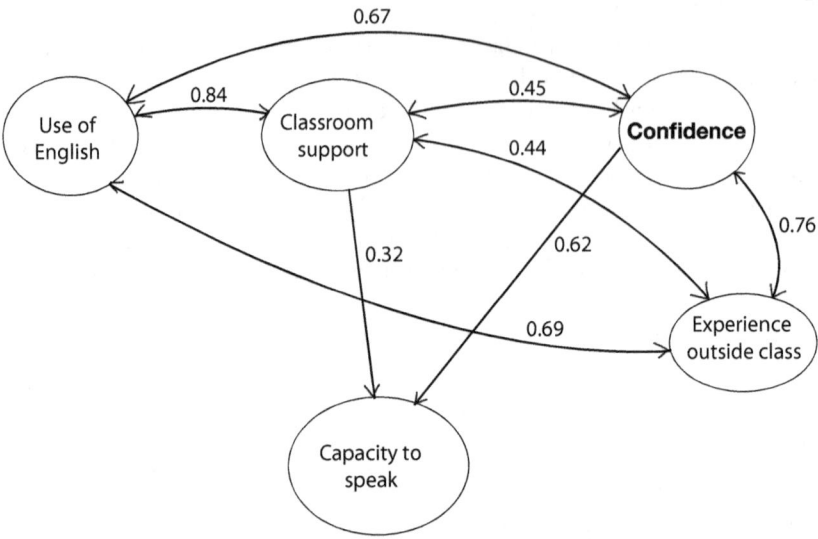

Figure 7.2 Model 2: Standardised model of underlying factors that fits the data

Unfortunately, Model 1 did not fit; therefore, we used the bootstrapping function in AMOS to find the best pathways, which resulted in Model 2 (Figure 7.2). After removing the motivation and anxiety variables, the root mean square error of approximation (RMSEA) value was 0.069, which indicates a good model fit (MacCallum et al., 1996; Steiger, 2007) (see Table 7.4 for more detail). All four remaining variables (i.e. use of English, classroom support, confidence and experience outside class) have significant correlations with each other. Confidence and, to a slightly lesser extent, classroom support were the two latent variables that had significant direct correlations with students' perceived CTS in English. 'Experience outside class' (0.76) had the strongest correlation with confidence, followed by 'use of English' (0.67) and 'classroom support' (0.45).

Table 7.4 Goodness-of-fit indices

Model	X^2	d.f.	p	X^2/d.f.	GFI	AGFI	CFI	IFI	RMSEA
Model 1	1320.7	242	<0.001	5.46	0.742	0.699	0.759	0.761	0.090
Model 2	496.2	222	<.001	2.24	0.856	0.821	0.900	0.901	0.069

Note. X^2/d.f.: relative chi-square; GFI: goodness of fit index; AGFI: adjusted GFI; CFI: comparative fit index; IFI: increment fit index; RMSEA: root mean square error of approximation.

Discussion

Teachers tended to use activities that corresponded with higher CTS for the students (the only exception is the high frequency of speeches, which students indicated as lower CTS). These high-CTS activities (gap-filling skits, reading aloud from the textbook, repeating after the teacher/CD and replying to a simple question) are all what Robinson (2005) would class as low complexity in the resource-directing dimension. In other words, these are activities that are unlikely to push learners to improve the accuracy or complexity of their grammar. Practising these activities could help students to speak correctly with limited language, but it will not improve their fluency in spontaneous conversations. Practising discussions ought to help students prepare communicatively, but they indicated a low CTS, which means that such activities are likely to cause silence. Therefore, when teaching English as a compulsory subject at a secondary school, where the goal would be to pass written entrance examinations, it is understandable that teachers would use the low-risk, low-complexity activities. We would recommend caution and patience from teachers who aim to increase the complexity of activities in an EFL context. Harumi (2011), citing the work of Gray and Leather (1999), recommends a balanced step-by-step approach to build the confidence of learners.

Regarding the underlying factors influencing CTS, it is interesting that motivation and anxiety, which are two of the most researched affective factors in SLA, do not correlate with CTS. Despite studies indicating that young Japanese people recognise the importance of the English language for their future (Yashima, 2002), this motivation does not seem to impact on their present classroom reality for breaking silence. Instead, these motivations are likely to translate into more effort in their written tests, as this will help to shape their more immediate futures.

We are more surprised that anxiety did not correlate with CTS, but our results are similar to Woodrow's (2006), who reported a weak negative correlation between anxiety and oral performance. In her study, taking part in group discussions was the least anxiety-inducing speaking activity, but in our study, respondents rated discussions as low CTS. It would appear, therefore (at least in the case of discussions), that the intrinsic complexity of the activity is more influential than anxiety. Discussions require more effort from students on Robinson's resource-directing dimension (reasoning), and the resource-dispersing dimension (lack of planning time) has a strong influence. It is difficult for students to think quickly and respond to others.

In contrast, the third psychological variable, confidence, has the strongest correlation with CTS. This finding mirrors WTC studies such as Yashima (2002) and MacIntyre and Charos (1996). Teachers' efforts to nurture confidence can give students a sense of progress in speaking

English. Experience outside class had the strongest correlation with confidence; therefore, it is worth encouraging learners to experience English outside the classroom, for example through study-abroad programmes (Isabelli-Garcia et al., 2018) and making use of technology to watch movies and read articles (Jones, 2018).

Regarding sociocultural variables, we intended to measure school context and classroom support. Unfortunately, school context proved to be an unreliable construct and was omitted from the final model. The school context construct was measured by contrasting items (e.g. classes conducted in English versus classes in Japanese); however, it is possible that some students experienced different types of class, which might have led to similar (rather than opposite) scores for each item.

In contrast, classroom support has a strong correlation with CTS. This finding mirrors other studies indicating that students care about how they are perceived by others (Humphries et al., 2015; King & Smith, 2017). This variable correlates with confidence and experience outside class, but it has the strongest correlation with use of English. Therefore, developing a positive English-speaking culture in the classroom looks important for breaking silence. Although it might appear undemocratic, it can also be a good idea to force all the students to speak, because it removes the pressure to be silent and develops equality (Shea, 2017).

It is also important to develop a good atmosphere in the class and a good rapport between the teacher and students. Edge and Garton (2009) recommend using humanistic activities that call on students to share personal information, but they warn that teachers should be sensitive to students' feelings. They also recommend thoughtful use of the teaching environment – particularly the use of space – to encourage students to move around and sit in groups. In an intervention in the Greek EFL context, Tsiplakides and Keramida (2009) introduced a collaborative atmosphere where students worked in small groups to complete projects, which replaces the competitive error-correction tendency found in many EFL classes. They reported improvements in students' willingness to participate in speaking activities. In the Japanese context, Asakawa et al. (2016) outline the need for four cooperative learning principles (positive interdependence, equal opportunity to participate, individual accountability and maximum peer interactions) supported by a list of useful expressions to help students maintain conversations. King, Yashima, Humphries, Aubrey and Ikeda, in Chapter 4 of the present volume, describe how interventions such as out-of-class social events can help students to speak. Teacher-researchers can develop a positive rapport with students through classroom-based action research (Burns, 2010). In an interesting Japan-based study, Murphey et al. (2014) surveyed students about their ideal classmates, developed 16 descriptors and then returned these categories to students for feedback. The authors suggest that this approach 'enabled students to imagine further how they could help their classmates' learning' (Murphey *et al.*, 2014: 242). Their study could be adapted into a group-work exercise, where students reflect and agree on important principles to support each other.

Although this study captures the attitudes of a range of Japanese high school students, there are some limitations. In particular, this is a snapshot of students' feelings at one point in time. Qualitative studies that triangulate the findings by using observations and student interviews over time can develop deeper understanding of the situations that cause silence. In particular, stimulated recall, where students watch and comment on the recording of a silent episode after the class, could provide rich insightful data. Due to changing speaking dynamics in relation to context and learner development, more longitudinal studies are needed, such as that presented by King *et al.* in Chapter 4, where silence is studied for changes after interventions. We would warn against generalising our study to other contexts; for example, English majors and Asian countries with closer ties to English are likely to yield different results.

Conclusion

Silence in Japanese classrooms is a widely reported phenomenon that the government has tried to address through various policy initiatives for the last 30 years. The need to solve this problem increased with Tokyo's hosting of the Olympics in 2020. To date, most studies have focused on university students and the opinions of JTEs; therefore, this study fills a gap by collecting data from high school students. Results indicate that student confidence followed by classroom support are the most important underlying factors causing classroom CTS, whereas, anxiety and motivation do not seem to have a significant influence. In contrast to an abstract notion of motivation, conceptualised as instrumental orientation and international posture, classroom realities have a stronger influence in keeping learners silent.

One direct classroom reality stems from the actual activities employed. In providing classroom support, teachers can consider aspects such as the level of cognitive load and the amount of planning time provided when selecting activities, so that students' confidence in speaking can be encouraged. Finally, it would be interesting if this study were replicated for English majors in Japan and English students in other Asian contexts, particularly where communicative activities such as discussions are used.

Self-reflection/Discussion Questions

(1) In our study, the questionnaire topics were derived naturally from our reading and previous studies; however, the number of question items and number of Likert responses proved to be problematic. What factors need to be considered when designing the number of questions

and Likert responses? You might consider your participants' backgrounds and the depth you need for your study. You could read Lee *et al.* (2002) for background on Likert scales and the different cultural responses.)
(2) The results from this study indicated a higher CTS for 'mechanical' activities that were unlikely to push learners to improve the accuracy or complexity of their language. In contrast, activities that ought to improve students' communicative skills had a lower CTS, which indicated a higher likelihood of silence. In your classroom, which of these two types of activities would you prioritise? What strategies could you use to reduce silence in the second type of activities?
(3) We were surprised that motivation and anxiety did not correlate with CTS in this study. We estimated that other influences took precedence, such as task complexity and the immediate need to prepare for written examinations. Do you agree or can you suggest other factors? Think about one or two of your students who seem extremely demotivated or highly anxious. Try to find time to talk with them and find ways to boost their motivation or reduce their anxiety. Keep a research journal to record any changes you notice in their CTS after the intervention.
(4) The strongest factors influencing CTS in this study were confidence and classroom support. How could you plan a classroom intervention study designed to develop one of these two factors in a class where you want to reduce silence?

Recommended Reading

Humphries, S., Burns, A. and Tanaka, T. (2015) 'My head became blank and I couldn't speak': Classroom factors that influence English speaking. *Asian Journal of Applied Linguistics* 2 (3), 164–175.

This earlier qualitative study asked students to write the causes that facilitated and hindered their CTS. The themes that developed formed the foundation for the questions in the current study.

Lee, J.W., Jones, P.S., Mineyama, Y. and Zhang, X.E. (2002) Cultural differences in responses to a Likert scale. *Research in Nursing and Health* 25, 295–306.

This study compared the responses of Chinese, Japanese and Americans to questionnaires containing either four, five or seven responses. It is worthwhile reading for researchers to develop their cultural awareness for the design of studies using Likert scale responses.

Shea, D.P. (2017) Compelled to speak: Addressing student reticence in a university EFL classroom. *Asian Journal of Applied Linguistics* 4 (2), 173–184.

After outlining the reasons for silence in Japan, Shea proposes an innovative and practical classroom approach that encourages students to volunteer to speak.

Wen, W.P. and Clément, R. (2003) A Chinese conceptualisation of willingness to communicate in ESL. *Language, Culture and Curriculum* 16 (1), 18–38.

This paper challenges the large body of research from a Western perspective into students' willingness to communicate. Although the authors focus on the Chinese context, their insights can be applied to other teacher-led classroom cultures.

Acknowledgement

This work was supported financially by JSPS KAKENHI grant number 17K02995 and the Kansai University Fund for Domestic and Overseas Research, 2018–2019.

References

Amano, I. and Poole, G.S. (2005) The Japanese university in crisis. *Higher Education* 50, 686–711.
Asakawa, M., Kanamaru, A., Plaza, T. and Shiramizu, C. (2016) Useful expressions for implementing cooperative learning in English. *TESL-EJ* 19 (4), 1–16.
Basso, K. (1970) 'To give up on words': Silence in Western Apache culture. *Southwestern Journal of Anthropology* 26, 213–230.
Burns, A. (2010) *Doing Action Research in English Language Teaching: A Guide for Practitioners*. New York: Routledge.
Butler, Y.G. (2011) The implementation of communicative and task-based language teaching in the Asia-Pacific region. *Annual Review of Applied Linguistics* 31, 36–57.
Carless, D.R. (2012) Task-based language teaching in Confucian-heritage settings: Prospects and challenges. Paper presented at the TBLT in Asia Conference, Osaka.
Dewaele, J.-M. (2017) Are perfectionists more anxious foreign language learners and users? In C. Gkonou, M. Daubney and J.-M. Dewaele (eds) *New Insights into Language Anxiety: Theory, Research and Educational Implications* [Kindle version]. Bristol: Multilingual Matters.
Dörnyei, Z. (1990) Conceptualizing motivation in foreign language learning. *Language Learning* 40 (1), 45–78.
Edge, J. and Garton, S. (2009) *From Experience to Knowledge in ELT*. Oxford: Oxford University Press.
Goh, C.C.M. and Burns, A. (2012) *Teaching Speaking: A Holistic Approach*. Cambridge: Cambridge University Press.
Gorsuch, G. (2000) EFL educational policies and educational cultures: Influences on teachers' approval of communicative activities. *TESOL Quarterly* 34 (4), 675–710.
Gray, P. and Leather, S. (1999) *Safety and Challenge for Japanese Learners of English: A Resource Book for Teachers*. Guildford: ETP/DELTA Publishing.
Harumi, S. (2011) Classroom silence: Voices from Japanese EFL learners. *ELT Journal* 65 (3), 260–269.

Horwitz, E.K. (2017) On the misreading of Horwitz, Horwitz and Cope (1986) and the need to balance anxiety research and the experiences of anxious language learners. In C. Gkonou, M. Daubney and J.-M. Dewaele (eds) *New Insights into Language Anxiety: Theory, Research and Educational Implications* [Kindle version]. Bristol: Multilingual Matters.

Horwitz, E.K., Horwitz, M.B. and Cope, J. (1986) Foreign language classroom anxiety. *Modern Language Journal* 70 (2), 125–132.

Humphries, S. (2013) Western-published versus MEXT-mandated: A comparative textbook analysis. *Doshisha Studies in English* 90, 217–238.

Humphries, S. (2014) Factors influencing Japanese teachers' adoption of communication-oriented textbooks. In S. Garton and K. Graves (eds) *International Perspectives on Materials in ELT* (pp. 253–269). New York: Palgrave Macmillan.

Humphries, S. and Stroupe, R. (2014) Codeswitching in two Japanese contexts. In R. Barnard and J. McClellan (eds) *Codeswitching in University English-Medium Classes: Asian Perspectives* (pp. 65–91). Bristol: Multilingual Matters.

Humphries, S., Burns, A. and Tanaka, T. (2015) 'My head became blank and I couldn't speak': Classroom factors that influence English speaking. *Asian Journal of Applied Linguistics* 2 (3), 164–175.

Isabelli-Garcia, C., Bown, J., Plews, J.L. and Dewey, D.P. (2018) Language learning and study abroad. *Language Teaching* 51 (4), 439–484.

Jones, R.H. (2018) Learning through technology. In A. Burns and J.C. Richards (eds) *The Cambridge Guide to Learning English as a Second Language* (pp. 319–326). Cambridge: Cambridge University Press.

Kikuchi, K. and Browne, C. (2009) English educational policy for high schools in Japan: Ideals vs. reality. *RELC Journal* 40 (2), 172–191.

King, J. (2013) Silence in the second language classrooms of Japanese universities. *Applied Linguistics* 34 (3), 325–434.

King, J. and Smith, L. (2017) Social anxiety and silence in Japan's tertiary foreign language classrooms. In C. Gkonou, M. Daubney and J.-M. Dewaele (eds) *New Insights into Language Anxiety: Theory, Research and Educational Implications* [Kindle version]. Bristol: Multilingual Matters.

Kitano, K. (2001) Anxiety in the college Japanese language classroom. *Modern Language Journal* 85 (4), 549–566.

Kizuka, M. (2006) Professionalism in English language education in Japan. *ELTED* 9 (1), 55–62.

Lamb, M. (2012) A self system perspective on young adolescents' motivation to learn English in urban and rural settings. *Language Learning* 62 (4), 997–1023.

Lee, J.W., Jones, P.S., Mineyama, Y. and Zhang, X.E. (2002) Cultural differences in responses to a Likert scale. *Research in Nursing and Health* 25, 295–306.

Littlewood, W. (2007) Communicative and task-based language teaching in East Asian classrooms. *Language Teaching* 40 (3), 243–249.

Liu, M. and Jackson, J. (2008) An exploration of Chinese EFL learners' unwillingness to communicate and foreign language anxiety. *Modern Language Journal* 92 (1), 71–86.

Lortie, D. (1975) *Schoolteacher: A Sociological Study*. London: University of Chicago Press.

MacCallum, R.C., Browne, M.W. and Sugawara, H.M. (1996) Power analysis and determination of sample size for covariance structure modeling. *Psychological Methods* 1 (2), 130–149.

MacIntyre, P.D. (1994) Variables underlying willingness to communicate: A causal analysis. *Communication Research Reports* 11 (2), 135–142.

MacIntyre, P.D. (2007) Willingness to communicate in the second language: Understanding the decision to speak as a volitional process. *Modern Language Journal* 91 (4), 564–576.

MacIntyre, P.D. (2017) An overview of language anxiety research and trends in its development. In C. Gkonou, M. Daubney and J.-M. Dewaele (eds) *New Insights into Language Anxiety: Theory, Research and Educational Implications* [Kindle version]. Bristol: Multilingual Matters.

MacIntyre, P.D. and Charos, C. (1996) Personality, attitudes, and affect as predictors of second language communication. *Journal of Language and Social Psychology* 15 (1), 3–26.

MacIntyre, P.D., Noels, K. and Clément, R. (1997) Biases in self-ratings of second language proficiency: The role of language anxiety. *Language Learning* 47 (2), 265–287.

MacIntyre, P.D., Clément, R., Dörnyei, Z. and Noels, K. (1998) Conceptualizing willingness to communicate in a L2: A situational model of L2 confidence and affiliation. *Modern Language Journal* 82 (4), 545–562.

McCrostie, J. (2017) Spoken English tests among entrance exam reforms Japan's students will face in 2020. *Japan Times*, 5 July. At https://www.japantimes.co.jp/community/2017/07/05/issues/spoken-english-tests-among-entrance-exam-reforms-japans-students-will-face-2020/#.XQ3s-y2ZN0s (accessed 22 June 2019).

MEXT (2014) *On Integrated Reforms in High School and University Education and University Entrance Examination*. At http://www.mext.go.jp/en/news/topics/detail/1372628.htm (accessed 22 June 2019).

Murphey, T., Falout, J., Fukuda, T. and Fukada, Y. (2014) Socio-dynamic motivating through idealizing classmates. *System* 45, 242–253.

Nagasawa, K. (2004) Teacher training and development. In V. Makarova and T.S. Rogers (eds) *English Language Teaching: The Case of Japan* (pp. 280–295). Munich: Lincom.

Nakane, I. (2007) *Silence in Intercultural Communication: Perceptions and Performance*. Amsterdam: John Benjamins.

Negishi, M., Sakai, H., Shigematsu, K., Takagi, A. and Kudo, Y. (2016) *Chuukou no Eigo Shidou ni Kansuru Jittai Chousa 2015 [Survey of Actual English Teaching Situation in Secondary Schools 2015]*. Tokyo: Benesse Educational Research and Development Institute.

Nunan, D. (1987) Communicative language teaching: Making it work. *ELT Journal* 41 (2), 136–145.

Papi, M. and Abdollahzadeh, E. (2012) Teacher motivational practice, student motivation, and possible L2 selves: An examination in the Iranian EFL context. *Language Learning* 62 (2), 571–594.

Robinson, P. (2005) Cognitive complexity and task sequencing: Studies in a componential framework for second language task design. *International Review of Applied Linguistics in Language Teaching* 43 (1), 1–33.

Sakui, K. (2004) Wearing two pairs of shoes: Language teaching in Japan. *ELT Journal* 58 (2), 155–163.

Sakui, K. (2007) Classroom management in Japanese EFL classrooms. *JALT Journal* 29 (1), 41–58.

Shea, D.P. (2017) Compelled to speak: Addressing student reticence in a university EFL classroom. *Asian Journal of Applied Linguistics* 4 (2), 173–184.

Shigemitsu, Y. (2007) A pause in conversation for Japanese native speakers: A case study of successful and unsuccessful conversation in terms of pause through intercultural communication. *Academic Report, Tokyo Polytechnic University* 30 (2), 11–18.

Sinclair, J.M. and Coulthard, M. (1975) *Towards an Analysis of Discourse: The English Used by Teachers and Pupils*. London: Oxford University Press.

Steiger, J.H. (2007) Understanding the limitations of global fit assessment in structural equation modeling. *Personality and Individual Differences* 42 (5), 893–898.

Swain, M. (1995) Three functions of output in second language learning. In G. Cook and B. Seidlhofer (eds) *Principal and Practice in Applied Linguistics* (pp. 125–144). Oxford: Oxford University Press.

Tahira, M. (2012) Behind MEXT's new course of study guidelines. *The Language Teacher* 36 (3), 3–8.

Thompson, G. and Yanagita, M. (2017) Backward yakudoku: An attempt to implement CLT at a Japanese high school. *Innovation in Language Learning and Teaching* 11 (2), 177–187.

Thornbury, S. (1996) Teachers research teacher talk. *ELT Journal* 50 (4), 279–289.

Tsiplakides, I. and Keramida, A. (2009) Helping students overcome foreign language speaking anxiety in the English classroom: Theoretical issues and practical recommendations. *International Education Studies* 2 (4), 39–44.

Tsui, A.B.M. (1996) Reticence and anxiety in second language learning. In K. Bailey and D. Nunan (eds) *Voices from the Language Classroom* (pp. 145–167). Cambridge: Cambridge University Press.

Underwood, P.R. (2017) Challenges and change: Integrating grammar teaching with communicative work in senior high school EFL classes. *SAGE Open* 7 (3), 1–15.

Van Lier, L. (1996) *Interaction in the Language Classroom: Awareness, Autonomy and Authenticity*. London: Longman.

Warden, C.A. and Lin, H.J. (2000) Existence of integrative motivation in an Asian EFL setting. *Foreign Language Annals* 33 (5), 535–545.

Wedell, M. (2003) Giving TESOL change a chance: Supporting key players in the curriculum change process. *System* 31, 439–456.

Wen, W.P. and Clément, R. (2003) A Chinese conceptualisation of willingness to communicate in ESL. *Language, Culture and Curriculum* 16 (1), 18–38.

Wong, J. and Waring, H.Z. (2009) 'Very good' as a teacher response. *ELT Journal* 63 (3), 195–203.

Woodrow, L. (2006) Anxiety and speaking English as a second language. *RELC Journal* 37 (3), 308–328.

Yashima, T. (2002) Willingness to communicate in a second language: The Japanese EFL context. *Modern Language Journal* 86 (1), 54–66.

Yashima, T., Zenuk-Nishide, L. and Shimizu, K. (2004) The influence of attitudes and affect on willingness to communicate and second language communication. *Language Learning* 54 (1), 119–152.

Yashima, T., Ikeda, M. and Nakahira, S. (2016) Talk and silence in an EFL classroom: Interplay of learners and context. In J. King (ed.) *The Dynamic Interplay between Context and the Language Learner* (pp. 104–126). London: Palgrave Macmillan.

Yashima, T., MacIntyre, P.D. and Ikeda, M. (2018) Situated willingness to communicate in an L2: Interplay of individual characteristics and context. *Language Teaching Research* 22 (1), 115–137.

Yoneyama, S. and Naito, A. (2003) Problems with the paradigm: The school as a factor in understanding bullying (with special reference to Japan). *British Journal of Sociology of Education* 24 (3), 315–330.

8 Willing Silence and Silent Willingness to Communicate (WTC) in the Chinese EFL Classroom: A Dynamic Systems Perspective

Jian-E Peng

Introduction

Second language (L2) learning inevitably necessitates plenty of speaking practice, and in contexts where English is learned as a foreign language (EFL), opportunities for such practice are mostly created in the language classroom. Students' active participation in class can not only promote individual psychological wellbeing (Yoshida, 2013) but may also contribute to a pleasant classroom environment at the group level (Peng, 2014). However, learners in EFL or Asian cultural contexts have often been reported to exhibit low willingness to communicate (WTC) or even silence (Jackson, 2002; King, 2013a) in L2 classrooms, squandering their already limited opportunities for authentic L2 communication.

WTC and silence are related yet distinct concepts. L2 WTC, which is 'the final step before starting to speak in the L2' (MacIntyre et al., 2001: 370), is a non-observable psychological construct, whereas silence is a behavioural consequence that can be observed. More specifically, L2 WTC directly predicts communication using the L2 (MacIntyre et al., 1998), which is the opposite of silence. Nevertheless, these two concepts share the same features of being dynamic and responsive to contextual influences (King, 2016; MacIntyre & Legatto, 2011; Yashima et al., 2018).

Given the relatedness of L2 WTC and silence, it is worthwhile to explore students' WTC vis-à-vis silence across classroom communication situations. Researching the two concepts in an integrative instead of separate manner can explore their theoretical connections and, moreover, reveal the delicacy and complexity of students' communication psychology in the L2 classroom. This line of enquiry can benefit from a dynamic systems theory (DST) perspective (De Bot et al., 2007; Larsen-Freeman

& Cameron, 2008). The DST approach views a host of factors as interdependent and interacting systems that are complex, dynamic, self-organising and constantly evolving (Larsen-Freeman & Cameron, 2008). EFL learners' L2 WTC and silence in class can be viewed as two dynamic systems that interact to bring out specific communication behaviour in certain situations, research into which may open a window on EFL students' psychological states, which are often unnoticed within fleeting teaching moments.

Willingness to Communicate

L2 WTC research necessitates a clarification of the theoretical underpinnings of WTC. L2 WTC has been conceptualised as 'a readiness to enter into discourse at a particular time with a specific person or persons, using a L2' (MacIntyre et al., 1998: 547). This conceptualisation recognises the trait-like and situational characteristics of L2 WTC. Trait WTC is generally measured by scale items, whereas situational WTC is captured through micro-level methods such as learners' self-reports made synchronously (e.g. Pawlak et al., 2016) or retrospectively (e.g. MacIntyre & Legatto, 2011). More importantly, L2 WTC refers not only to an intention but also to a 'readiness' to take action, which is central to the analyses in the present study. Wen and Clément (2003: 25) made an important distinction between desire to communicate (DC) and WTC, and stated that DC refers to 'a deliberate choice or preference' whereas WTC means 'the readiness to act'. They pointed out that in the Chinese cultural context, although many students possess DC, their DC fails to develop into WTC due to culturally rooted factors such as deference to the teacher as the authority, and concerns about the judgement and verdicts of others or the public (see also Cortazzi & Jin, 1996; Peng, 2014).

L2 WTC has been found to be subject to the influence of many factors, which can be roughly classified into two categories: (1) individual factors, such as attitudes and motivation, language anxiety (Yashima, 2002), psychological conditions (i.e. excitement, responsibility and security) (Kang, 2005), emotions (Khajavy et al., 2017) and learner beliefs (Peng, 2014); and (2) contextual factors, such as topic, task, interlocutor and teacher (Cao & Philp, 2006) and classroom environment (Khajavy et al., 2017; Peng & Woodrow, 2010).

The past decade has witnessed a shift in focus to the dynamic changes in L2 WTC, in which WTC is viewed as complex, momentary and non-linear (MacIntyre & Legatto, 2011; Yashima et al., 2018). MacIntyre and Legatto (2011) video-taped the performances of six female adult learners in eight communication tasks, and in follow-up stimulated interviews the participants viewed the recordings and simultaneously rated their L2 WTC (on a scale from −5 to +5) on a moment-to-moment basis using specifically designed software. Their results showed great variations in learners' L2 WTC, with searching for vocabulary being one major influential factor. Adopting complex dynamic systems theory, Yashima *et al.* (2018) audio-recorded whole-class discussions in a language class and reported that students' self-initiated turns emerged in differing ways as a joint function of students' enduring characteristics and contextual influences such as group-level talk–silence patterns.

With a focus on naturally-occurring English classes (rather than laboratory settings) in Poland, Mystkowska-Wiertelak and Pawlak (2017; see also Pawlak *et al.*, 2016) used a grid for the participants to rate their L2 WTC within a range from +10 (extreme willingness) to −10 (extreme unwillingness) every five minutes in response to a computer-generated beep. Similarly, the results showed that L2 WTC was in continual flux and reactive to individual and contextual factors, such as familiarity with interlocutors, topics, the mastery of requisite lexis and planning time.

Silence in the EFL Class

Contrary to students' WTC, which is welcomed and applauded, students' silence in class generally causes concern for L2 teachers and researchers since second language acquisition (SLA) requires learners to 'talk in order to learn' (Skehan, 1989: 48). Silence is considered to be an elusive concept that cannot be consensually defined. Although one's intuition may suggest that silence is a state void of speech (Granger, 2004), researchers have argued that silence is ambiguous and loaded with multiple communicative meanings (Liu, 2002; Sobkowiak, 1997). For instance, silence is not simply an absence of sound, but can also be a communicative strategy for handling power disparities (Jaworski & Sachdev, 1998), showing respect to superiors such as the teacher (Liu, 2002), signalling learners' attentiveness (Liu, 2002) or even reconstructing one's identity in a transition from first language (L1) to L2 ego (Granger, 2004). Researchers have also noted that the interpretation and tolerance of silence is often specific to cultures. Granger (2004: 5) has pointed out that Western cultures 'favour performance over contemplation, participation over inaction', and 'speech over silence', whereas in Asian cultures, particularly those under Confucian influence, silence is acceptable, if not highly embraced. Liu (2002) articulated that Chinese students' culture-nurtured silence, which functions to show respect, politeness and modesty and to avoid face-threatening situations, may cause cross-cultural conflicts in American classrooms.

Recent research on silence in L2 classrooms has also subscribed to the DST approach. King (2013b: 339) measured macro-level silence in English classrooms among 924 students from nine Japanese universities, and found that a fifth of class time had no oral participation from all parties, which led him to conclude that student silence in the Japanese context has developed into 'a semi-permanent attractor state'. Yashima *et al.* (2016) conducted an interventional study over 12 weeks. In each lesson, the students engaged in a 20-minute discussion during which the typical initiation–response–feedback patterns (i.e. the teacher initiates, the student responds and the teacher gives feedback) (Sinclair & Coulthard, 1975) were deliberately avoided. Through analysing audio-recordings of the verbal participation of the teacher and students, they identified the salient existence of students' silence.

The literature shows that WTC and silence are two learner factors significant to L2 classroom communication, one being latent and the other being overt and readily observable. They were also found to share similar influential factors, such as linguistic competence, language anxiety, face-saving concerns or showing respect for others (Liu, 2002; MacIntyre *et al.*, 1998; Wen & Clément, 2003), which suggests that L2 learners' WTC and silence may be intricately interlinked. Recent research in these two areas from the DST perspective has provided valuable insights into the situated and dynamic nature of these two concepts. Exploring the interplay of WTC and silence as two complex dynamic systems in the L2 class can unveil a fuller picture of students' classroom communication psychology. Such a DST perspective is briefly presented in the next section.

A Dynamic Systems Theory Perspective

Dynamic systems theory views chaotic and messy real-life events as interconnected and interdependent. In a broad sense, according to Larsen-Freeman and Cameron (2008: 26), a system is 'produced by a set of components that interact in particular ways to produce some overall state or form at a particular point of time'. In a complex system, a large number of components or elements interact to form a unity (Larsen-Freeman & Cameron, 2008). Therefore, DST defies simplistic and linear explanations and recognises interrelatedness and the ever-changing nature of a complex system, which features 'a theory of process not state; becoming not being' (Larsen-Freeman, 2015: 12).

A dynamic system's attractor states, variation and non-linearity have received particular attention from SLA researchers (De Bot *et al.*, 2007; Hiver, 2015; Larsen-Freeman, 2007). Attractor states refer to the patterned outcomes towards which dynamic systems self-organise to settle down over time (Hiver, 2015). Hiver (2015) clarified that attractor states are not necessarily appealing to individuals, but rather are simply the likely outcomes that a system arrives at. This was often typologically described as a ball rolling over many basins and settling into the deepest one with the steepest sides, with the depth and steepness of a basin indicating the strength of an attractor (Larsen-Freeman & Cameron, 2008). A dynamic system also displays variation and is always in a state of flux and development; therefore, each step 'creates the conditions for the next one' (Larsen-Freeman & Cameron, 2008: 2). Moreover, a dynamic system develops in a non-linear fashion, which cannot be fully accounted for by isolating a few factors and working out their causal relationships. This non-linearity results from the complex and constant interaction between elements within a dynamic system (Larsen-Freeman & Cameron, 2008).

The present study draws on a DST perspective to explore how L2 WTC and silence interact to bring out variation, non-linearity and different attractor states of students' communication behaviour. The word 'interact' here is used to refer to the complex entangled states of WTC and silence when, for instance, students wish to communicate but are not ready to do so and thus remain silent, or when they are silent but are actually ready and eager to be nominated by the teacher. The DST perspective allows such complexities to be captured, which have seldom been explored in previous studies, as these have prioritised isolating causal reasons for students' communication behaviour.

Methods

This study explored Chinese university students' silence in the English classroom, and examined the interaction of L2 WTC and silence in classroom communication by focusing on four students' observed behaviour and their reflections in follow-up stimulated recalls. In order to capture students' fleeting silence and momentary changes in WTC, this study adapted the instruments used by King (2013a) and Mystkowska-Wiertelak and Pawlak (2017). It may be considered a partial replication of King's (2013a) study, in which Japanese students' silence was observed and interpreted as attractor states using DST. However, this study differs from King (2013a) in that its focus was not just silence but, more importantly, the interaction between L2 WTC and silence. The following questions are addressed in this study:

(1) To what extent are the participants silent in class?
(2) How do L2 WTC and silence interact with each other in naturally occurring classroom communication?

Participants

This study was conducted in a provincial university in southern China. This university emphasised the development of students' communicative competence in English, and thus student participation in class was highly promoted. College English was a mandatory course for non-English major freshmen and sophomores.

The study involved a group of 26 non-English major sophomores who had received formal English instruction for about 10 years and who could be viewed as intermediate English learners. They took a compulsory English class twice a week, each lasting 90 minutes excluding a 10-minute

Table 8.1 Demographic information of the four focal students

Name	Gender	Age	WTC	Major
Qian	Female	20	High	Interaction Design
Huan	Female	19	Medium	Business Administration
Kui	Male	19	Medium	Mathematics and Applied Mathematics
Tong	Male	20	Low	Biological Technology

break. The teacher was a native Chinese-speaking woman in her mid-twenties. She had an overseas master's degree in English language teaching and had been teaching English for three years since gaining her qualification. English was used as the only medium of instruction in her class.

Data were collected from 23 students, since two students did not consent to participate and another did not complete the WTC ratings; their data were therefore removed. Of the 23 students, 11 were male (47.8%) and 12 were female (52.2%), and they were aged between 18 and 20 years ($M = 19.26$, $SD = 0.619$). They came from several disciplines: Business Administration ($n=3$), Public Administration ($n=3$), Accounting ($n=2$), Law ($n=3$), Journalism ($n=2$), Interaction Design ($n=1$), Mathematics and Applied Mathematics ($n=3$), Computer Science and Technology ($n=4$) and Biological Technology ($n=2$).

Four students from this group were invited to be focal cases. Purposive sampling (Neuman, 2014) was employed to select those with high, medium and low levels of WTC. This was executed by administrating Peng and Woodrow's (2010) WTC scale to the group, with those who scored the highest, the medium and the lowest on the scale being approached and invited to participate. Table 8.1 shows the four students' demographic information. All names in this chapter are pseudonyms, for ethical reasons.

Instruments

Student silence was observed using King's (2013a) Classroom Oral Participation Scheme (COPS), with minor modifications made after a pilot study (described under 'Data collection', below). The modified COPS contains two sections: the first measures nine categories of the whole group's behaviour, and the second records 11 categories of the focal students' behaviour. Table 8.2 details these categories and their explanations (see also King, 2013b). The scheme was divided into 90 one-minute segments to correspond to the 90-minute lesson.

In each observed lesson, the students were invited to rate their WTC on thermometer-shaped figures adapted from Mystkowska-Wiertelak and Pawlak's (2017) WTC grid. Their WTC grid consisted of horizontal lines with a five-minute-interval timeline, on which students rated their

Table 8.2 Categories of observed behaviour in the modified Classroom Oral Participation Scheme (COPS)

Section	No.	Category	Brief explanation
The whole group's behaviour	W1	Teacher-initiated talk	Talk to the whole class initiated by the teacher
	W2	Teacher talk in response to student questions	The teacher's talk to the whole class in response to students' questions
	W3	Student self-initiated talk	Unsolicited talk by a student to which the whole class is exposed
	W4	Student talk in response to teacher prompts	A student's self-selected or teacher-nominated talk in response to the teacher's question
	W5	Student talk in a single pair/group	Talk in a single pair or group to which the whole class is exposed
	W6	Student talk in multiple pairs/groups	Talk in different pairs/groups that simultaneously perform speaking tasks
	W7	Choral activity	Talk in choral speaking activities
	W8	Off-task melee	The majority of the class not being on-task (e.g. laughter, chatting in L1)
	W9	Silence	No oral interaction, including moments of silent reading or while audio/video is played
The focal students' behaviour	F1	Self-initiated talk	See W3
	F2	Talk as a response	See W4
	F3	Talk in a pair/group	See W5 and W6
	F4	Talk in choral activities	See W7
	F5	Talk at desk	Talk at desk with audible volume in response to the teacher's prompts
	F6	Listening to the teacher	Activities of listening to the teacher
	F7	Listening to peers	Activities of listening to the peers
	F8	Listening to audio/video materials	Activities of listening to audio/video materials
	F9	Reading silently	Performing reading tasks silently
	F10	Writing	Performing writing
	F11	Off task	Not on task (e.g. sleeping, checking a mobile phone)

WTC on a scale from −10 to +10 at the prompt of a pre-recorded beep. The scale used in this study was reduced to a range of −5 to +5, because after the pilot the focal students all reported that differentiating so many options was difficult and distracting. The figures were printed on a sheet of paper and given to the students before each lesson.

Three rounds of interviews were conducted with the focal students. General questions were asked in the first interview to elicit the four students' interest in English and their perceptions of their communication tendencies. The focus of each interview was the students' reflections on their communication behaviour and their underlying reasons in conspicuous silent scenarios identified in the observation data and the recordings of classroom interactions.

Data collection

The students and their English teacher were first informed of the research purposes and the confidentiality of their identifiable information. Prior to the study, a pilot observation and an interview with each focal student were conducted at the beginning of the autumn term in the academic year 2017–18. The pilot observation showed that while most students were attentive and engaged, none of them self-initiated talk to the teacher, and student talk in response to teacher prompts was generally brief, with only a few long utterances. This may be because whole-class discussions were led by the teacher and followed typical initiation–response–feedback patterns. In addition, no long or marked student silences were observed because the teacher usually called on students shortly after she had raised a question (i.e. after 5–10 seconds). Therefore, following King (2013b), it was decided to tally instances of student talk and student silence when these two categories of behaviour occurred and lasted more than five seconds, and to code the other categories when they took up the majority of a minute-long observation segment. Although using five seconds as a threshold for tallying student talk and silence was somewhat arbitrary, it was arguably reasonable and feasible for the research purposes, given the markedness and short duration of these two categories in the current context.

Three sessions were observed and audio-recorded: at the beginning, middle and end of the term. The observations were made by tallying the occurrence of the categories of the behaviour in the scheme (Table 8.2) within each one-minute timeframe. In addition, the students rated their WTC on the thermometer-shaped figures at the prompt of a buzzer at five-minute intervals. The teacher's PowerPoint files were also obtained to facilitate interviews and data analyses.

Stimulated recall interviews were conducted in Chinese individually with the four students on the day after each observation; beforehand, conspicuous silent scenarios were identified and the four students' WTC ratings were analysed. To enhance the validity of the students' recall, three measures were taken in the interviews: (1) playing the recorded scenarios where their silent behaviour was observed; (2) referring them to their WTC ratings at moments close to the specified scenarios; and (3) showing them the teacher's PowerPoint slides.

Data analysis

The observations were analysed by adding the tallies (i.e. the total duration in minutes) for each behavioural category in the scheme for each lesson. The number of minutes for each category was then divided by the total lesson time (i.e. 270 minutes – see Table 8.3) to obtain the percentage of time for each category within the total duration of the observation.

Table 8.3 Oral participation of the whole group

Lesson observed	Teacher initiated (W1)	Student response (W4)	Students pair/group multiple (W6)	Choral activity (W7)	Silence (W9)	Total
First (beginning of term)	31	12	26	5	16	90
Second (middle of term)	42	3	20	8	17	90
Third (end of term)	29	12	34	6	9	90
Total (min.)	102	27	80	19	42	270
Mean per class	37.78%	10%	29.63%	7.04%	15.56%	100%

The interplay of the focal students' situational WTC and silence over the 90 minutes observed in the three lessons was analysed by synthesising the observation data, students' WTC ratings and interview transcriptions. More specifically, instances of marked silence were first identified, and the focal students' self-ratings of L2 WTC at or near those silent moments were examined. The students' elaborations on these moments in the interviews were then content-analysed in order to allow the interaction between silence and L2 WTC to be interpreted. Due to space constraints, this chapter reports only the analytic results of the first class session observed.

Findings and Discussion

Silence in class

The first research question concerns the extent to which the participants were silent. As observed, each lesson contained three to five occurrences of students' group discussions, each followed by a teacher-led whole-class discussion. Table 8.3 shows the observation results for the whole group's oral participation. Since no instances of four behavioural categories were observed (W2, W3, W5 and W8), only five categories are shown. On average, teacher-initiated talk took up 37.78% of the lesson time, and three types of student talk (W4, 10.00%; W6, 29.63%; and W7, 7.04%) amounted to 46.67%. The category of 'Silence' took up 15.56%. In such silent periods students mainly performed tasks such as reading and writing. Thus the majority of lesson time featured talk in one form or another, and silence was not salient.

Table 8.4 shows 10 categories of performance among the focal students. The category of student self-initiated talk (F1) is not shown since no instance of it was observed. As Table 8.4 illustrates, the majority of the focal students' time was spent listening to the teacher (41.85%) or to peers (21.20%). Their talk mostly happened in pairs/groups (14.44%), and only 0.74% of their talk was in response to the teacher in front of the

Table 8.4 Focal students' classroom performance (on average)

Lesson observed	Talk response (F2)	Talk in a pair/ group (F3)	Talk choral (F4)	Talk desk (F5)	Listening to teacher (F6)	Listening to peers (F7)	Listening to audio (F8)	Reading silent (F9)	Writing (F10)	Off task (F11)	Total
First (beginning of term)	1	13.75	5	1.5	34.5	19	0	10	0	5.25	90
Second (middle of term)	0.25	4.75	7	0.25	46.5	17	7.75	0	3	3.5	90
Third (end of term)	0.75	20.5	6	0	32	21.25	2	6.25	1.25	0	90
Total (min.)	2	39	18	1.75	113	57.25	9.75	16.25	4.25	8.75	270
Mean per class	0.74%	14.44%	6.67%	0.65%	41.85%	21.20%	3.61%	6.02%	1.57%	3.24%	100%

class. The absence of student-initiated talk in this study (F1) suggests that the students all followed the teacher's lead, talking only in response to the teacher's prompts.

Dynamic interaction between WTC and silence

This section presents the analyses of the interaction of L2 WTC and silence by focusing on five silent scenarios observed in the first lesson. The goal of this lesson was to practise interpreting intercultural encounters and to analyse individualist and collectivist cultures. The first 45-minute period started with a 10-minute warm-up activity in which students walked around and talked with peers about possible real-life dilemmas (e.g. which university to choose after their college entrance examinations). The teacher then led several rounds of whole-class discussion, each preceded by a group discussion lasting several minutes. During the second 45-minute period, the students first read two passages in the textbook and then discussed two concepts: individualism and collectivism. The latter half of this period involved students' quiet reading and writing activities, followed by the teacher wrapping up the lesson and announcing assignments.

Figure 8.1 shows the WTC fluctuations at the group and individual levels in this lesson. The WTC scores for the group were the average of the 23 students' self-ratings of WTC. The individuals' L2 WTC scores were based on the focal students' self-ratings. Figure 8.1 indicates that the four students and the whole group experienced constant fluctuations

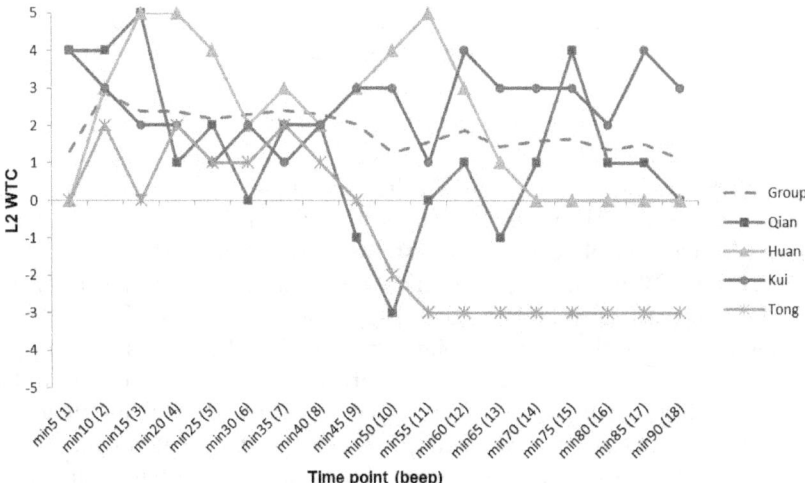

Figure 8.1 WTC fluctuations at group and individual levels in a 90-minute lesson

in L2 WTC. Huan's and Kui's WTC remained at zero or higher throughout the lesson, whereas Qian and Tong displayed more radical changes in WTC, with their highest level reaching +5 and the lowest −3. These results corroborated findings in other studies and confirmed the situated nature of WTC, which has been found to change dynamically over a semester (Yashima *et al.*, 2016, 2018), in a conversation class (Pawlak *et al.*, 2016) or even on a momentary basis (MacIntyre & Legatto, 2011). The less variable mean WTC of the whole group, as illustrated by the relatively smooth dotted line in Figure 8.1, was understandable since, as Larsen-Freeman and Cameron (2008: 145) argued, 'group averages can conceal a great deal of variability', which was clearly seen in the individual trajectories.

Five scenarios containing marked silence (i.e. lasting 5 seconds or more) were identified and are presented below. The transcriptions did not follow the conventions typical in conversation analysis but focused on recording students' silence. Hence, double parentheses were used to signal a silence, with its duration shown in seconds with the double prime symbol ("). Square brackets were used to signify a pre-recorded beep sounded (see Scenario B).

In Scenario A, the teacher was inviting students to talk about what they would do if they found it difficult to decide which university to choose after college entrance examinations. After a five-second silence, a student called Yanhong was invited to talk:

Scenario A
11:27–11:51
Teacher: All right. Let's imagine it is a difficult decision. If you found it very difficult to decide, what would you do? And how would you feel? Anyone? ((silence 2")) Anyone? ((silence 2")) No? ((silence 3")) Anyone would like to share? ((silence 5")) Yanhong, please.

The focal students gave different accounts regarding their silence and WTC in this scenario. While Qian was at a state of high WTC (between +4 and +5, as shown in Figure 8.1), she ended up remaining silent because she had misunderstood the teacher's question and had been thinking about which disciplinary major instead of which university to choose. Grounded in Wen and Clément's (2003) perspective, Qian seemed desirous but not linguistically and/or cognitively ready to address the teacher's prompts. Put another way, although she perceived herself as 'willing' to talk, in fact she did not reach the state of 'readiness' that is central to the conceptualisation of WTC (MacIntyre *et al.*, 1998). At this moment she seemed to reach an attractor state of 'being desirous but linguistically/cognitively unready, and thereby silent' (*desirous but silent*, henceforth).

Somewhat differently, the other three focal students, whose self-rated WTC around the 11th minute was also high (see Figure 8.1), all admitted that they had formulated their answer and could have instantly responded to the teacher if they had been called on. Huan reported that she did not volunteer because her intended answer (i.e. asking advice from parents and friends) was nothing novel. Tong emphasised that he would be the silence-breaker only when the silence became markedly long:

> I would wait to see, maybe if the [silent] time was double long, and if no one volunteered to reply, I would eventually do so.... Of course I would be able to answer the question if she called on me.

While the above excerpt seemingly indicates that Tong was unwilling to communicate, in fact two interpretations are possible. It may reflect that students' self-reported WTC does not always correspond to their actual behaviour (Cao & Philp, 2006). However, with WTC anchored in the definition of 'readiness' (MacIntyre *et al.*, 1998), it could also be argued that Tong's remark and similar excerpts presented below show that the students were linguistically and cognitively ready but lacked sufficient motivation to speak – or, in Peng's (2014: 155) term, they lacked 'motivational readiness'. Therefore, in this scenario the three students could be viewed as arriving at an attractor state of 'being linguistically/cognitively capable but willingly silent' (*capable but silent*, henceforth).

Scenario B
14:50–15:01
Teacher: If in this situation, if your mum asks you to do the tutoring, would you do it? If yes, please raise your hand. If no, please raise your hand. Why not? ((silence 5")). [beep 3] Jiashan, why not?

In Scenario B, the salient silence happened when the teacher asked the students what they would do if their mother asked them to tutor their brother during a holiday when they had already made a plan to travel. At the end of this scenario a beep sounded (beep 3, in the 15th minute), at which point Qian and Huan rated their WTC at +5 and Kui at +2, which were high levels. In the interview, Qian explained her silence as follows:

> I wanted to speak up very much at that moment and I also raised my hand. But the teacher did not pick me. If the teacher called on me, I would talk a lot.... I saw some other students were also raising their hands. I could not just speak up, you know. That would affect the teaching.

Qian's narration indicates that she was linguistically and cognitively ready and eager to express her opinion, but refrained from speaking up because she was not given the floor. That is, despite her silence, Qian was yearning to speak. At that moment the interaction of L2 WTC and silence as two systems seemed to lead her to an attractor state of 'being silent but ready and yearning for nomination' (*silent yet yearning*, henceforth). This attractor state and the previous one (*capable but silent*) both indicate students' linguistic and cognitive readiness to take action, but the former implies a strong motivation or an impulse to speak up whereas the latter indicates a lack of such an impulse.

Huan and Kui seemed to remain at the attractor state of *capable but silent*, and they both affirmed their ability to answer the teacher's question if called on, but instead they habitually remained silent:

> I had this habit and don't want to answer questions in public.... If I stand up and speak English, since my pronunciation is not accurate and I don't know whether what I am going to say is correct, it is quite embarrassing. (Huan)

The reported habit of being silent, as is further manifested in the reflections by Huan and Tong in Scenario C, may be attributed to the entrenched culture of learning in China, whereby children from primary schooling onwards are oriented to obey rules and speak only when they are spoken to by the teacher, and they are often afraid of giving 'wrong' answers or making a fool of themselves (Cortazzi & Jin, 1996). Therefore, their linguistic and/or cognitive readiness to speak often needs to be triggered by the teacher's nomination.

In contrast, in this scenario Tong seemed to land in an attractor state of 'unwillingness coexisting with silence' (*unwilling and silent*, henceforth). He explained that his reluctance to talk was due to his misunderstanding of the case being discussed:

> I misunderstood the case. I didn't notice the 'had a plan for travelling' part. In the preceding group discussion I shared my opinion that I would help with tutoring my brother. But I paid no heed to the 'already had a plan for travelling' part.... Because I got the situation wrong, I did not want to talk.

Scenario C
22:08–22:12
Teacher: I mean, if the old man is not trying to cheat you, are you going to help him across the street? ((silence 2")) Are you? ((silence 4")) When you see him in the middle of the road, are you going to help him? ((silence 5"))
Qian: I can't help him by myself. I will call the policeman.

In Scenario C, the teacher was inviting the class to express their ideas about whether they would help an old man who was crossing the street slowly but had become stuck in traffic. This topic was interesting since helping a stranger in such circumstances could be tricky if the person in fact intends to fake an accident for blackmail purposes. In this scenario, Qian self-initiated a response to the teacher's question after a five-second silence. Qian reflected on this moment and attributed her talk to her interest in the topic and her cognitive and linguistic readiness:

> I liked this topic.... After the teacher raised this question, some students murmured a few words but none of them replied. I had organised my language but had been holding back from volunteering. After holding back for five seconds, I couldn't do so any longer and then I spoke up.

Based on Qian's account, it could be inferred that at this moment Qian's silence was overpowered by her WTC, which pushed her to an attractor state of 'WTC overtaking silence' (*willing and breaking silence*, henceforth). This attractor state, which was seldom observed in this study, seemed to be contingent on several factors at that moment, such as an interesting topic and Qian's linguistic and cognitive preparedness.

Huan and Tong seemed to enter to the attractor state of *capable but silent* in this scenario. Huan recalled that she enjoyed a good discussion in her group and thus would have been ready and 'comfortable' to answer the question if the teacher had picked her. Tong also expressed his capacity to respond to the teacher. He was silent because he thought that his idea (i.e. 'to secretly help the old man by walking behind him and signalling to the traffic to slow down') was too unique and off-track:

> I didn't know whether my idea could be counted as giving help, and the teacher kept asking whether we would help the old man ... I didn't want to interrupt the teacher's pace. I didn't want to over-express my unique point of view. If at that moment she happened to call on me, I would be willing to talk about my point.

The remaining student, Kui, seemed to get to the attractor state of *unwilling and silent.* He reported feeling confused about the given case, not knowing whether the class was discussing the old man being at the side or in the middle of the street. This confusion made him unwilling to engage in the whole-class discussion.

Scenario D
24:41–24:52
Teacher: All right. You are going to be very moved. And what else? ((silence 2")) Are there any other feelings? ((silence 2")) Are there any feelings? ((silence 5")) Are you going to be quite grateful? ((silence 3"))

In Scenario D, the teacher asked the students how they would feel if their classmates helped them with their luggage on their first day at university.

One nominated student answered that he would be moved, upon which the teacher pursued this topic. It can be seen that the teacher was trying to phrase her prompt in different ways, but each attempt was met with silence. Eight seconds after this scenario there was a beep (beep 5), at which point the four students rated their WTC at: +2 (Qian), +4 (Huan), +1 (Kui) and +1 (Tong). When reflecting on this moment, Qian gave two reasons for her silence: uncertainty about her idea and difficulty in expressing herself:

> The first reason was that I didn't quite agree with many of my classmates – that is, feeling moved. I would feel weird if an upper schoolmate was especially nice to me. I found my opinion different from others', so I was not sure whether I should express it. The second reason was that I couldn't organise my language to express myself. I meant to express *wu shi xian yin qin* [someone who pleases you out of the blue must be up to something], but didn't know how to express it in English.

It appeared that while Qian might remain desirous of talking, as indicated by her self-rated WTC, her silence again got the upper hand due to her linguistic inadequacy and concern about deviating from the group view. The attractor state where she was situated at that moment was again *desirous but silent*.

The other three students appeared to slide into the attractor state of *unwilling and silent*, according to their retrospections. Huan admitted that she was distracted by the topic under discussion and her attention had wandered back to the days when she was a newly arrived freshman. Kui said he had nothing novel to contribute, except saying 'feeling warm'. They both admitted to feeling tired at that moment. As for Tong, he was unwilling to talk because he anticipated that his answer would be frowned upon:

> Because my response would be 'not feeling moved', if I said so others would think bad of me – others offer help to you but you are not moved. So I did not speak up.

Scenario E
67:04–67:30
Teacher: Alright, let's see. Who can tell me? What can you see in this picture and how is it related to the concepts of individualism and collectivism? Describe what you see and what you think of the relation between the picture and these two concepts. ((silence 5")) Anyone? ((silence 3")) Anyone? ((silence 3")) Ruifeng, please.

Scenario E happened in the second period, when the teacher prompted students to talk about their understanding of individualism and collectivism by showing them several pictures related to the two concepts. For instance, one picture showed a person with the word 'Me!' appearing in a speech bubble and a group of people with the word 'We?' appearing in another bubble. Qian recalled that in this scenario she had wanted to speak up but remained reticent because she felt she would be unable to make herself understood by the teacher:

> I couldn't make my opinion clear to my partner and she looked quite confused at what I said. So although I wanted to tell the teacher my opinion because mine was different from others', I didn't know how to explain it clearly to her.

In other words, linguistic difficulties stopped Qian from contributing, and again she rested in the attractor state of *desirous but silent*. The other three students all seemed to sink into the attractor state of *unwilling and silent* in this scenario. Coincidently, they all pointed to the same major reason, which was that they did not know or were not sure of the meaning of the two words (i.e. individualism and collectivism), and thus could not relate the two words to the pictures shown in the PowerPoint slides:

> I didn't know the meaning of the two words, neither did my deskmate. I was wondering whether individualism is the noun of 'invade'.... Later I gradually guessed their meanings when seeing the pictures. But I was not sure of my guess, and at that moment I certainly could not express myself in English. (Huan)

> I was not clear about the meanings of the two concepts or their association with the pictures. I was silent because I didn't know what to talk about. (Kui)

The above descriptions and the students' accounts show the complex and dynamic entanglement between L2 WTC and silence in response to many elements in the larger dynamic system of classroom communication, which drove the four students to different attractor states. Table 8.5 presents the attractor states and their frequencies in the five scenarios, and episodic factors underlying these states. The factors summarised in Table 8.5 resonate with many previous findings. For instance, topical interest and linguistic and cognitive readiness have been widely reported to enhance L2 WTC (Cao, 2014; Pawlak & Mystkowska-Wiertelak, 2015; Peng, 2014; Yashima *et al.*, 2016). The important role of vocabulary knowledge was identified by MacIntyre and Legatto (2011), and here it also functioned to nudge the students into certain attractor states. The students expressed concerns about disturbing the teacher's pace or about others' judgements, reflecting what Wen and Clément (2003) called a submissive way of learning and an other-directed self rooted in Chinese

Table 8.5 Attractor states in the interaction of WTC and silence

Attractor state	Scenario (frequency)	Total frequency	Factors
Unwilling and silent	B (1), C (1), D (3), E (3)	8	Misunderstanding, concern about no novel contribution, fatigue, insufficient vocabulary knowledge
Capable but silent	A (3), B (2), C (2)	7	Not being called on, habitual silence, linguistic and cognitive readiness, short silent time
Desirous but silent	A (1), D (1), E (1)	3	Misunderstanding, confusion, concern about others' judgements
Silent yet yearning	B (1)	1	Topical interest, linguistic and cognitive readiness, concern about disturbing teacher's pace
Willing and breaking silence	C (1)	1	Topical interest, linguistic and cognitive readiness

culture. These findings also confirm Liu's (2002) argument that for students with a Chinese cultural heritage, silence can function as a communication strategy to show respect and politeness in class.

The attractor states originating in the interaction of L2 WTC and silence may be typologically illustrated as being situated in a three-dimensional landscape of classroom communication, as shown in Figure 8.2. Multiple factors in this landscape compete, resulting in various attractor states, of which *unwilling and silent* and *capable but silent* seem stronger and more stable in the current context, as reflected by their higher frequencies (shown in Table 8.5); they therefore have steeper sides than *desirous but silent, silent yet yearning* and *willing and breaking silence*. This implies that when the interaction of L2 WTC and silence leads to the former two attractor states, stable communication tendencies may develop, and it may require great force to change them. It should be

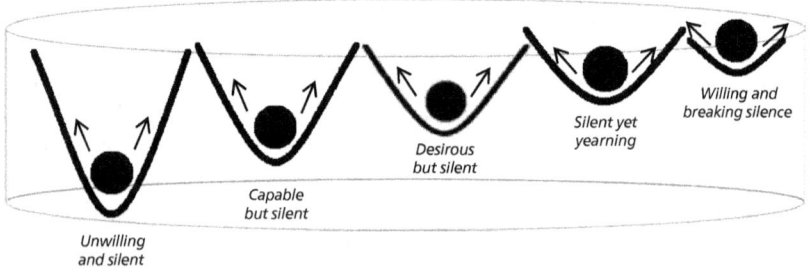

Figure 8.2 Attractor states of interplay of WTC and silence (based on Thelen & Smith, 1994: 60)

noted that the five attractor states are neither exhaustive nor clear-cut, but should be viewed as examples of a multitude of attractor states, varying in depth and steepness, which emerge from momentary contingencies.

Conclusion

This study has adopted the DST perspective to investigate L2 WTC vis-à-vis silence among university students in the Chinese EFL classroom. It was found that in the live English class the students engaged in talk for almost half of the lesson time, although this was mostly in pairs or groups. However, no instance of student-initiated talk to the whole class was observed. The analysis of the five scenarios with marked silence showed that the four focal students mostly remained in the attractor states of *unwilling and silent* and *capable but silent* (i.e. being linguistically/cognitively capable but willingly silent). Fewer instances were observed of *desirous but silent* (i.e. being desirous but linguistically/cognitively unready, and therefore silent), *silent yet yearning* (i.e. being silent but ready and yearning for nomination) and *willing and breaking silence*. Many factors were found to contribute to the students' attractor states in L2 classroom communication.

It is noteworthy that the current analyses were necessarily interpretive, and the findings may require more compelling research evidence. Also, the use of a buzzer to prompt students' self-ratings of WTC could have caused distraction. Nevertheless, the current findings suggest certain implications. It is important for teachers to recognise that students' silence can be intertwined with complex communication psychology such as various degrees of WTC. Students may often remain silent due to problems with comprehension or expression, but at other times, even though they may be prepared to speak, they tend to stay in their 'comfort zone' without venturing to speak up. Hence, teachers need to be observant and skilled in diagnosing students' *in situ* communicative responses. Then, teachers may develop students' linguistic and cognitive readiness by giving them sufficient language input and time for pair or group discussions, and expend more effort to boost students' desire to speak. This may help to push students away from the attractor states of *desirous but silent* and *capable but silent* and towards the state of *silent yet yearning*. When moments of *silent yet yearning* are observed, teachers need to trigger students' action – for example, by lengthening the pause time or opting for immediacy behaviour (e.g. smiling and making eye contact) (Wen & Clément, 2003). Once some students arrive at a state of *willing and breaking silence*, teachers should acknowledge and praise them so as to keep the momentum and spread it to the whole group – especially given the relative instability of this attractor state. In sum, in an L2 class the teacher is not just transmitting knowledge, but is also orchestrating various elements in many dynamic systems embedded in the complex system of classroom communication to promote students' L2 practice.

L2 WTC and silence have garnered great research attention, particularly in Asian contexts. This study has shown that they are not two opposite sides of the same issue. Rather, they operate simultaneously and compete to drive individual students towards attractor states of varying strength and stability. Drawing on the DST, this study has contributed fresh insights into the dynamic interplay between Chinese students' L2 WTC and silence, which is central to their psychological tapestry in class. The findings may inspire language instructors to make informed decisions or develop pedagogical interventions by attending to the many factors operating to bring out students' situational communication behaviour.

Self-reflection/Discussion Questions

(1) In this study, markedly long student silences were not observed, which might be because the teacher often nominated students shortly after she had raised a question. What could be inferred from this finding regarding the teacher's attitudes towards silence in class? What other techniques could be employed to handle student silence?
(2) What were the focal students' attitudes towards silence reflected in this study? In a language class, which type of students does the teacher prefer to have, those who are willingly silent or those who are silently willing to communicate? Why?
(3) When the students reported their levels of WTC, did their understanding of the term 'L2 WTC' correspond to the conceptualisation of L2 WTC in MacIntyre et al.'s (1998) model? While L2 WTC is a latent variable and only a few signs, such as hand-raising (MacIntyre et al., 1998), could be viewed as its indicator, could other multimodal signs such as facial expressions and gaze signal students' L2 WTC?
(4) From a DST perspective, complex systems are interrelated, variant and ever-changing. How do the dynamic systems of L2 WTC and silence self-organise to settle in the attractor state of *unwilling and silent*? How could researchers pinpoint the many dynamic systems pertinent to students' communication behaviour in the language classroom so as to offer implications for teaching practice?

Recommended Reading

Larsen-Freeman, D. and Cameron, L. (2008) *Complex Systems and Applied Linguistics*. Oxford: Oxford University Press.

Larsen-Freeman and Cameron present and elucidate the conceptual underpinnings of the complexity theory, its key concepts and its pertinence in language and language learning. They further demonstrate the application of the complexity theory in the development of a first and of a second language, in discourse analysis and in language teaching. This is the seminal work that guides researchers to understand and empirically employ the complexity theory in applied linguistics research.

Lauzona, V.F. and Bergerb, E. (2015) The multimodal organization of speaker selection in classroom interaction. *Linguistics and Education* 31, 14–29.

Lauzona and Bergerb draw on conversational analysis to provide a nuanced description of how turn allocation is managed in classroom interaction. Of particular interest is their findings that students used multimodal signals such as gesture and gaze in the teacher's direction to display their availability or willingness to speak prior to the teacher's nomination of a speaker; conversely, students signalled their unavailability by withdrawing gaze, looking out of the window or displaying being busy with something. The authors highlight the subtlety of embodied displays of availability of students and argue that classroom interaction is not controlled by the teacher but instead is a result of collaborative adjustments from all parties. This study may have implications for tapping L2 WTC with observation data besides relying on students' self-reports.

Liu, J. (2001) *Asian Students' Classroom Communication Patterns in U.S. Universities: An Emic Perspective.* Norwood, NJ: Ablex.

This monograph reports on a multi-case ethnographic study of Asian students' participation in American classrooms. Liu identifies among the participants four classroom communication patterns (i.e. total integration, conditional interaction, marginal participation and silent observation) and reveals the factors that influence the students' participation, which are classified into five categories (i.e. cognitive, pedagogic, affective, sociocultural and linguistic) that have three types of functions (i.e. facilitating, debilitating and neutral). Liu further interprets Asian students' silence in the classroom settings from an Asian perspective. This work has profound significance for understanding unbiasedly Asian students' silence in class.

References

Cao, Y. (2014) A sociocognitive perspective on second language classroom willingness to communicate. *TESOL Quarterly* 48 (4), 789–814.
Cao, Y. and Philp, J. (2006) Interactional context and willingness to communicate: A comparison of behavior in whole class, group and dyadic interaction. *System* 34 (4), 480–493.
Cortazzi, M. and Jin, L. (1996) Cultures of learning: Language classrooms in China. In H. Coleman (ed.) *Society and the Language Classroom* (pp. 169–206). Cambridge: Cambridge University Press.

De Bot, K., Lowie, W. and Verspoor, M. (2007) A dynamic systems theory approach to second language acquisition. *Bilingualism: Language and Cognition* 10 (1), 7–21.

Granger, C.A. (2004) *Silence in Second Language Learning: A Psychoanalytic Reading*. Clevedon: Multilingual Matters.

Hiver, P. (2015) Attractor states. In Z. Dörnyei, P.D. MacIntyre and A. Henry (eds) *Motivational Dynamics in Language Learning* (pp. 20–28). Bristol: Multilingual Matters.

Jackson, J. (2002) Reticence in second language case discussions: Anxiety and aspirations. *System* 30 (1), 65–84.

Jaworski, A. and Sachdev, I. (1998) Beliefs about silence in the classroom. *Language and Education* 12 (4), 273–292.

Kang, S.-J. (2005) Dynamic emergence of situational willingness to communicate in a second language. *System* 33 (2), 277–292.

Khajavy, G.H., MacIntyre, P.D. and Barabadi, E. (2017) Role of the emotions and classroom environment in willingness to communicate: Applying doubly latent multilevel analysis in second language acquisition research. *Studies in Second Language Acquisition* 40 (3), 605–624.

King, J. (2013a) *Silence in the Second Language Classroom*. Basingstoke: Palgrave Macmillan.

King, J. (2013b) Silence in the second language classrooms of Japanese universities. *Applied Linguistics* 34 (3), 325–343.

King, J. (2016) Classroom silence and the dynamic interplay between context and the language learner: A stimulated recall study. In J. King (ed.) *The Dynamic Interplay Between Context and the Language Learner* (pp. 127–150). Basingstoke: Palgrave Macmillan.

Larsen-Freeman, D. (2007) On the complementarity of chaos/complexity theory and dynamic systems theory in understanding the second language acquisition process. *Bilingualism: Language and Cognition* 10 (1), 35–37.

Larsen-Freeman, D. (2015) Ten 'lessons' from complex dynamic systems theory: What is on offer. In Z. Dörnyei, P.D. MacIntyre and A. Henry (eds) *Motivational Dynamics in Language Learning* (pp. 11–19). Bristol: Multilingual Matters.

Larsen-Freeman, D. and Cameron, L. (2008) *Complex Systems and Applied Linguistics*. Oxford: Oxford University Press.

Liu, J. (2002) Negotiating silence in American classrooms: Three Chinese cases. *Language and Intercultural Communication* 2 (1), 37–54.

MacIntyre, P.D. and Legatto, J.J. (2011) A dynamic system approach to willingness to communicate: Developing an idiodynamic method to capture rapidly changing affect. *Applied Linguistics* 32 (2), 149–171.

MacIntyre, P.D., Dörnyei, Z., Clément, R. and Noels, K.A. (1998) Conceptualizing willingness to communicate in a L2: A situational model of L2 confidence and affiliation. *Modern Language Journal* 82 (4), 545–562.

MacIntyre, P.D., Baker, S.C., Clément, R. and Conrod, S. (2001) Willingness to communicate, social support, and language-learning orientations of immersion students. *Studies in Second Language Acquisition* 23 (3), 369–388.

Mystkowska-Wiertelak, A. and Pawlak, M. (2017) *Willingness to Communicate in Instructed Second Language Acquisition: Combining a Macro- and Micro-Perspective*. Bristol: Multilingual Matters.

Neuman, W.L. (2014) *Social Research Methods: Qualitative and Quantitative Approaches* (7th edn). Boston: Pearson.

Pawlak, M. and Mystkowska-Wiertelak, A. (2015) Investigating the dynamic nature of L2 willingness to communicate. *System* 50, 1–9.

Pawlak, M., Mystkowska-Wiertelak, A. and Bielak, J. (2016) Investigating the nature of classroom willingness to communicate (WTC): A micro-perspective. *Language Teaching Research* 20 (5), 654–671.

Peng, J. (2014) *Willingness to Communicate in the Chinese EFL University Classroom: An Ecological Perspective*. Bristol: Multilingual Matters.

Peng, J. and Woodrow, L.J. (2010) Willingness to communicate in English: A model in Chinese EFL classroom context. *Language Learning* 60 (4), 834–876.

Sinclair, J.M. and Coulthard, M. (1975) *Towards an Analysis of Discourse*. Oxford: Oxford University Press.

Skehan, P. (1989) *Individual Differences in Second Language Learning*. London: Edward Arnold.

Sobkowiak, W. (1997) Silence and markedness theory. In A. Jaworski (ed.) *Silence: Interdisciplinary Perspectives* (pp. 39–62). Berlin: Mouton de Gruyter.

Thelen, E. and Smith, L.B. (1994) *A Dynamic Systems Approach to the Development of Cognition and Action*. Cambridge, MA: MIT Press.

Wen, W.P. and Clément, R. (2003) A Chinese conceptualisation of willingness to communicate in ESL. *Language, Culture and Curriculum* 16 (1), 18–38.

Yashima, T. (2002) Willingness to communicate in a second language: The Japanese EFL context. *Modern Language Journal* 86 (1), 54–66.

Yashima, T., Ikeda, M. and Nakahira, S. (2016) Talk and silence in an EFL classroom: Interplay of learners and context. In J. King (ed.) *The Dynamic Interplay Between Context and the Language Learner* (pp. 104–126). Basingstoke: Palgrave Macmillan.

Yashima, T., MacIntyre, P.D. and Ikeda, M. (2018) Situated willingness to communicate in an L2: Interplay of individual characteristics and context. *Language Teaching Research* 22 (1), 115–137.

Yoshida, R. (2013) Learners' self-concept and use of the target language in foreign language classrooms. *System* 41 (4), 935–951.

9 Conclusion: Silence in EFL Classrooms Revisited

Amy B.M. Tsui and Rintaro Imafuku

Introduction

For a long time, silence in the classroom where English is learned as a foreign language (EFL), or in fact in all classrooms, had been seen as a phenomenon which was pedagogically problematic and something to be avoided. In the last three decades or so, as the editors of this book have pointed out in their Introduction (Chapter 1), research on silence in EFL classrooms has thrown light on the multiple meanings that underlie silence and the multiple ways in which it can be interpreted, how it may be shaped by different contexts, its underlying factors (including linguistic, psychological, sociocultural and pedagogical ones), the complex interplay among these factors and how it can be usefully exploited and managed for better language learning. The chapters in this volume, with a focus on Asian learners, make an interesting contribution to the elucidation of this phenomenon from different perspectives and in different contexts.

Research on Asian learners' classroom learning has found their classroom behaviours to be distinctly different from those of their Western counterparts, their tendency to remain silent being one of them. This tendency has been substantiated by a number of studies, both qualitative and quantitative, as well as by studies reported in this volume. The phenomenon of 'silence' refers to the absence of sound, noise or voice. 'Silence in the classroom' generally refers to the absence of speech by the learners or the teachers. In the research literature, such silence has been interpreted to cover a range of phenomena, from students doing individual seat work (such as reading, writing, listening to audio-tapes and reflecting on their learning experience) and a lack of engagement by learners in group work or pair work, to the intentional withholding of speech by the teacher to achieve the pedagogical goal of enabling learners to formulate their response, commonly referred to as 'wait time'. To avoid confusion, 'silence in the classroom' in this chapter refers to students remaining silent when they are expected to provide a response. In other words, it refers to 'reticence' on the part of the learners as expounded in Tsui (1996).

Reticence of Asian Learners and Sociocultural Values

Asian learners have been referred to as learners from 'Confucian heritage cultures' (CHC). The assumption is that there are common cultural values that are shared by Asian learners rooted in Confucian philosophy. While this seems to be a sweeping generalisation and it is questionable whether some of the sociocultural values are indeed rooted in Confucian philosophy, investigations of the underlying factors that shape Asian learners' classroom behaviours have shown that there are indeed sociocultural values and associated psychological states that are widely shared. The chapters in this volume pertain mostly to Chinese and Japanese learners and teachers, except for Chapter 2, where the participants included also Korean and Mongolian learners. The findings reported in these chapters have provided further evidence to substantiate this claim.

Bao in Chapter 2 noted learners' tendency to exercise more caution in spoken participation. He argued for the need to investigate the impact of context on the tendency of Asian learners to be reticent. His study showed that for most of his participants (consisting of Chinese, Korean, Japanese and Mongolian students), in the context of learning in an overseas (Australian) university where verbal participation was expected and silence was viewed unfavourably, sociocultural values such as 'face-saving' and 'cultural harmony' and psychological state such as 'shyness', which would have been important to them in their home cultural context, became less important and his students became much more participative.

His study further showed that task design, including content and whether it is challenging, peer dynamics, teacher support, expectation and context, had an impact on students' oral participation. The findings demonstrated the interplay between different factors that impinged on their reticence. What is interesting is that when the task contents were 'controversial, sensitive, embarrassing or offensive', learners tended to resort to silence to 'evade discomfort'. Similarly, when group members were 'aggressive, talkative and domineering', his participants would resort to silence. In other words, the findings showed that there are certain sociocultural values that are more deeply rooted than others, in this case, social harmony, and have stronger impact on learners' participation.

Humphries *et al.* in Chapter 7 noted that learners' tendency to remain silent in the classroom was prevalent in Japan, particularly in high schools. They cited similar cultural values shared by Chinese and Japanese learners, including 'face' protection, avoidance of disagreement with and disapproval of the teacher and peers, fear of negative evaluation by peers, and deference to authority. Their online survey of the factors that underlay students' capacity to speak (CTS) showed that classroom support and confidence were the factors that were most strongly correlated with the respondents' CTS, compared with other factors such as school context, motivation and anxiety. The survey items pertaining to classroom support were all related to the cultural values of social harmony, teacher approval and support, and fear of negative evaluation, suggesting that those were the cultural values which were more strongly held by learners. (The survey items are not provided in Chapter 7 but interested readers can contact the authors.)

Adopting a cognitive-behavioural approach, Maher focused in Chapter 5 on a single Japanese learner who exhibited a high level of anxiety as manifested by her body language, silence and avoidance strategies in the EFL classroom. She conducted several interviews to elicit the student's thoughts, emotions and beliefs underlying her behaviours in order to understand the contributing factors. The findings echo those reported in the research literature and in this volume, with fear of negative peer evaluation (or lack of peer approval) and fear of imperfect self-presentation being the dominant factors. What is interesting is that the fear of negative peer evaluation was so overpowering that it kept surfacing even in an intervention activity which aimed to induce balanced thinking in the student.

Peng's study of Chinese learners in a university in China, presented in Chapter 8, cited the use of silence in Chinese culture to denote values such as respect for the teacher, politeness, modesty and avoidance of threats to face. Adopting a dynamic systems theory as an analytical lens, she examined the dynamic interplay between the willingness to communicate (WTC) and silence of four focal students during several episodes of 'marked' silence (five seconds or more) in a lesson. The data showed interesting changes in students' WTC as the lesson progressed. The reasons cited by these students for remaining silent, irrespective of whether their WTC was negative or positive, though different, converged on similar cultural values, including teacher approval, deference to teacher authority, fear of embarrassment if their answers were incorrect or 'nothing novel' or their pronunciation was inaccurate (fear of negative evaluation, face saving), fear of disrupting the pace of the lesson set by the teacher and fear of their opinion being different from that of the rest of the group (groupism).

From the perspective of teachers, Harumi studied their pedagogical strategies to deal with silence in EFL tertiary classrooms as an 'interactional resource' (Chapter 3). Her questionnaire survey findings and classroom data analysis of tertiary teachers' strategies when encountering learners' silence in a Japanese EFL context demonstrated their awareness of cultural values such as groupism and group pressure among the students, the importance of peer approval and support (changing from 'one-to-one' to 'peer-oriented interaction'), teacher support, both linguistic and affective support, including 'avoid putting students on the spot'.

Also from the perspective of teachers, Karas and Faez investigated Chinese teachers on a pre-service teacher education programme at a Canadian university (Chapter 6). Reasons for students' reticence mentioned by the teachers were remarkably similar: fear of embarrassment and losing face, feeling unsafe, and language anxiety due to lack of language ability. Functions of silence mentioned by the teachers included to show respect for the teacher, to allow other voices to be heard, to indicate disagreement and to serve as a safe space for cognitive processing and rehearsing answers before speaking. In their discussions and reflections on the unsuitability of communicative language teaching (CLT) in Chinese contexts, which represented the majority view, deference to the teacher's authority figured prominently as a major deterrent to the implementation of a methodology which encourages learners to argue and challenge the teacher.

In Chapter 4, King, Yashima, Humphries, Aubrey and Ikeda reported a longitudinal intervention study of three EFL teachers over one term to tackle learner reticence and anxiety in a Japanese university. Stimulated recall interviews conducted with learners on episodes of silence and their own self-reports again revealed similar cultural values, including fear of making mistakes and negative evaluation by peers, negative self-image and self-evaluation of English competence compared with their peers, need for teacher approval before actively speaking in class ('Don't speak too much') and power relationship between senior and junior students. The post-intervention findings showed the out-of-class activity intervention to be minimally effective, if at all. By contrast, the in-class intervention activities to address students' feelings of anxiety and inhibition showed that some students were able to speak up more in class because they were able to 'throw away the shame' and they became 'more confident than usual'. For a number of learners, task complexity and difficult discussion topics continued to be inhibiting factors. The findings confirmed that cultural values that impact on learner reticence are deeply rooted and that sustained efforts are required, on the part of both the teachers and the learners themselves, to bring about changes in their perceptions of the relative importance of these values.

The above brief summary does not do justice to the rich discussion in the chapters in this volume. It merely serves to show how similar the sociocultural values are that underlie learner reticence in the classroom. It is remarkable that even the wordings in which these values were expressed by the learners across the volume were similar.

To advance research on this phenomenon, further investigations of the dynamic interplay between these values and factors which impinge on learners' reticence and their relative impact on learners' classroom behaviours would be necessary. Complexity theory, or complex dynamic systems theory (CDST), provides a powerful theoretical framework for this purpose because silence is highly contextual and learner behaviour in relation to silence may be influenced by a number of coexisting variables, both internal and external to the learner, whose influence may change over time. Recent studies have drawn on CDST to make sense of the phenomenon of silence in the classroom (see for example King, 2016; MacIntyre & Legatto, 2011; Smith & King, 2017; Yashima *et al.*, 2016; and Peng in Chapter 8 of the present volume). In the following section, we shall briefly outline the basic tenets of complexity theory and the methodologies that are aligned with it.

A Dynamic View of Silence in the Classroom: Complexity Theory and Research Methodologies

The application of CDST to studies of classroom silence has been influenced by the pioneering work of Larsen-Freeman (1997) which pointed out that similar to natural systems, language acquisition is a dynamic, complex and non-linear process. Complex systems, as Larsen-Freeman has observed, often comprise a large number of components (or subsystems). The behaviour of a complex system is, though, not just the product of the behaviour of its individual components: it emerges from the interactions among those components. Any change in one component will result in changes in other components; they are interdependent. The development of dynamic systems is characterised by non-linearity in that the effect may not, and is often not, proportional to its cause. Citing the analogy of the 'butterfly effect', Larsen-Freeman observed that a slight difference in the input can result in vast differences in the output (Larsen-Freeman, 1997: 144). Complex systems are adaptive, that is, they are sensitive to feedback and will change themselves accordingly (see also Larsen-Freeman & Cameron, 2008). Complexity theory argues for a holistic approach to investigations of phenomena rather than an atomistic approach in which measurable variables are isolated and controlled, as the latter will not unravel the dynamic interactions between the component parts and will miss the significance of the whole (see Cohen *et al.*, 2018). Furthermore, the study of processes emerging over time and critical incidents in evolving situations is central to such investigations (Byrne & Callaghan, 2014).

In order to capture the dynamic and multifaceted nature of silence in language-learning situations, it is important that the research methodologies adopted are aligned with complexity theory. The candidate methodologies include action research, case study, narrative enquiry and participatory forms of research, all of which allow for interactionist and multi-perspectival accounts. They are not mutually exclusive, however. One can be embedded in another and multiple methods can be used for data collection and analysis. It is increasingly recognised that mixed methods research (i.e. combining qualitative and quantitative approaches) provides a better understanding of the research problem under investigation. Cohen *et al.* (2018) observe that the adoption of mixed methodologies has been 'meteoric', so much so that it has been referred to as the 'third methodological movement', the 'third paradigm' or the 'third path' (Cohen *et al.*, 2018: 31). Due to the limit of space, we shall briefly discuss only action research and case studies below.

Action research is aligned with the basic tenets of complexity theory: systems are seen as open, complex and dynamic, and the outcomes and processes of action research are understood as unpredictable and non-linear. Action research celebrates the emergence of new states and situations from the dynamic interactions among the participants (Morrison, 2008). In fact, it has been argued that action research and complexity theory are deeply complementary (Phelps & Graham, 2010), and that action research itself can be considered a complex system (Luttenberg *et al.*, 2017).

Action research has been widely adopted in research on the teaching of English as a second language (ESL) and EFL teaching, and guidebooks have been produced for practitioners (for example, Burns, 2010; Wallace, 1998). In general, action research involves four main stages, planning, acting, observing and reflecting, with variations. These stages are a cyclical process in which reflections will lead to another cycle of action research. The open and dynamic nature of action research is evidenced by the fact that each stage of the cycle is open to modification on the basis of the outcome of the previous stage. Increasingly, mixed methods are adopted in data collection and analysis relating to the pre- and post-intervention, as mentioned above. In studying the phenomenon of silence, the use of action research requires careful and sensitive planning of the intervention based on prior understanding of learners' psychological states relating to verbal participation and the underlying reasons. Equally important is the evaluation of the intervention and reflection in which multiple perspectives of the processes and outcomes should be obtained. Unfortunately, the majority of action research reported in the literature is limited to only one cycle. In fact, it is often in the second and subsequent cycles that the emergence of new states or situations becomes more prominent and the dynamic and multifaceted nature of the phenomenon under investigation can be more fully understood. In other words, there should be more action research involving sustained intervention over time and analyses of longitudinal data on the dynamics of the associated changes over time.

Case studies, being in-depth studies of individuals, groups or organisations in a natural setting and focusing on the unfolding processes of interactions and relationships in the context in which the participants operate (see Denscome, 2014b), are particularly suited to the study of phenomena such as silence in the classroom. The thick description (Geertz, 1973) of the lived experience of learners will yield a better understanding of its complex, dynamic and multifaceted nature.

A case study can be 'snapshot' or longitudinal. The former collects data on a single occasion, whereas the latter requires the researcher to be immersed in the world of the participants over a period of time and to collect data at different points during that period to track the changes. Snapshot studies suffer the weakness of presenting a relatively static view of the phenomenon under investigation. Examples of snapshot studies are questionnaire surveys, such as the study reported by Humphries *et al.* in Chapter 7 of this volume, and recordings of learner participation in a single lesson, for example the study by Peng in Chapter 8, although there is some interesting evidence of the dynamic interplay between WTC and silence on the part of the learners over several points in a single lesson. Had the author provided findings of the entire longitudinal study with three data collection points over a whole term, the study would have provided further insights into the dynamic processes. King *et al.* present in Chapter 4 the only longitudinal study in this volume. As the authors point out, sustained pedagogical intervention and further exploration of the dynamic interplay of the underlying factors over time are much needed. We would add that longitudinal case studies which track changes, or the lack of change, of the *same learner* over an extended period of time would yield more powerful insights than those which are focused on learners as a group because each learner's lived experience of the phenomenon is different.

In the next section of this chapter, we shall report on a longitudinal case study of Japanese learners' participation in problem-based learning (PBL) tutorials. Due to the limit of space, the findings reported are for illustrative purposes, and are based on a subset of a larger data set.

Japanese Learners' Participation in PBL Tutorials

The study was conducted in a private medical university in Japan where interdisciplinary PBL tutorials were conducted over the course of an academic year to encourage first-year students from different professional schools to work together. There were altogether four tutorials: two in the first term (April–July) and two in the second term (September–December). Each tutorial consisted of two sessions over two weeks and were conducted in L1 (i.e. Japanese). The tutorials were theme-based and a scenario relating to environmental issues and medical issues was provided to students for discussion. There were six tutorial groups in each tutorial and three of these groups were randomly selected for study. Each tutorial group consisted of nine students from different professional schools, including medicine, dentistry, pharmacy, nursing, occupational therapy and physical therapy. There was a change of group membership after two tutorials to enable students to get to know each other. Each tutorial was chaired by a student volunteer with another student volunteer serving as the scribe for note-taking and a tutor serving as the facilitator. Students were encouraged to identify their learning objectives through group discussions and solve the problems together.

A mixed-methods approach was adopted, consisting of quantitative analyses of learner participation and qualitative analyses of interviews with learners on their background and their lived experience in these tutorials. All four PBL tutorial sessions were video-recorded, transcribed and analysed.

On the basis of the quantitative analysis of the initial session, nine focal learners showing different levels of participation were selected from the three tutorial groups for in-depth investigation. Stimulated recall interviews were conducted with these students after each tutorial on their own participation in terms of roles and responsibilities in the discussion group and their thinking processes during the discussion. In these interviews, the students were encouraged to comment on what was happening during a particular event of the discussion, using video recorded data as a prompt. Interviews were also conducted with their group members to solicit their comments on how the discussion went as well as on the participation of these nine focal students. All the interviews were conducted in Japanese and lasted around 25–45 minutes.

Learners' participation trajectories

The participation trajectories were plotted on the basis of the percentage of 'moves' (Sinclair & Coulthard, 1975) made by the participants in relation to the total number of moves made by the whole group in each tutorial session. For illustration, Table 9.1 provides the participation trajectories of four of the nine focal learners. As can be seen, the learners' participation trajectories were quite different. In this chapter, because of the limit of space, we will present briefly the findings from two out of the nine learners, Aya and Rina. (For a more detailed discussion of the data, see Tsui & Imafuku, 2019). Aya's participation demonstrated an upward trajectory, whereas Rina's participation rate demonstrated a fluctuating trajectory, from upward to downward and then upward again.

Table 9.1 Participation trajectories (percentage participation rate*) of four Japanese learners in PBL tutorials

	First tutorial (April/May)	Second tutorial (May/June)	Third tutorial (Sept./Oct.)	Fourth tutorial (Nov.)
Aya	3.6%	7.3%	19.5%	23.8%
Rina	6.0%	24.9%	7.4%	14.5%
Miu	19.3%	26.6%	15.1%	9.2%
Hiroko	3.0%	5.0%	3.4%	2.2%

*The percentages were calculated according to the number of 'moves' made by a learner over the total number of moves made by all learners in the tutorial group; each tutorial had eight other participants.

Learners' reflections on participation

Aya

In the first PBL tutorial, Aya's participation rate was low, only 3.6% of the total contribution. She knew that PBL required students to take control of their own discussion and that she could not learn anything without active participation. In the interview, she said, 'That's why I found PBL very challenging for me. I wanted to have more instruction from the facilitator to guide our learning.' She also felt that active participation was not her personality trait. She said, 'Frankly speaking, it was so hard because I am not the kind of person who actively express my opinion in front of people.' She knew that she was expected to participate actively and she was worried that she might get a low mark from the facilitator, who seemed to base her assessment of each student on their frequency of participation. She was also aware of the expectation of her group members but she was apprehensive about negative evaluations from her peers. She said, 'I think that everyone would want me to be more active in the group discussion.... I know I am a very quiet member, so I need to become a participant who could more actively express opinions without any anxiety about other members' critical reaction.'

In the second tutorial, which was one month later, her participation rate increased somewhat, to 7.3%, but she felt that she 'could not make enough contribution to the discussion'. When she did participate, she tried to make sure that her comments were based on evidence and her own experience. Even then, she was still 'worried about others' negative response to my opinion, and [also that] it might disrupt the flow of the discussion'. That is, in addition to the fear of negative evaluation by her peers, she was also concerned about her contribution being irrelevant. When she was asked during the discussion whether she had any ideas about the learning objectives, she said she wanted to suggest studying the nutritional value of cup noodles but she did not. She explained that that was because enough learning objectives had already been suggested. In fact, the same topic was also suggested by another member but it was considered not relevant by most members and so she gave up the idea. She said, 'Most members seemed to think cup noodles were not relevant to the main theme. That's why I couldn't express my opinion in this discussion.' In other words, for her, if most members felt it was not relevant, then it would not be acceptable to still put forward the opinion.

In the third tutorial, which took place in the second term, her participation increased substantially, to 19.5%. Reflecting on her experience in the first semester, she said, 'In the first semester I observed that no matter how trivial [the point is], members frankly expressed what they thought. So, I became aware that I could express my thoughts even though it might be unimportant.' When she was asked whether other group members' participation had positively influenced her participation, she said,

'Exactly.... Probably, this group had an atmosphere where all members felt comfortable and free to share their ideas. They had an open attitude to any opinions. Like, whatever I said, they tended to attentively listen to me. Their attitudes made me remove my anxiety to communicate.' Not only did she contribute more actively, but she also felt that because of the positive group dynamics, she should play the role of encouraging quieter members to contribute. She said, 'I think I could more actively contribute to discussions than in the first semester. So, to understand the group situation, I have to encourage quiet members to make contributions to the discussions and to create a supportive climate in the group. I think that discussions should be achieved by not a part of but all members.'

In the fourth tutorial, Aya's contribution continued to increase, reaching 23.8%. The interview data revealed that she focused more on the content of her contributions rather than just the number of contributions, which was what she did in the first semester. She said, 'I attempted to offer more fruitful suggestions in the discussion.... I was conscious of doing like this in my mind, such as sharing knowledge related to the theme and opinions from different perspectives which others didn't notice ... in the first semester, I only focused on increasing the number of contributions, whereas now I am much more focusing on enhancing the content of my contributions.'

The positive group dynamics that she had experienced clearly had a strong impact on Aya's attitude towards her own participation. She said, 'I've realized that any opinions can contribute to the development of group discussions.' Furthermore, it also enabled her to see what was necessary for group discussions to thrive. She said, 'It is important for the group to establish an atmosphere where all members feel free to express any opinions. In order to do so, everyone needs to respect other members' contributions.... So, in discussions, active listening is very important. For example, I think that listeners need to properly make eye contact and nod, because this non-verbal behaviour will alleviate anxiety of communication.' Looking back at her own participation, Aya said that she strongly felt that she could not have done that in the first tutorial.

We can see that the factors mentioned by Aya which contributed to her minimal participation in the first two tutorials were very similar to those reported in the literature and the chapters in this volume. They include her perception of reticence being her own personality trait, her anxiety about giving wrong information, and her fear of being criticised by her group members and also of being negatively assessed by her facilitator. They also pertained to her concern about the relationship of self to group, that is, the 'interpersonal self', which is a cultural value that came through strongly in the interviews with other learners (see also Itakura & Tsui, 2004). The positive and non-face-threatening relationship that she had experienced over two tutorials seemed to have had a critical impact on her participation and had rendered less important other cultural values which had inhibited her participation. Her perception of the 'interpersonal self' also changed from seeing herself in relation to the group as a passive, non-disruptive member to an active facilitative one. This had a further impact on her attitude towards learning. She said, 'Through learning in PBL tutorials I think I became a little bit more of an autonomous learner compared with my attitude in the first semester. In PBL, students need to take the initiative to study a topic, so that it can also be useful in terms of knowledge acquisition. We can't just rely on the teacher's instruction.'

Rina

Rina's participation rate in the first tutorial was 6%, and she was described as a quiet member by her group. However, she described herself as somebody who readily spoke her own mind: 'I tend to say whatever I want to say'. Nevertheless, her participation was inhibited by her perception of what was expected of group members in a PBL tutorial, and also her observation of group members contributing 'opinions which were useful for deepening the discussion when it got stuck'. She said, 'I want to enhance the quality of my contributions to the discussion, but I'm not this kind of person [that is, a member who can make effective contributions to the discussion]'. It is interesting that, similar to Aya, she attributed her reticence to her personality trait. Her perception of her own contribution was actually contrary to the comments from her group members, who said that her contribution was 'insightful'.

In the second tutorial, her participation rate rose to 24.9%. She volunteered to chair the discussion, to the surprise of her group members. She explained that she did so because she had not offered to be the chair or the scribe in the first tutorial, when nobody else seemed willing to be the chair. When asked to reflect on her participation, she felt that the chair should form a collective opinion by eliciting individual opinions from the members. She said, 'When I disagreed with a member's opinion, I tried not to interrupt his/her turn and listen carefully to him/her till he/she finished his/her talking. I value active listening and full understanding of members' opinions more than just saying what I thought.' An analysis showed that about 60% of her moves in this tutorial were 'follow-up moves' which provided acknowledgement of members' responses, elicitation of responses, and agreeing with members or developing a member's response. She did, however, interrupt members who were chatting during the discussion. Upon reflection, she felt that this was not conducive to creating a friendly and relaxed atmosphere. Further, she felt that the group could get useful ideas from what seemed to be irrelevant to the main theme of the discussion.

In the third tutorial sessions, her participation rate dropped substantially, to 7.4%, which was just slightly more than her participation in the first tutorial sessions. One factor was that she was no longer chairing the meeting. A major factor was the change in group membership in this tutorial. In this group, there was a medical student, Yuri, whose opinions she valued highly, not only because of her self-confidence and assertiveness but also because of her field of study. She said, 'When the medical students firmly insisted on their opinions, I would be convinced that their opinions were definitely correct. I couldn't say anything and take the first step to express a different opinion today.... I tended to think that the medical students' opinions were somewhat "better" than those of students from other schools [in the university].' (The original wording of 'first step' in Japanese was *ippo o fumidasu*, which means 'take action to do something in a courageous manner'.) Rina subsequently disclosed that she was afraid of Yuri's critical response to her opinion. Rina was clearly intimidated by Yuri, as can be seen from the use of 'first step'. She said: 'I strongly felt that I couldn't frankly express what I thought at the first meeting [referring to the first tutorial in the second term]. Probably, this feeling might not change in the future tutorial.' She continued, 'I need to be sensitive to the atmosphere of the group and be aware of the members' personalities so as to show *my true feelings* in this group *in an appropriate manner*.... To cultivate a group atmosphere in which *I feel free to express my opinion*, it is necessary to establish a good relationship with them and to obtain a better understanding of each member's position in the group' (emphasis added). Rina's feeling was shared by other group members interviewed, who described Yuri's attitude as 'arrogant', and they pointed out that she talked too much and did not give enough opportunities for the quiet members to speak, and that the chair should have moderated the situation.

Another factor that contributed to Rina's reduced participation was her continued concern for the quality of her contribution, which was probably exacerbated by the negative group dynamics. She was keen that her contribution would enhance critical thinking, which she defined as the ability 'to analyse a phenomenon from different angles'. She elaborated thus: '[W]hen another member gives a different opinion of a subject from mine, first, I need to accept and respect the different viewpoint. Then, it is necessary for me to be able to provide an *appropriate* and *productive* response to that member's opinion from my own viewpoint.' Not only that, she also wanted to make sure that the information she shared with her group members was accurate, and she tried to 'strike a balance between the *frequency* of my participation and the *accuracy* of information I shared' (emphasis added). While self-presentation, through providing 'accurate' information, and establishing a good relationship among group members, through providing 'appropriate' and 'productive' responses, continued to be important factors, the unequal power relationship between Yuri and herself and the negative group dynamics had the strongest impact on her participation.

In the fourth tutorial, Rina's participation rate almost doubled, rising to 14.5%, though it was still considerably lower than that in the second tutorial, when she had been the chair. Taking into consideration the fact that 60% of her moves in the second tutorial consisted of providing acknowledgement and eliciting responses from group members, Rina's participation in this tutorial was substantially different from the previous tutorial. The quality of her contribution continued to be an important factor. She spoke about the need to carefully organise her thoughts, to consider whether her opinion was relevant to the topic of discussion before expressing it, and to listen to other group members in order to fully understand them. She still found it difficult to clearly express her thoughts. She said, 'Although I had a certain idea in my mind, I couldn't find the right way to express it to the members.' However, because of the better relationship within the group, brought about by a change in Yuri's behaviour in the group (see below), she managed to share her thoughts even though she was worried that her question might be off the point. She further elaborated as follows:

> Basically, I could frankly share what I thought, even though I was uncertain of the accuracy of the information, partly because I feel that this group has the sort of good relationship. After sharing the information that I was uncertain of, I always asked for members' opinions and confirmation, like saying 'what do you think?' … In this tutorial, it was the first time for me to really feel like actively participating to obtain substantial knowledge from this scenario. That's why I think I was able to ask questions which explored the essence of the subject content [under discussion].… It was the first time for me to enjoy participating in the PBL tutorial.

While the presence of Yuri inhibited her participation significantly in the third tutorial, in her reflections on the fourth tutorial, she referred to Yuri, who acted as the chair, as a role model for leading a group discussion. She observed, 'I recognised that Yuri always did excellent work in this group. She led this group by expressing her thoughts succinctly and I didn't feel that she dominated the discussion [in this tutorial].… I felt that she was a leading member in this group.' The interviews with Yuri revealed that she actually reflected on her own participation after the third tutorial and felt that by talking too much, she might have prevented other members from contributing. So in the fourth tutorial, when she took on the chair, she tried to establish an atmosphere in which all members felt free to share their ideas. Taking on the role of the chair further made it necessary for her to do so.

The fluctuating trajectory of Rina's participation showed that the factors that shaped her participation were interrelated and fluid. Similar to Aya, a positive relationship among the group members, which she actually experienced, was a critical factor and it minimised the impact of values which she had firmly held, such as not making any contribution to the discussion unless it was of high quality and appropriate. However, power relationships, which are deeply respected in the participants' culture, critically affected the group relationship and it was not until the unequal power relationship was mitigated by Yuri's conscious effort to overcome her own assertiveness and to play a facilitative role as chair that Rina was able to enjoy actively participating in a PBL tutorial.

Concluding Remarks

Silence, or rather reticence, on the part of learners, is prevalent in Asian classrooms, especially in EFL contexts. The research literature and the interesting studies reported in this volume have demonstrated that there are certain commonly shared and deeply rooted sociocultural values underlying this phenomenon. These studies have also shown that the dynamic interplay between these values and related factors is still not fully understood. To address this, we have briefly outlined the basic tenets of complexity theory or CDST and proposed that the methodologies adopted should be aligned with this theory. We have briefly discussed two of the methodologies, action research and case study. We have argued for the need to conduct more longitudinal studies rather than snapshot studies, be they action research or case study, which track the changes in learners' attitudes, emotions, beliefs and behaviours that are brought about by the dynamic interplay of these sociocultural values and factors over time. We have provided a brief report on a longitudinal study of the participation trajectory of two Japanese learners over an academic year for illustration. We hope that the findings demonstrated to a certain extent how the complex, dynamic and multifaceted nature of silence can be unravelled through longitudinal studies of this kind.

Self-reflection/Discussion Questions

(1) Consider an EFL class you have taught or observed over a semester. Have you observed any changes in the oral participation of the learners? What are the possible reasons for these changes or lack of change?
(2) Identify several learners who have demonstrated fluctuations in their oral participation and conduct an interview with them. Compare the reasons that you have listed in (1) above and those disclosed by the learners, and see if there are any differences.
(3) Compare the learners you have interviewed and Aya and Rina in this chapter. Are there any similarities or differences in their beliefs, emotions and attitudes?
(4) What implications do the findings reported in this chapter and your own findings have for you as an EFL teacher or teacher educator?

Recommended Reading

King, J. (2013) *Silence in the Second Language Classroom.* Basingstoke: Palgrave Macmillan.

This book is the first detailed empirical study to investigate the prevalent phenomenon of silence in second language classrooms. Although the data collected are specifically from Japanese EFL classrooms, the cultural and socio-psychological reasons that underlie this phenomenon are highly relevant to learners in the region. Readers who are interested in exploring the sociocultural dimensions of classroom phenomena will find this volume interesting and useful.

Larsen-Freeman, D. (1997) Chaos/complexity systems and second language acquisition. *Applied Linguistics* 18 (2), 141–165.

This article is a pioneering piece of work which applies dynamic complex systems theory to second language acquisition. It outlines the features of complex non-linear systems in an accessible way and explains how language acquisition can be viewed as a dynamic, complex and non-linear process. It is an excellent introduction to CDST. Readers who are interested in pursuing this topic should also read the next recommended reading.

Larsen-Freeman, D. and Cameron, L. (2008) *Complex Systems and Applied Linguistics.* Oxford: Oxford University Press.

This is the first book-length exploration of how a complex systems approach can illuminate domains in applied linguistics, including first and second language development, discourse analysis and language teaching. The discussion of the key concepts of complexity theory is highly engaging and accessible.

Tsui, A.B.M. (1996) Reticence and anxiety in second language learning. In K.M. Bailey and D. Nunan (eds) *Voices from the Language Classroom: Qualitative Research in Second Language Education* (pp. 145–167). Cambridge: Cambridge University Press.

This is one of the earliest studies to discuss the prevalent phenomenon of reticence in EFL classrooms in the Asian context and draws on Horwitz's work on communication apprehension. It points out that speaking in a language that learners are still trying to master is a psychologically unsettling process and calls for teachers' empathy for ESL learners.

References

Burns, A. (2010) *Doing Action Research in English Language Teaching.* London: Routledge.

Byrne, D. and Callaghan, G. (2014) *Complexity Theory and the Social Sciences*. London: Routledge.
Cohen, L., Manion, L. and Morrison, K. (2018) *Research Methods in Education* (8th edn). London: Routledge.
Denscombe, M. (2014) *The Good Research Guide* (4th edn). Maidenhead: Open University Press.
Geertz, C. (1973) *The Interpretation of Cultures*. New York: Basic Books.
Itakura, H. and Tsui, A.B.M. (2004) Gender and conversational dominance in Japanese conversation. *Language in Society* 33 (2), 223–248.
King, J. (2013) *Silence in the Second Language Classroom*. Basingstoke: Palgrave Macmillan.
King, J. (2016) Classroom silence and the dynamic interplay between context and the language learner: A stimulated recall study. In J. King (ed.) *The Dynamic Interplay Between Context and the Language Learner* (pp. 127–150). Basingstoke: Palgrave Macmillan.
Larsen-Freeman, D. (1997) Chaos/complexity science and second language acquisition. *Applied Linguistics* 18 (2), 141–165.
Larsen-Freeman, D. and Cameron, L. (2008) *Complex Systems and Applied Linguistics*. Oxford: Oxford University Press.
Luttenberg, J., Meijer, P. and Oolbekkink-Marchand, H. (2017) Understanding the complexity of teacher reflection in action research. *Educational Action Research* 25 (1), 88–102. doi: 10.1080/09650792.2015.1136230.
MacIntyre, P.D. and Legatto, J.J. (2011) A dynamic system approach to willingness to communicate: Developing an idiodynamic method to capture readily changing effect. *Applied Linguistics* 32 (2), 149–171.
Morrison, K.R.B. (2008) Educational philosophy and the challenge of complexity theory. In M.M. Mason (ed.) *Complexity Theory and the Philosophy of Education* (pp. 16–31). Chichester: John Wiley and Sons.
Phelps, R. and Graham, A. (2010) Exploring the complementarities between complexity and action research: The story of Technology Together. *Cambridge Journal of Education* 40 (2), 183– 97.
Sinclair, J.M. and Coulthard, M. (1975) *Towards an Analysis of Discourse: The English Used by Teachers and Pupils*. London: Oxford University Press.
Smith, L. and King, J. (2017) A dynamic systems approach to wait time in the second language classroom. *System* 68, 1–14.
Tsui, A.B.M. (1996) Reticence and anxiety in second language learning. In K.M. Bailey and D. Nunan (eds) *Voices from the Language Classroom: Qualitative Research in Second Language Education* (pp. 145–167). Cambridge: Cambridge University Press.
Tsui, A.B.M. and Imafuku, R. (2019) Intercultural communicative competence revisited. Plenary presentation, 17th Asia TEFL International Conference, Bangkok, 27–29 June.
Wallace, M. (1998) *Action Research for Language Teachers*. Cambridge: Cambridge University Press.
Yashima, T., MacIntyre, P.D. and Ikeda, M. (2016) Situated willingness to communicate in an L2: Interplay of individual characteristics and context. *Language Teaching Research* 22 (1), 115–137.

Index

active listening 90, 175, 176
active participation 7, 143, 174
affective support 44, 52, 168
Anglo-American 4
anxiety 7, 8, 9, 10, 11, 51, 52, 60, 61, 62, 63, 64, 69, 70, 72, 74, 75, 76, 77, 80, 81, 82, 83, 84, 86, 88, 89, 90, 91, 93, 97, 98, 99, 100, 101, 108, 112, 125, 126, 127, 130, 133, 134, 135, 137, 138, 168, 169, 174, 175, 180
Athabaskan 4
attractor state 86, 145, 146, 147, 154, 155, 156, 157, 158, 159, 160, 161, 162
Australia 4, 5, 20, 22, 30, 107, 127
Australian 5, 7, 20, 21, 22, 30, 56, 167
authority 5, 116, 118, 128, 144, 167, 168, 169
avoidance 3, 4, 9, 27, 33, 61, 62, 71, 73, 75, 86, 92, 94, 96, 97, 128, 145, 167, 168

barrier 2, 90, 91, 127, 128
bullying 128

Canada 10, 106, 110, 120, 125
capacity to speak (CTS) 7, 11, 124, 125, 130, 131, 132, 133–134, 135, 136, 137, 138, 167
China 10, 106, 108, 109, 110, 114–116, 117, 118, 119, 127, 147, 156, 168
Chinese 5, 7, 10, 12, 21, 25, 28, 29, 30, 34, 106–110, 111, 112, 113, 114–115, 117, 118, 119, 120, 127, 138, 139, 144, 145, 147, 148, 150, 159–160, 161, 162, 167, 168, 169
Classroom Oral Participation Scheme (COPS) 12, 65, 66, 67, 68, 72, 87, 148
cognitive-behavioural theory (CBT) 7, 9, 10, 80–81, 83–84, 88–89, 91–99, 100, 101, 168

cognitive
 load 132, 137
 processing 10, 25, 113, 169
collective
 opinions 176
 silences 39
 thinking 127
collectivism 153, 159
comfort zone 161
communication psychology 12, 146, 161
communicative activities 82, 96, 109, 114, 115, 117, 120, 137
comprehension
 comprehension deficiency 48, 52
 comprehension difficulty 51
confidence 9, 11, 26, 32, 40, 46, 50, 62, 69, 81, 88, 92, 96, 97, 98, 99, 100, 112, 124, 125, 126, 130, 131, 133, 134, 135, 136, 137, 138, 167, 177
Confucian 127, 145, 167, 182
Confucian heritage cultures (CHC) 127, 128, 167
confusion 20, 107, 108, 113, 115, 157, 159, 166,
cooperation 4, 26, 32, 64, 65, 73, 76, 136
coping strategies 8, 31, 99
cultural expectations 4, 8, 37
cultural misconceptions 4

desire to communicate (DC) 144
discomfort 8, 27, 72, 75, 87, 167
distraction 87, 158, 161
Dynamic Systems Theory (DST) 143–144, 145, 146–147, 161, 162, 168, 169-170, 179, 180

embarrassment 27, 62, 70, 72, 73, 74, 76, 77, 112, 117, 156, 167, 168, 169
emotion 9, 22, 28, 44, 62, 67, 80, 83, 84, 86, 88, 89, 91, 97, 98, 99, 112, 144, 168, 179

Index 183

emotion regulation 77
encouraging learners 3, 10, 11, 44, 52, 61, 64, 90, 98, 117, 118, 128, 136, 139, 175
exams 10, 82, 115–116, 118, 126, 128, 129, 135, 138, 154
experience outside class (*see* overseas study, study abroad) 130, 131, 133–134, 136
experienced teachers 31, 43, 63

face (*see* losing face) 30, 62, 127–128, 145, 146, 167, 168, 175
fear
  of making mistakes 70, 72, 73, 84, 92, 100, 108, 128, 130, 169
  of negative evaluation 62, 82 ,97, 108, 128, 167-169, 174
feelings 64, 65, 67, 69, 70, 71, 72, 94, 98, 99, 136, 137, 157, 158, 177
Finnish 4, 14
foreign language anxiety (*see* language anxiety) 9, 62, 69, 81–82, 88,
frustration 4, 5, 29, 30, 33, 44, 48, 52, 80, 89, 92, 97

Garrwa language 4
group cohesiveness 64–65, 75
group dynamics 9, 21, 54, 62, 64, 68, 72, 76, 125, 128, 175, 177
groupism 44, 52, 168
group pressure 44, 168
group psychological processes 75

habit 18, 120, 129, 156
harmony 20, 29, 30, 167, 168
Hong Kong 81

identity-based fears 84
individualism 153, 158–159
initiation–response–feedback (IRF) 39, 55, 62, 129, 146, 150
inner speech 7, 18, 19, 27, 113
interpersonal dynamics 8, 64, 71, 72, 73
interpersonal self 175–176

Japan 9, 20, 60, 62, 63, 64, 66, 68, 77, 82, 84, 86, 87, 91, 92, 118, 124, 126, 127–128, 129, 130, 136, 137, 139, 167, 172
Japanese 4, 5, 7, 8, 9, 11, 12, 20, 21, 25, 28, 29, 30, 31, 34, 37, 38, 39, 44, 51, 54, 56, 57, 60, 61, 62, 63, 66, 67, 69, 70, 71, 73, 75, 77, 80, 81–83, 84, 86, 87, 90, 91, 96, 97, 100, 101, 107, 108, 123, 124, 125, 126, 127-128, 130, 131, 135, 136, 137, 138, 145, 147, 167, 168, 169, 172–173, 177, 179, 180

Korea 30, 31, 127
Korean 7, 21, 25, 26, 27, 28, 30, 34, 108, 167

language anxiety (*see* foreign language anxiety) 9, 62, 81, 86, 90, 99, 101, 112, 117, 144, 146, 169
learning mode (*see* mode of learning) 18, 20, 22, 23, 25, 26, 30–31, 32, 33
learning opportunities 6, 38, 39, 41, 42
learning strategies 31, 107
linguistic support 8, 44, 45, 52, 98
losing control (of the class) 124, 129
losing face (*see* face) 112, 129, 169

mental processing 18, 19, 30, 35
mental rehearsal 19, 32
mode of learning (*see* learning mode) 6, 7, 17, 27, 33, 34, 39
modesty 145, 168
Mongolian 7, 21, 25, 28, 29, 30, 167
motivation 11, 84, 91, 96, 113, 120, 125–126, 129, 130, 133–134, 135, 137, 138, 144, 155, 156, 168

New Yorkers 4
non-linguistic cues 41, 54
non-participation (*see* silence – non-participatory) 3, 37–38, 112
non-talk 61, 87
non-verbal behaviour 17, 87, 97, 105, 107, 108, 112, 175

off-task
opportunity to speak
oral participation 6, 7, 9, 10, 11, 12, 60, 61, 62, 63, 64, 65, 66, 67, 68, 69, 72, 73, 74, 75, 81, 84, 96, 145, 151, 167, 179
overseas study (*see* experience outside class, study abroad) 29, 106, 120, 148, 167

participation rate 173, 174, 176, 177
passivity 2, 5, 66, 107, 115, 128, 176

pauses 3, 4, 47, 52, 61, 65, 83, 100, 124, 128, 161
peer dynamics 27, 28, 167
peer evaluation 8, 82, 85, 95, 98, 128, 167, 168, 169, 174
peer support 28, 44, 48, 54, 96, 99, 168
personality trait 124, 125, 174, 175, 176
politeness 14, 116, 145, 160, 168
power 71–72, 116, 129, 145, 169, 177, 179
problem-based learning 172
pre-service teachers 10, 106, 109–110, 112, 117, 168
pressure 28, 44, 116, 125, 126, 136
processing time 19, 28, 29
proficiency 18, 38, 40, 41, 53, 75, 108, 116, 126
proficient students 81, 108, 117

resistance 11, 19, 106, 124
respect 10, 28, 31, 96, 108, 113, 116, 145, 146, 160, 168, 169, 175, 177, 179
reticence 3, 6, 12, 34. 39, 56, 60, 62, 63, 81, 107, 108, 109, 110, 112, 117, 127, 138, 159, 166, 167, 169, 175, 176, 179, 180

safe space 113, 169
safety behaviour 86, 97
scaffolding 34, 43, 45, 46, 49, 52, 53, 54
self-doubt 92, 96, 97
self-image 62, 70, 169
silence
  breaking silence 61, 135, 136, 155, 157, 160, 161
  communicative function of silence 105, 113, 118
  and disengagement 20, 77, 105, 107
  and engagement 13, 18, 31, 48
  facilitative silence 3, 6, 8, 13, 37, 39, 61
  inhibitive silence 6, 13, 61, 76
  as interactional resource 1, 8, 38, 39, 40, 41, 49, 54, 168
  involuntary silence 117
  macro silence 3, 10, 145
  marked silence 5, 150, 151, 154, 155, 161, 162, 168
  micro silence 3, 8, 10, 38, 61
  negative silence 4, 13, 37, 61, 108
  non-participatory silence (see non-participation) 6, 8, 61, 63, 72, 75

positive silence 1, 10, 13, 113, 117, 119
productive silence 6, 10, 17, 31, 32, 34, 117, 119
shared silence 31
silent engagement pedagogy (SEP) 34
silent learning strategies 10, 39, 111, 113, 118
silent processing 18, 25, 29, 30, 31, 33
social anxiety 62, 80, 81, 88, 97, 101
social inhibition 8, 9, 60, 61, 63, 75
spontaneous speech 18, 21, 26, 28, 37, 83, 108, 125, 135
stereotype 2, 4, 107
student-initiated talk 65, 68, 75, 81, 124, 150, 153, 161
study abroad (*see* experience outside class, overseas study) 63, 70, 82, 87, 89, 92, 97, 100, 136

talk-heavy classes 105, 110
task challenge 27–28
task complexity 7, 75, 125, 138, 169
task design 7, 8, 17, 20, 21, 23, 31, 32, 167
teacher-centred 107, 109, 111, 114, 116, 118, 124, 129
teacher-fronted classes 38, 43, 45, 54
teacher cognition 3, 109
teacher support 7, 8, 11, 32, 43, 53, 54, 167, 168
teaching style 44, 45, 116
tolerance 3, 4, 20, 77, 129, 145
training teachers 40, 109, 114, 116, 124, 129
turn-taking 4, 8, 38, 40, 44, 52, 53, 56, 107, 120

verbal involvement 20, 28
verbal participation 7, 9, 12, 30, 34, 72, 82, 146, 167, 171
Vietnamese 34, 108, 127

wait time 3, 8, 11, 25, 29, 31, 38, 39, 40, 41, 42, 43, 44, 45, 46, 48, 50, 52, 53, 54, 61, 62, 90, 129, 166
whole-class silence 71, 72, 73, 75
willingness to communicate (WTC/L2 WTC) 3, 5, 7, 12, 40, 41, 69, 108, 109, 124, 125, 126, 127, 135, 139, 143, 144–145, 146, 147, 148, 149, 150, 151, 153-155, 157, 158, 159, 160, 161, 162, 163, 168, 172
willingness to speak 27, 71, 163

For Product Safety Concerns and Information please contact our EU Authorised Representative:

Easy Access System Europe

Mustamäe tee 50

10621 Tallinn

Estonia

gpsr.requests@easproject.com